Living Through Mourning

Also by Harriet Sarnoff Schiff

The Bereaved Parent

Living Through Mourning

Finding Comfort and Hope When a Loved One Has Died

Harriet Sarnoff Schiff

Viking

VIKING
Viking Penguin Inc., 40 West 23rd Street,
New York, New York 10010, U.S.A.
Penguin Books Ltd, Harmondsworth,
Middlesex, England
Penguin Books Australia Ltd, Ringwood,
Victoria, Australia
Penguin Books Canada Limited, 2801 John Street,
Markham, Ontario, Canada L3R 1B4
Penguin Books (N.Z.) Ltd, 182–190 Wairau Road,
Auckland 10, New Zealand

First published in 1986 by Viking Penguin Inc.
Published simultaneously in Canada

LIBRARY OF CONGRESS CATALOGING IN PUBLICATION DATA
Schiff, Harriet Sarnoff.
    Living through mourning.
    Bibliography: p.
    Includes index.
    1. Death—Psychological aspects.   2. Bereavement—
Psychological aspects.   I. Title.
BF789.D4S33   1986   155.9′37   85-40801
ISBN 0-670-80028-7

Printed in the United States of America by
R. R. Donnelley & Sons Company, Harrisonburg, Virginia
Set in Baskerville
Design by Beth Tondreau

To the memory of
   Robby
   Helen Sarnoff
   Rose Schiff
   Meyer Schiff
   Phyllis Winograd Gordon
   Manny Gorman

My child, parents and friends who
will always be remembered.

Contents

Preface

In the course of my life I thought very little about what happens within a family after a special person dies. I thought very little about it until our ten-year-old son Robert died in 1968 following open-heart surgery. It was then, at the worst moment in my life, that I discovered I lacked direction, lacked purpose, and most of all had an overwhelming fear that my pain would never ease. I would try to imagine my life twenty and thirty years down the road and never, not for a moment, did I picture that time *not* fraught with hurt and despair.

Yet miraculously, with the passage of time and the employment of whatever meager help was available nearly twenty years ago, I found the wonder of knowing I could continue with my life and enjoy my husband and two surviving children as well as my special relationship with my daughter-in-law.

Perhaps the most undermining experience I've ever had occurred shortly after Robby died. An inveterate reader, I went to the public library to get books that would help me survive the dreadful pain I was experiencing. To my dismay there were no books. Certainly there were nonfiction sagas people had written about their own dead children—books that served as memorials. But that was not what I needed. I needed something that would tell me I would survive today and tomorrow, and no such works were available.

It was then I began my interviewing and thinking about filling this need. As a reporter with the *Detroit News* I came across many stories dealing with the fallout of a death in the family. Each story carried its own weight and pain. Each was cataloged on paper or in my memory and eventually resulted in *The Bereaved Parent*.

Since that time more attention has been given to how to cope when a special person dies. More literature is available now. What I hope to accomplish with this work is to identify those who grieve and their problems. It is long past due that stepparents and former spouses and friends be included in a work on grief. They have been included here.

There is also a section introducing a proven support group technique. In a world in which people are becoming more and more isolated, support groups take on the character of surrogate families. The section details how to run meetings effectively and productively and gives outlines for their implementation.

Most of all, it is my wish that this become a book of hope for you. I assure you that even though you know great tragedy, there is hope. The future can still be bright and full, providing you allow it to be that way.

Please find comfort because it is there to be had. Please use pencils and paper where I have asked you to. Write me and let me know how you are coming along. I care.

—HARRIET SARNOFF SCHIFF

Acknowledgments

In the years since the publication of *The Bereaved Parent* I have met thousands of people who have been hurt by the death of a special person in their lives. These people—bereaved parents, widows, widowers, surviving children, surviving siblings, friends, grandchildren, grandparents—have had stories to share that simply begged for publication so that all might have the opportunity of knowing they are not alone.

These people, who spoke so readily during my workshops and lectures, who were willing to bare their souls with the hope of not only easing their own pain but helping the pain of those who heard them, are to be honored, for they are survivors with courage and integrity. They come from all parts of this country and Canada. They have shared their stories by mail, by telephone and in public forums.

I thank them.

Also to be commended for going beyond the nine-to-five mentality they could so easily have adopted are the men and women who make up the mental health community in this country. Many of them have come to understand the very special needs of those who grieve. They have made themselves available day and night, worked to form support groups, invited speakers such as myself to help organize these support groups, and in general displayed a high degree of decency toward vulnerable people. These men and women, who have made easing bereavement their careers, have been gracious through the years and have unstintingly shared their thoughts and observations and insights with me.

I thank them.

Acknowledgments could not be complete without recognizing The Compassionate Friends everywhere; all Sudden Infant Death Syndrome Parents; parents of newborns who die and all the widowed people organizations nationally who have proven so helpful in offering insights. I thank you. Also, my thanks to the people who are involved in MADD. They, along with Candy Lightner, have done much to help families victimized by drunk drivers to begin to feel that there might at least be justice.

Although the list is long, I hope it is as complete as was their openness with me: Association of Pediatric Oncology Social Workers; Ohio Funeral Directors; National Association of Funeral Directors; International Order of the Golden Rule; Professional Association for Retardation in Ohio; Bronston Methodist Hospital, Kalamazoo, Michigan; Western Ontario Funeral Service Association, Ontario, Canada; Ingalls Memorial Hospital, Harvey, Illinois; Harvard Medical School–Massachusetts General Hospital–Eunice Kennedy Shriver Center; Memphis Funeral Directors, Memphis, Tennessee; North Carolina Funeral Directors Associaton; Burton Funeral Homes, Erie, Pennsylvania; Pennsylvania Funeral Directors; Northeast Kingdom Mental Health Service, Vermont; Riverbend Center for Mental Health, Florence, Alabama; Villa Maria College, Erie, Pennsylvania; Alabama Funeral Directors Association; Community House, Birmingham, Michigan; Michigan Funeral Directors Association; Ohio Chapter, National Sudden Infant Death Syndrome Foundation; National Organization of Compassionate Friends; Houston Medical Center, Houston, Texas; Touro Infirmary, New Orleans, Louisiana; St. Francis Center, Washington, D.C.

Along with the many people in the mental health field such as Marilyn Gilbert, M.A., among the first bereavement counselors in the country to work directly for a funeral home, I would like to extend a special note of appreciation to Dr. Philip R. Muskin, deputy director of Consultation-Liaison Psychiatry at Columbia Presbyterian Medical Center in New York City. Dr. Muskin is assistant clinical professor of psychiatry at Columbia College of Physicians and Surgeons and is on the faculty of the Psychoanalytic Center of Columbia University.

Also to Dr. William Jones a well-deserved thank you. Dr. Jones, formerly department chairman of psychology at Oakland University, Rochester, Michigan, serves as associate professor of counseling at that university. He is a counseling therapist in private practice who has lectured and taught lay people and professionals throughout the country how to cope with significant loss.

Thank you to Dr. Ned Poponea who has so ably taught grief-counseling techniques not only within the Veteran's Administration but to many in the health care field. Of course, my thanks to Roy V. Nichols and Patrick Lynch for their insights into the grief process.

And, in general, an across-the-board thank you to the countless psychiatrists and psychologists and social workers who have opened their thinking and offered guidance to me in my work.

My deep thanks go especially to Phil Donahue and his remarkable staff who trusted in the topic of coping with a death and allowed a most special bereavement, the death of a child, to become a national issue, thereby opening many doors for *all* who grieve and wish to share. A very special thank you to the people on the *Today Show* for airing the topic of the Bereaved Parent.

A special appreciation to wonderful Ellen Levine, my friend, agent, and sounding board, for believing in this project. To Nan Graham, my friend and editor, whose suggestions were solid and leant an added dimension to this work, thank you.

On a personal level, there are family and friends who helped with their moral support. My sister, Roz Rope, who became involved early with this project. My children, Dale, Sharon, and Stacie, who were so concerned; and most of all, to Sander, my husband and friend. Thank you.

Living Through Mourning

Introduction

There once was a mighty king who owned the finest diamond in all the world. People came from far and near to see the precious stone, which sat glowing in a display case.

One day the king passed the case and decided he wished to hold the stone that had given him such pleasure. As he stood gazing at it, a flash of sunlight happened to strike at a certain angle and the king noticed for the first time that his diamond had a flaw.

So precious had the jewel become to him that the ruler was distraught. He called for his advisers to tell him what to do. The advisers pondered and could arrive at no solution. Finally, by consensus they agreed the king should offer a reward to anyone who could come forward and ease the ruler's pain.

The reward was duly posted and the amount was substantial. Word traveled quickly and soon jewelers from throughout the land lined up to offer their suggestions. Each viewed the stone and shook his head. No, the stone was permanently flawed and the only alternative offered to the sad king was to cut the diamond at the flaw line and make two smaller stones. To this the king would not agree.

Finally, all the jewelers had been heard. Left standing was a poor bedraggled man who had been pushed to the end of the line by all the others. Eyeing him, the king asked if he, too, were a jeweler.

"No, I am not, your highness. I do lapidary work. I see beauty not only in precious jewels but in stones from the ground, as well."

The king hesitated a moment and thought carefully. He nearly turned the lowly man away, but there was something that glowed in the lapidist's eyes that caught and held the king's attention, some sureness.

"Your highness, if you will permit, I can not only restore the jewel, but I can bring it to even greater beauty than it had before. Please trust me."

The king stood quite still, his hands behind his ermine-bedecked velvet robes. Finally, after what seemed an eternity to all who listened, he ordered the lapidist to begin his work.

His advisers were aghast.

"How can you trust such a man with such a jewel?"

"No! Sire, please reconsider."

But the king held firm.

"You may proceed," he said, "but be aware that if you fail you will die."

"I understand, sire," said the little man.

He was given a special room in which to work, one that glowed in the sunlight from many sides. The king watched as the man examined the stone and began chiseling around the imperfection. Startled, the king demanded to know why the lapidary was further damaging the stone.

"Please, your highess," he said, "wait until I am done and you shall see I have not damaged the diamond."

A week went by, and then another. Frequently the king would stop into the workshop, and each time the lapidist would assure him and then reassure him that all was going well.

Finally, the great day came. With a look of pride the poor man entered the king's chamber and, kneeling, presented the ruler with the finished jewel. The king loved his diamond so greatly that he actually feared what he might see.

Finally, after saying a small prayer to his god, he looked down at the gem now glowing in the palm of his hand. What he saw brought such an aura of joy to him that it matched the happiness on the lapidist's face.

What the man had done was to engrave a rosebud around the imperfection and in creating the rosebud he used the flaw as its stem.

The king was truly awed for the poor man had kept his word. Not only did he have his precious stone but it was now even more special as the flower glistened from every angle.

In his joy the king asked the lapidist to name any reward and his wish would be granted. The lapidist declined gracefully, explaining that he feared wealth and fame would blur the inner vision that helped him to see the rosebud.

There is a lesson in the story of the flawed diamond that can help us all when we are hurting and sorrowing. Just as the king saw the stone as ruined beyond repair and a joyless thing, so many of us view our lives following the death of a special person.

When we are in pain we cannot comprehend, nor do we wish to, that a rosebud may be carefully carved out of a flaw. That a new life, not better but different, can be carved out by us when we have had to deal with the catastrophe of the death of someone special.

The burden, and it is a heavy one for building this new life, generally comes at a time when we are least able to carry it. That certainly heightens our distress. When the mere business of existing in a harsh and cruel world is such an uphill struggle, how can we ask ourselves to look toward a better time? No, the burden as we see it is heavy and it is one that weighs us down as we attempt to go forward.

Perhaps the most important thing we can know is that it is possible to shift the weight, to balance it more effectively so that we are not pulled backward but can indeed take small, slow steps toward healing.

The author Thomas Mann once said, "A man's dying is more the survivor's affair than his own."

At first those words sound incongruous. After all, when someone dies it is his own death. But those who have endured the death of a dearly loved child, husband, wife, parent, sibling, friend know too well the accuracy of Mann's observation. Being a survivor brings with it a sense of being intimately involved with death because a part of the survivor has died, too. And to rebuild without that part is indeed work for the strong and determined.

How to develop that strength, how to become determined to continue on with a life, and a quality life at that, is something countless people have explored through the generations.

Grieving certainly is not new. Pain is not new. Separation is not new. They have gone on since the beginning of time. Yet there are differences in our world today that make grieving more difficult. There is no automatic long-term family cushioning when people are scattered halfway around the country and indeed the world. That issue, of our mobility, requires some exploration and thought.

We live in a world of instant coffee, instant breakfast, instant communication. We can dial a telephone number and be in touch with nearly anyone in the world. We no longer have to wait months to receive a letter. All this instant gratification, while in some cases helpful, has culturally conditioned us to be afraid of pain and mourning. Pain and mourning do not lend themselves to instant solutions. Healing is a long-term process that gradually, if well and carefully nurtured, will alleviate pain and mourning. We are no longer practiced in the art of patience. Instead, if we are not feeling "all better" in a short period of time we panic. The panic further exacerbates our pain, and rather than gently seeing ourselves through the catastrophe and nurturing ourselves, we tend to feed on the panic, making ourselves more and more distraught.

It seems the modern American asks God, "Dear God, I pray for patience . . . and I want it *right now!*" How true and how destructive that is. Aside from our hurt, therefore, we are confronted with many issues that test our sense of whether we are behaving appropriately under the worst stresses we can possibly confront.

Life has been likened to a series of collisions with the future;

it is not a sum of what we have been but of what we yearn to be. How devastating, therefore, when a child dies. Not only do parents feel the pain of surviving, they feel an additional sense of catastrophe because with the death of their child they have lost their future, their sense of posterity, their investment in life when they, too, are dead.

Widows discover all too quickly what being a survivor is all about. Without choosing to do so—and perhaps that is the worst part—widows learn the dreadful lesson of aloneness. Webster defines being alone as being solitary; separate from others or from the mass; without the presence or aid of another; by oneself. How apt a definition of the widowed state.

Widowers discover this same sad fact. They too come to internalize the definition of being alone because they too are separate from others, no longer part of humanity at large. Cultural conditioning comes into play as well. Men have been led to believe that they will not have to endure the agonies of being a survivor. Check every life insurance chart: all of them indicate women will outlive men. Men who find themselves widowed generally seem bewildered by the world and the things around them, and not without reason. After all, they have defied the laws of probability of this world. What an uncomfortable position in which to find oneself.

There is a saying that a boy may be a brilliant mathematician at the age of thirteen but that there has never been a child of thirteen who had anything useful to say about an end of human life. The person who made that observation must never have spoken to a child whose parent had died. Not having a mother or father any more makes children feel they are no longer part of the mainstream of life. Far too many young people feel deep within themselves that "he really couldn't have loved me or he wouldn't have died." It is very rare that a widow or other relative will take the time when it is needed most to sit down with surviving children and explain that their parent's death was not voluntary, that they, the children, have not been abandoned by choice. Because so few adults take the time to have such a discussion, many youngsters grow up feeling their own father or mother did not care enough about them to live. What kind of self-image and self-esteem does this encourage? How do these children conduct themselves as they grow older?

Older children already away from home when their parents die also bear deep regrets. There is a sense in many adult children that they will really not be terribly affected if their parent dies. In recent years we have been turning back to our origins, our beginnings, and parents are our immediate past. When a mother or father dies we feel the sharp pangs of a severing with that past, and we know with a humbling acceptance that one day we too will be considered the past.

Siblings suffer greatly when a sister or brother of any age dies. That age-old biblical question, "Am I my brother's keeper?" looms large indeed when we survive the death of a sibling. The anxieties run deep within us. The questions "Why him and not me?" "Did I wish him dead because I was jealous of the attention he got?" haunt surviving children. They are questions often left unanswered because no one takes the time to ask a youngster what he is feeling.

When adult siblings die, sisters and brothers feel a deep loneliness because of their absence. There were times they shared from long ago that can no longer be shared. There are family occasions from which an important family member is now absent. There is deep within many people the idea that blood is thicker than water and no friend, no matter how dear, can take the place of a sister or brother.

There are others who would argue this point fiercely. While to many no one can be closer than a sister or brother, there are others who invest their emotions in friends, friends who become confidants and companions. When such a friend dies the loss is often catastrophic yet rarely is the surviving friend's pain acknowledged by those who come to the funeral. Only the family is recognized, thereby adding yet another layer of hurt—a sense that no one else knows the magnitude of loss.

A family has been described as a group of people whose trouble is that the youngsters grow out of childhood, but the parents never grow out of parenthood. How true that is, and how painful when one is a grandparent whose grandchild has died. Grandparents carry dreadful burdens that are frequently never mentioned. They are the secret mourners, the unacknowledged grievers. When a child dies, grandparents bear the grief of the death of a loved boy or girl compounded by the pain of watching their own adult child, the dead child's parent, writhe in an agony they are powerless to ease. It is a double grief.

While the ages and relationships of those who grieve may vary, there are common threads that bind us all: the thread of pain; the thread of confusion; the thread of isolation.

An optimist has been described as someone with a cheery frame of mind, like a tea kettle that still sings although it is up to its ears in hot water.

If you are mourning, this book will not turn you into an optimist. You *are* in hot water. You cannot be expected to sing. You are not a tea kettle. You are a real person who thinks and feels and knows pain.

Instead, this book will bring with it some understanding of what you are enduring and, equally important, a sense that you are not alone in your suffering. For assuredly you are not. People from one end of this country to the other share your pain, your disillusion, your questioning. Sometimes just to know that can be helpful. You are not different. You are still part of humanity, but it is the part that has come to know and recognize suffering.

In order even to begin thinking of living through mourning it is important to know the issues you will be confronting and the pathways you may follow. You will of course confront sorrow. There will be times you will think "This is really not happening to me." Anger may temporarily overtake you as will guilt. There will be times you will feel completely depressed and wonder why you should go on. Many people experience a destructive sense of powerlessness. You may be such a person and may experience that emotion. It is a feeling that you no longer can control anything about your life. You may grapple with issues involving God. Do you still believe? Is your faith stronger? Less strong? Finally when you have traveled the road to healing you will arrive at that most desired place—acceptance. There is a great comfort to be gained in knowing these issues have been identified, labeled. Much fear may be removed when you know that you are not floating around at sea without an anchor. You do indeed have an anchor and that anchor is knowledge. Understanding is the cornerstone upon which you may rebuild your life. It is in not knowing, in feeling you are the first one, that you may be tempted to allow yourself to go down in defeat.

To further assure you that you are not alone we will also discuss groups: groups for those who are widowed, whose babies have died, whose parents have died. These groups in many instances have proven a lifeline to those who have moved from their family and those who do not have strong alternative support systems. There is probably no luxury to equal that felt by a hurting person who sits down with a group of strangers and hears his feelings coming out of someone else's mouth. There is security in this and comfort that cannot be measured.

Perhaps the most important message of all is that if you allow yourself to sink, there will be a double tragedy, for there will have been more than one death. You, the survivor, will also have died. Died mentally. Therein lies a tragedy you can avert.

This does not mean you will come from your special person's funeral and begin tap dancing around the house. It does mean that you can and will make a commitment to go on with your life to the best of your ability.

You alone know how high that level can be and what you may aspire to while living through mourning.

Bereavement

For Parents

Most people have been conditioned to believe that they will grow
up, marry, have children and eventually be buried by those
children. This is the way things generally proceed and it is the
pattern by which most of us live. In a changing world there is
comfort in knowing that such a pattern exists. But what happens
when the pattern changes? What happens when you suddenly
find yourself burying the being you brought into this world? A
being filled with all your hopes and aspirations? Not only are
you griefstricken because you see a part of yourself lying in a
coffin and lowered into the ground, you are also stunned because you have lived through the trauma of a reversal of nature!

Age plays no part whatsoever in these emotions and hurts.
Many elderly men and women now living in nursing homes will
say they have lived too long. How can their statement be dis-
puted when they tell us that they have buried at least one of
their children? To defy nature's law and feel you are merely
surviving alone in a nursing home may be very painful, especially when you have endless hours to dwell on the past. When
someone in this situation challenges why *he* lived so long while
his child died before him it is important not to question his

reasoning. There are times when statements such as these are not invalid just because they are uncomfortable to hear.

If your child lived to be old enough to show signs of different talents you probably projected these into a glowing future for him. How many budding artists lie in a parent's imagination when a nursery school teacher sends home a note saying your child has artistic instincts? When that child dies you are not only bereft of him and his presence, but you are also bereft of all the promise he might have developed into true accomplishments. No, you are not imagining the frustration you feel. It is real and something most bereaved parents experience. Hold onto that thought. While it cannot bring back your dead child, at least you can know your thinking and frustration are shared by many other bereaved parents.

As a bereaved parent you may feel you are swimming in a stream whose current suddenly shifts and you find yourself swimming upstream for dear life. You may paddle about frantically at first, but as you begin to tire and to think about all the energy needed to make this great attempt to survive you begin to wonder why. What is the point? You feel so tired, so weary, there is nothing you wish for more than a welcoming blackness to encompass you.

Bereaved parents come in all ages. Some are young and appear terribly vulnerable. We have a sense that they are nothing more than children themselves trying to make some sense out of an unreasonable world. After all, newspaper stories daily tell tales of babies left in trash cans who still manage to live despite exposure to the elements. How do you feel, you, who have done everything possible to keep your child alive without success when another baby, unwanted, uncared for, lives? There is certainly room for bitterness and anger and a feeling of powerlessness in your heart when such things occur.

Thinking practically, why shouldn't these emotions be present? You, the young parents, have indeed been dealt a blow from which there is no total recovery. Certainly you will learn to live again and function again and hopefully stay married to one another, but the hurt and the loss of that child's life and future will remain for all time.

People make comparisons when a young child dies that can be most offensive. One woman whose fifty-year-old daughter died suddenly told another mother whose child died at age eight that the death of the fifty-year-old was worse. Worse? How does the mother of an eight-year-old explain what she would have given to have shared in the additional four decades in which her child might have married, in which grandchildren might have been enjoyed? If you have been "victimized" by comparison-makers you certainly have the right to show your displeasure at the comparison or simply to tell whoever has been so insensitive that you find their conversation offensive. No one has the right to diminish your loss unless you give them that right.

When a young child dies there are multiple small deaths that accompany the tragedy. First of all, you feel cheated of all that might have been. Perhaps your child lived long enough to walk and talk and enjoy the friendships of other youngsters. Then he died and you still see those youngsters outside laughing and playing. You may feel discomfort because the sight of these others fills you with envy and perhaps some bitterness. Know that you are not alone. Most bereaved parents have felt the same bitterness.

At the opposite end of the spectrum a baby has been called a perfect example of minority rule. When a child dies of a disease such as Sudden Infant Death Syndrome (SIDS), how do young parents learn to trust themselves once again, to sleep through a night in peace knowing that though this event occurred once, they are not immune from having it occur again? Fortunately progress has been made with SIDS and hospitals now provide monitors in some cases when there has been a SIDS death in the family. But in spite of these advances countless parents berate themselves for any harsh thoughts they might have had when their baby woke them in the middle of the night. What seemed perfectly normal then, the annoyance of having a disturbed sleep, takes on different connotations when that child dies. If you are the parents of a baby who died of SIDS you might suddenly view yourself as an ogre. How monstrous that you could have felt annoyance at a helpless baby, or so you might think. When your baby died you may have lost perspective and also lost the innate honesty that tells you all children can be good, bad, annoying, and wonderful, sometimes all at the same time.

Rarely given their place on the ladder of grief or any room along the pathway through pain are the parents whose children are stillborn. The grief of these parents is rarely acknowledged by society. People tend to turn from them without sharing words of comfort.

The idea that there is no intense grief for mothers and fathers of children who are stillborn, who have miscarried, whose children died soon after birth is both cruel and false. There is a general overtone that such deaths are not the end of the world.

One of the worst difficulties such parents face is the sense that no one wishes to hear about their pain, their loss.

"It was strange for me to go out in public," said one young mother whose baby died at birth. "I would run into people I knew and no one, not a single person, ever said they were sorry about my baby's death. What they did instead was to look away or start talking too loud or rush off.

"I felt so isolated."

This woman is not alone as hundreds and thousands of parents who have lived through this situation will verify.

One father who is furious about the way he and his wife were received when their child had been stillborn pounded his fist on the table and said, "All we kept hearing was well, you're young. You'll have other children. No one gave a thought to the fact that our baby had died. Somehow just because he had not yet lived he had lost his humanness."

After saying this he wiped his eye with his fist. Was the tear pain? Frustration? Perhaps both.

Young couples can indeed have more children but it is wrong to trivialize the death of the child they had. Remember that child was real to them. It was a wanted baby. They had nine months of hopes and wishes for a long and satisfactory future poured into it. Both the mother and father felt it move before it was born.

Sometimes there is an immediate denial that is shared by the couple when told of a stillbirth. "This is really not happening" is frequently the first reaction. Some new ideas about how to help a mother and father face the reality of the situation are currently in use in hospitals with high-risk pregnancy units.

One nurse who works in such a facility said the most difficult problem a young couple faces is coming to terms with the fact that the baby is indeed dead and also, to some degree, that the baby actually existed. Since this particular hospital does extensive follow-up work they are able to chart just how well the couple is coping six months to a year after a stillbirth.

"In general, we have found that those who leave the hospital without seeing the dead baby have the hardest time dealing with reality," she said. "After all, how well and effectively can you mourn when you never even saw the child you conceived and delivered? You are not mourning an actual being, you are mourning a concept. That is harder to do."

Another nurse in a Midwestern high-risk unit shared her approach to helping families face this problem. "The mother had delivered a stillborn child. Since we know a bit more about how people mourn than we did years ago, I went to both parents and asked if they wished to see the baby. I told them it was deformed but it was their child."

She said both parents emphatically rejected the idea of seeing their dead girl. In fact, they displayed anger at being asked if they wished to do so. The nurse, believing that it is most important to view the body, asked the hospital's morgue to retain the baby in hopes that the parents would change their minds.

She could not have been more correct; early the next day she went into the mother's room and saw both parents sitting there holding hands and tearful. "We have decided to see our baby," said the mother, pulling out yet another tissue with which to wipe her eyes.

The father, according to the nurse, sat stone-faced, not saying a word. The nurse told the couple she would be back as soon as she could. She went to the morgue, used an elecric blanket to slightly warm the child, and then wrapped the baby in a yellow blanket, the same type of blanket used at that hospital for all babies.

She called ahead and asked that the couple be taken into a small doctor's lounge where they would have privacy. When she walked into the room she said first, "Here, Mother," and gave the baby to the young woman. The mother held the child and cried and rocked back and forth with her. Then, after a time, she was ready to relinquish the tiny bundle. The nurse then took the baby and said, "Here, Father."

The stone-faced father took the child and held it and cried and sobbed for what seemed an eternity. He simply did not wish to let go. But ultimately, tears drained dry, he gave the child back to the nurse without saying a word.

When it was time for the mother to leave the hospital some days later, the father sought out the nurse to thank her. "This is our second stillbirth and the first time anyone let us see the baby and the first time anyone called me father. Even though the baby is dead, I want to thank you for calling me that."

The nurse, although saddened, felt she had done an appropriate bit of nursing work. Now the couple could go home having touched and seen their baby without having phantom images that foster denial. They knew they were parents and that their child was dead.

Perhaps the greater service was done for the father. People who have united into support groups around this country and Canada say when a couple is given the opportunity to hold the dead baby it is invariably the father who has the most difficulty relinquishing it, perhaps because he hasn't carried it for nine months.

This difficulty in relinquishing the dead baby may well indicate society's need to rethink this problem. There is a general sympathy for the mother, the idea being that she carried the child. One father said his wife was the more fortunate because she knew the baby more intimately. Perhaps in this more enlightened world it is time both fathers and mothers were seen as separate but equal mourners.

There are other aids now being used by informed high-risk hospitals to help these parents. Most take a picture of the dead baby. They offer it to the parents before the couple leaves the hospital. Sometimes the parents say they do not want the picture, but come back six months later begging for it. The hospitals make it a point to keep those pictures on file for just that reason.

Another thing these hospitals have found to be helpful is to keep the baby's identification bracelet when the child has lived only briefly. Again, not every parent is ready at the time of impact to take the bracelet home. The hospitals also store these bracelets knowing that more often than not they will be wanted at some time along the line.

Still another way in which hospitals and mental health people are trying to help couples work through the death of an infant is by encouraging the couple to name the baby. Instead of being "it" there is a sense of identity when the child has a name. The naming says to the couple and the world at large that, however briefly, this person did live, even if only in the mother's womb.

Perhaps one of the more significant changes that has occurred in helping these couples is having a funeral for the baby. It is no longer uncommon for funeral directors to be asked to come to the hospital in order to include both parents in the arrangements, and it is something they are generally willing to do.

When an infant has died and there is a funeral, it becomes more difficult for people to look away and change the subject. Somehow they must acknowledge the event; they must offer condolences. After all, the death notices printed in every newspaper make it impossible to avoid. These formal acknowledgments help immensely in teaching others how to deal with the bereaved couple.

Although not as widely as could be hoped, support groups are being formed for parents of stillborn children. They gather generally in homes and, with both husbands and wives attending, talk out their pain and frustration and the fears they experience as they become pregnant once again. Such groups hold a valid purpose in assuring these bereaved people they are not alone.

Whether in the early months or later in the pregnancy, when a woman miscarries, that, too, is a loss and a death. There was a fetus that she hoped to deliver safely and watch grow into adulthood, and that fetus died. Parents who experience miscarriage receive even less societal nurturing than those who experience stillbirth. Almost never is anything mentioned about their loss of hopes and wishes. They are not given their due by anyone except by one another and even then, in most cases, the father does more caretaking of the mother than she of him.

In any discussion on living through mourning certain situations must be acknowledged because they carry with them an additional level of tragedy than has already been presented.

There are parents whose loss is nearly indescribable. They are the parents unable to conceive again, who have an only child die. To bring some life or purpose to these people is perhaps the hardest task a mental health professional or a friend will ever face. These people are not part of any Zero Population Growth movement; they did not elect not to have more children. Quite the contrary. They wanted a child badly and when that child died they had no other children who could even begin to draw the parents' interest in another direction. Perhaps such parents should think of adoption, of big brother and big sister organizations. Certainly they will not be able to take away the hurt but at least they may help another human being who is hurting through no fault of his or her own. If you are faced with this type of death, do not try to go it alone—each step will be too painful. Some professional input is necessary whether it be psychiatric help or a support group of others with a similar problem. Find a support group, preferably one that does not have its entire focus on bereaved parents because in most cases they will discuss surviving children, a subject likely to cause you greater pain. Rather, find a mixed group of grieving people; one that includes the widowed, siblings and some bereaved parents as well. The mixture will help add insight and perhaps some new perspective to what you already are beginning to understand.

When your child dies as a result of suicide a sense of utter hopelessness and despair can overtake you. It is hard to think rationally when you are convinced you could not or did not do enough to help him. Yet many people who work with suicides now have changed their language, and with the change has come a new attitude toward those who have suffered this type of death. No longer do all professionals call it "commiting suicide." Many now say "died of suicide," much as a person dies of cancer or any other terminal ailment. The thinking now is that there are people who simply cannot live. Although it sounds brutal it is no less true for its harshness; just as there are cancer patients who cannot live though the finest care has been given them.

There are parents who are overwrought because despite running from psychiatrist to social worker for any number of years their child still died of suicide. One woman whose daughter had attempted to take her own life more than once still cries at any mention of her daughter although four years have elapsed since the suicide. She finds no solace in knowing she tried everything and asked everyone she knew to help her daughter. "I knew something like this would happen eventually. I just knew. But I tried and tried. I used to tell her I loved her. She was special. Some doctors acknowledged she could possibly take her own life. But when she did I felt like I should have done more. Maybe it meant just one more doctor—that one special man who would have known how to save her." As time goes forward some of the pain might ease for this tragic mother but she most of all needs to become involved with other parents whose situation is the same, or perhaps see a therapist, or perhaps both.

The other parents who suffer greatly after a child's suicide are those who feel there was no warning. Many bewildered parents ask themselves how and why this could have happened.

One man, a lawyer whose son hanged himself while away at college, seems dazed by the tragedy. He maintains there was no warning, nothing to indicate deep-seated pain in his child. "He was a happy-go-lucky kid," said the father. "He always seemed so content with his life. He was a good athlete and a good student." The young man left no note, nothing by way of explanation. The father said that after the funeral he went to his son's school and talked to his roommates and friends. No one could enlighten him. As shocked as the father, the friends simply had nothing to offer. "At least if I knew the reason maybe I could rest. It's the not knowing that is hurting me so!"

In the final analysis whether a parent is forewarned or not the shock of a child's death by suicide is immense and will have a lifelong effect upon the mother and father. The questions that have no answer, the fear that not enough was done, all compound themselves as time goes on. No parent who has endured such a tragedy can afford the idea of self-help. Some form of mental health support is urgent if only to find a place in which to ventilate feelings and hidden fears.

How does a parent rationalize the death by homicide of a loved child and come to terms with it? How do you, as many clergymen suggest, learn to turn the other cheek and begin rebuilding your life when you know the killer will be set free in a few years or has not yet been caught? It makes a great tragedy all the greater when a death occurs under such circumstances. The need, the urge for vengeance, grows as time passes. One father whose daughter was raped and killed carries a printed slogan, "No release without resurrection," and he means it. He said as long as his daughter is dead he will fight and fight to keep behind bars the man convicted of the killing.

But when all is said and done the bottom line is that the child is dead and the parents must go about rebuilding their lives after such a tragedy. Although we are always accompanied by pain along the journey, the path we take and how we move along it can make all the difference in achieving a healthy recovery.

When a child dies there are generally two tragic courses that have the potential of creating mayhem. Often surviving siblings are overlooked and their grief not addressed. Parents are so focused on their own pain they neglect the pain of their other children unless forcefully reminded by a knowledgeable third party. The other potential tragedy is the separation or divorce of the parents which occurs in numbers out of all proportion to society at large after the death of a child. Some studies indicate that three out of four marriages are in crisis within months after a child dies. Then we have tragedy compounded with tragedy.

Despite feeling vulnerable and out of control when a child dies there are some things parents may do as a couple to help themselves and their relationship with each other.

• Find new activities that might be shared. One couple, both lawyers, took up upholstery. Another couple became involved in church by regularly attending mass together. From there it was a simple step to become active in a couples club at the church. The important point is to do something *new* and do it *together*.

• Schedule a talking time when hurts and thoughts may be shared. That time may be daily or several times a week. Once you have developed the timetable, stick to it. This will prevent small annoyances from building into great rage. Make certain this is private time. Take the phone off the hook, go into your bedroom and shut the door, or go for a drive. While you may wish to have a "talking time" with your children do not make it part of your husband-wife sessions.

• Become involved in a support group. To hear an outsider verbalize what your spouse says may make it less irritating to you the next time he or she says it.

For Widows

Between grief and nothing I will take grief.
—WILLIAM FAULKNER

Perhaps you walked down the aisle in a flowing white gown or in a cocktail dress. Perhaps you got married in a reverend's study or a judge's office. Regardless of where and when, you married with hope in your heart and the joy of knowing you had at long last found your special person, your closest friend. Never, unless he had some diagnosed terminal illness at the time of the marriage, did you discuss the possibility of his dying. Your plans always revolved around how you two would live and grow and prosper.

Of course there are other plateaus you reached during your years together. Perhaps you took special vacations. There might have been a big promotion that came through after you both worked so hard to achieve it. Certainly you shared sad times. One of you might have been fired from your job. Together the two of you weathered this crisis and somehow survived. Then of course you might have shared the joy of having children. What joy! During your years together you probably shared all these things and many more because they are the peaks and valleys that make up the terrain of a life shared.

The knowledge that statistically you would eventually experience widowhood had not prevented you from marrying anyway. You, like most other women, possessed a certain type of eternal optimism which enables society to remain intact. You made plans and had dreams; you did not allow the possibility of widowhood to deter you.

Afterward, even when you found some of your dreams were merely fantasies that would never come about, you still retained the sense of striving with a partner to achieve emotional and financial goals.

But then the dreadful moment came, the moment that statistically is borne out. Your husband died. Even knowing the marriage vow in some churches includes the words "till death do us part" did not bring any solace. You knew the facts. You knew the statistics. Yet your beloved husband is dead and you are left unbelieving.

Young wives often have great difficulty in accepting their husband's death because *becoming a widow is something that happens to someone else . . . someone much older.* Such young women, like most of us, visualize a widow as a shadowy figure, old and faceless. They simply do not see themselves in that remote role.

Widows, however, do come in all ages. Young women frequently feel an additional sense of outrage because ladies with dead husbands are not supposed to be strong and vital and the mothers of young children.

These young women speak frequently about sexual frustration as well, although certainly this problem is not limited to the young. In general, the need for gratification does not come about immediately. For many, in the beginning at least, there is a sense of "something having died inside of me as well" as one widow said. But after a reasonable period of time during which she begins her pathway to acceptance her feelings and desires will once again return. It is often suggested for those women who do not believe in sex outside marriage that a regime of physical fitness be introduced. Swimming, jogging and bicycling can release some of the pent-up tension that had previously been released by the sex act.

If you are experiencing such difficulty, it might be wise to talk with a therapist who may help you defuse or learn to satisfy those feelings. Also, in an intimate setting, members of a support group may discuss such longings. Above all, the group may offer the comfort of knowing these urges are natural and not a betrayal of a recently dead mate.

Business women who work long and hard to rise within their professions rarely see themselves as becoming widows either. The women who have managed to move up the corporate ladder and now manage to pull themselves out of the morass of mourning and attempt to go forward generally throw themselves into their work. If you are such an individual, it is to be admired that you still have the drive to fight for your corporate position, but your pain at being alone may be as strong as your drive for success.

At the end of a day, even if that day includes dinner or cocktails with co-workers, it is still necessary to face going home. Widowed executives enter their homes and are shocked anew because the person with whom they shared their successes and failures is no longer there. A sense of outrage at this turn of events is not uncommon. These women must now use the telephone if they are fortunate enough to have someone, friend or family, who cares about their day. Of course, the caller must be aware of interrupting even if she is calling a parent or sibling or close friend.

Sometimes, again, the physical aspects of your relationship make you think all the harder about what you lost. Physical includes more than sex. Physical is touching and holding and feeling warm. Along with your business acumen there is a need in you, as there is in all people, to feel the warmth that emanates from someone special to you. One counselor said she hears more from widows about the loss of touching than the loss of actual sexual activity.

Widows frequently keep their husband's pajamas and do not buy new pillows. These are the things that bring physical contact to the fore. A pillow upon which his head rested can still be touched and a pair of pajamas can still be worn to try and remember a sense of closeness where real physical closeness is no longer possible.

And there are women who choose to remain at home with

the children and allow their husbands to be the sole provider. The women who fulfill the traditional role also feel all the rage and turmoil bereavement can bring. One woman has three sons, the eldest of whom is sixteen. She says they are now all completely out of control. The oldest is the worst and he "eggs on" the other two. "My husband was always the disciplinarian and I was always the easygoing one."

In many homes the parental roles are divided in just that manner. There is an old saying that to every son his father is a Republican and his mother a Democrat, the one being more conservative, the other more liberal. Perhaps there is truth in that. To be left with children to be raised and decisions that cannot be shared with an equally interested second party is a hardship of great magnitude, one that is destructive not only to the widow but to the children as well.

Another woman said that not only the decisions are painful. There are the special moments that parents should share when a little girl plays the princess in the school play, or an even younger child first begins talking or reading—these are the times that can be particularly painful when a mother, despite the best intentions of her support system, cannot share them with the other person who would have derived equal joy.

These women, the young, the vigorous, the active, often must fight their sense of disbelief. After all, in our imagination, widows are none of these things. They are the old, silver-haired women who use canes, walk slightly bent over, and always need a sweater. They are not young, vigorous *you*.

Although middle age is always at least ten years older than you are, you do not see yourself as being widowed between the ages of forty and sixty. Are these not the prime years? They are the years when the children are growing and often have left home. The years when the two of you have come together again and, as often happens, rediscovered one another. Frequently the financial burdens have even begun to ease somewhat so the two of you have been able to breathe more easily. You have begun to talk about retirement. You are still making plans. Then, whether slowly or suddenly, you are confronted with the death of your husband and you are bewildered. You are questioning how this could have happened to you, and you are feeling robbed of your future. The loss of future is no light matter. You may have heard the expression by Bovee "When all else is lost, the future still remains." But when you are widowed you no longer believe in your future. You believe that you have buried it in your husband's cemetery plot.

Older women who are widowed feel a sense of despair that younger women might not expect them to feel. If you are an older widow you have reached the sad plateau which includes far too many of your contemporaries. You may look about and see yourself surrounded by people who seem to exist without purpose, without aim. Just how important is that nightly poker game played for matchsticks if you are left with reduced funds? Just how enjoyable is any part of your social life regardless of how wealthy you are if there is no husband with whom to share the events of the evening?

We, in this country, have come to accept the concept of being widowed as a given. In the course of your life you, too, would probably have thrown the term around fairly loosely. "Oh, she's a widow." These words had little impact even to you, until you became one. Now, how the image changes. How sad to know the pain that sets in. How difficult to know what decisions to make in these circumstances. You may have paid all the bills and done much of the household work when your husband was alive but you always knew he could back you up. Now he is gone and you are truly left to stand on your own two feet, alone.

While each age group has its own set of woes and difficulties to surmount, there are some truisms that all widows confront. By and large we live in what has been described as a "Noah's Ark Society." We think in terms of two by two. Yet some statistics indicate there are hugely disproportionate numbers of widows as compared to widowers, so remarriage cannot be a realistic hope for most widows. Somehow we must rid ourselves of the notion that unless we are functioning two by two we are not functioning at all. Remember, in living through mourning, you are no longer volleying on the tennis court. Now you are hitting a ball against a backboard. You have the capability of existing, as do we all, but in addition you can decide to live your life to its fullest. If a backboard is the only way you can play tennis, that is far better than not playing at all.

Despite the odds many women do remarry at some point down the road, but you cannot allow yourself to let that be your life's goal. Rather, you must begin to reexamine what you are as an individual, something many women may not have done. There is also a tendency among the members of a couple to divide responsibility; one does the bills, the other the taxes, for instance. Now you will have to assume or resume all the responsibilities. When you are married and part of a couple you could be a quiet person with an outgoing husband and still maintain friendships. Now things are different and you must force yourself to become more outgoing. It is not reasonable to ask for total change, but modification is almost essential. If your husband was the person who always decided about cars and other large purchases, you are going to have to drag yourself into a car dealer eventually in order to make that purchase. If you choose to bring one of your adult children or a friend, that is acceptable so long as you do not diminish yourself by allowing the auxiliary person to make your decision. You, the newly single woman, will be making a strong statement of position by attempting to do some of these things in your own manner and also in your own time. Everyone has their own clock and what may seem slow to Mary may seem too quick to Anne. You must go at your own pace. That pace will vary as time goes on. Decisions will probably become easier for you. Certainly purchasing a car will not assume the proportion of selecting your husband's coffin. That was trauma. This is a difficult choice. In remembering the difference you may well be able to make the appropriate decisions in your new life with the right perspective.

As you begin to realize the importance of discovering once again who you are, you will find there is a different world out there. Even if you worked all the years of your marriage, that world will look different once you are widowed. Even jokes of co-workers may suddenly seem to have overtones that you ignored at a different time in your life. You may walk away wondering whether he was making a sexual overture or is this the way he always was. You may ask yourself whether people always avoided using the word "dead" or is that new because of your situation. In effect, now that you are a widow you do hear with a different ear. You cannot avoid so doing, but take a deep breath, give co-workers the benefit of the doubt and assume friendliness still exists where it always existed. You will come to recognize when a man makes a true sexual overture soon enough and, if it is not appreciated, simply tell him he is making you uncomfortable. This sort of honesty will allow you to remain friends and hopefully will make him more selective in how he speaks to you.

You will discover, too, there is another mainstream of people who are not coupled. You will have to search for your niche and you may well get lost a number of times before you find it.

One woman whose husband died when she was in her mid-forties decided her salvation lay in being busy. She volunteered for every project that came to hand, but as the time came for doing the actual work she invariably called in to say she was not well. After a while she felt foolish and those who knew her did not take her volunteering seriously. She was pushing herself in her frenzy to ease the pain. You cannot enter the mainstream or any part of society when you *think* it is time. It must be when you *feel* it is time.

When you begin to sense you are indeed moving forward, know it is urgent to help yourself go ahead. The statistic on the remarriage of widowers may help prod you along. Some studies indicate that 75 percent remarry within three years; they generally choose someone twenty years younger. Once again, these numbers should help serve as an impetus to make you understand the absolute necessity for developing your own life. While it has been said that second marriages are the triumph of hope over reality, the facts seem to indicate that there may well not be a second marriage in your future, especially if you are middle-aged or older. Yet that does not mean you must deprive yourself of a future. That future is still out there waiting for you to grab hold.

Women take different approaches to widowhood. For some there is a sense of anchorless drifting. Women who in their despair fall into this state are the ones for whom life no longer holds any promise, any solid earth beneath their feet, because they will allow no promise or anything steady to enter their worlds. These are the women who have simply given up and do not care whether they live or die. Ironically, they are not always alone. Often they do have caring friends and family but have chosen this sad route rather than the pathway that might ultimately help them stop floating.

Then there are the women to whom the past is everything. The good old days are painted in such rich hues that it is difficult for them to return to the bleak black and gray which they now perceive to be their lives. You may be such a widow, the type of woman who, when it is suggested you take a job or change your residence, responds by saying her husband would not have liked that. You must, in order to leave this glowing past, be able to say goodbye and mean it. You cannot go on being someone's widow when it is more important to become yourself. The idea of becoming entrapped in what *was* as opposed to what *is* will prevent you from being a part of your new reality.

Someone once compared widows who only look backward into the past to a driver who places newspapers on her front windshield and leaves the rear window clear. If you see yourself in this description perhaps you can take a small step and just pull a little piece of newspaper off the front windshield. By doing just a little at a time you may well find that after a while, much to your surprise, that front window has become as clear as the window in the rear, and what you see out of it is not so frightening.

Then there are women who have deliberately chosen to avoid reality. These are the women who have found themselves unable to meet their "today." These are the women who use alcohol and drugs and fattening foods to help keep reality at bay. They refuse to deal with their pain or attempt to work through it. Sometimes these women include shopping and frequently going to doctors as part of their grieving pattern. These remedies offer only Band-Aid therapy—they merely cover the wound rather than heal it.

You may be one of those women who, after time spent in each of these sad phases, now find themselves ready to take a long hard look at what is around them. You may use binoculars for that first look because you still have a tenuous sense of wishing to keep some distance from things that might cause you pain. Regardless of how you begin, you will eventually be able to leave the binoculars behind and see your world with honest, undistorted perception. If you are willing to take such a look you will find the world not a bad place after all. It can be a place that still offers reasons to live and enjoy. Things will not be easy. But you can find the world again. Hopefully you will take up with old friends, and perhaps join a support group of other grieving people. Such a group will induct you into a whole new world where there is automatic understanding of what you have endured.

If you are willing to leave your cocoon of grief and step into such a group you will find yourself in the most luxurious situation of all, that of being with knowing, loving people who do not require explanations about feelings and moods. People who merely want to be there for themselves and for you can be very comforting when you each must address many of the same painful issues.

It is important too to recognize financial limitations when attempting to reenter the world. If you do take up with your old friends or make new ones it is a good idea to suggest that everyone pay their own way. Old friends with limited funds have been known not to include a widow after she repeatedly does not offer to pay her share of a restaurant bill or movie ticket. If this has happened to you, you might make it clear at the outset that you insist on paying for yourself. You may suggest handing the gentleman your portion of the dinner check privately if you are with people who might view a woman's paying as a discomfort. But never allow yourself to be placed in the situation of not being included merely because you did not think about your financial responsibility. Never allow your old friends to feel discomfort because they have to pay for you when they simply cannot or don't wish to do so. This is in their best interest, but more important, it is in yours. Many widows who claim they are now ostracized can hold this simple issue to blame for the break in friendships. That is no more than a friendship lost by default.

There is a great irony to yet another pitfall that lurks in the background for many widows. Sometimes children should be seen and not heard, especially when they are older children. There is a tendency in many families for adult children to take charge when a father dies. Widows, feeling all too alone and frightened, are often glad to relinquish their roles as parents. Instead, a serious role reversal begins in which an adult child starts to make decisions that are rightfully left in the province of the widow.

This often begins with the funeral arrangements. The children, with the kindest of motives in wishing to spare their mother, take it upon themselves to make decisions, whether good or ill, that should have included input from the widow.

This issue is particularly important because so often precedents are set early on in the grief process and there is no going back. If Mother could not handle Father's funeral, we had better help her decide whether to remain in her house, what to do with her husband's clothing; when should she go out in public again; what friends to retain. The list is endless and precarious. If a widow who has been knocked nearly senseless by the devastation of her loss does not have the fortitude to look about her in the beginning she may suddenly find herself becoming a dependent child. Ironically when that occurs she is frequently considered an annoyance by her children and family members. Sometimes people create their own monsters.

Not too long ago one funeral director in Ohio looked about at the group of people who had come to make the decisions about their father's burial. "I asked them where their mother was and they said she was home absolutely prostrate with grief. I asked if they would mind my telephoning her and they agreed to allow me to do so.

"Although she was truly devastated and had been tranquilized, I asked what suit she wished her husband to be buried in. She told me his navy blue one. I thanked her for offering us some guidance."

While certainly this way of handling the situation was less than ideal, the director succeeded in reminding the widow that she still had a position in the family and the right to make a decision. Her children told the director they would have decided upon the same suit and wondered why he bothered to call. He explained the need to maintain their mother's status even though she was now a widow. He told them she was still their mother, their parent and their father's wife. The director said he was pleased at how the family has interacted with their mother since that time.

She has since become involved in a support group which he sponsors and is making steady headway into building a new life. The reason this takes on a measure of urgency is that ultimately the adult children will go back, and rightfully so, to their own lives. They will become busy socially with their contemporaries, their children and their jobs. It is the widow whose life has changed most drastically. It is her home and bed that are empty. Because no one should expect to replace a husband with a son, regardless of how good a son, it is urgent that the widow see her own options, make her own decisions and build on them, even if they are not the right decisions. Taking charge again would allow her to learn, to grow, to stand on her own without her child's hand in hers.

For many women this simply does not happen. They went from their father's home to their husband's home and now they go to their son's control! When will they be themselves?

If you see this happening to you, try a support group as a beginning, for it is there that you will hear other women either reflect your own sense of helplessness or discuss some of their own strengths. You might sit back and hear a woman simply throw her hands up in disgust at not being able to do or decide anything. Seeing a nonfunctioning human being—what you might become—may help you decide to make changes.

On the other hand, you may find a perfectly marvelous, sensitive widow who is a bit further along the healing path and who can serve as a role model. Frequently such women are willing to take newcomers under their wings and encourage them to go forward with their lives. Role models can be invaluable.

Sometimes widows develop almost desperate feelings about remarriage; given the statistics perhaps all that energy could be better channeled into some positive activity. The old saying about a watched pot never boiling may be modified to "Intense widows don't seem to meet marrying men." If you want to meet men but abhor the bar scene, you might help yourself by deciding to just go on with your life. Possibly taking a class in something of interest can start you in a new direction. Hobbies are important. Nothing can be sadder than to think you do not leave your house day after day because no one has called you to make plans. Since telephones operate both ways, why don't *you* initiate some plans? You never know. There may be another widow just down the street fretting and wishing someone would call her.

By the same token it is not always necessary to befriend widows exclusively. Sometimes a good mix is healthier. Getting perspective on how younger people live will offer you some balance. Becoming completely homogeneous can be the road to becoming boring. Mix your friends and you will have a nice blend that will keep you in touch with all the current thinking.

There are many widows who simply closed their kitchens after their husbands' deaths. If you have stopped inviting people to your home do not be surprised when they stop inviting you. Your new sad situation does not sit well for all time as an excuse to do nothing. There is a time when, even if you use paper plates to make it easier, you must begin to work on doing your fair share of the entertaining. Remember, people will go along for a time, but after a while they will see their efforts are not being reciprocated. They may begin to feel you are taking advantage of their good nature and slowly the invitations will decrease.

You became a widow through no choice or action of your own. That is a tragedy. By not acting or becoming involved you are furthering that tragedy for yourself. Although you were not widowed by choice how you function as a widow is certainly a choice. Make that choice in a way that will allow growth and a measure of peace.

It might be helpful for you, the widow, to take stock of just what is happening to you. Remember there is always a balance sheet in life. Take a sheet of paper and begin your inventory just as a businessman takes stock of his inventory. Write down what you know to be your problems. Loneliness? Despair? A sense of futility? Ask yourself on paper what remedies you might have for these problems. An example might be: "I am lonely. In order to ease this I will _____" and fill in an answer. Remember, today's answer might not suit your mood a month later, but deal with today. Your answer to the "I will _____" might include some of the following ideas:

- Attending church auxiliary meetings
- Becoming involved in civic functions
- Offering to do telephone work for an organization
- Taking a class in an adult setting

If you are having sexual difficulties discuss them with a counselor who might offer some suggestions. Since this is such a specialized area it might be wiser to see a mental health professional rather than a minister. Some women have found comfort and even a touch of warmth from things of meaning to their late husbands. Try these things:

- Holding his pillow when trying to sleep
- Wearing his pajamas
- Sleeping on his side of the bed

It is also most important to remember your role in the family. If you are a parent, regardless of the age of your children:

- Do not allow a role reversal. Do not turn into their child and allow them to make all your decisions.
- Attempt to become even more a part of your grandchildren's lives. In this busy society where most mothers and fathers are forever rushing, your involvement, if handled well, could be a blessing to all.

For Widowers

Death lies on her, like an untimely frost
Upon the sweetest flower of all the field.
—WILLIAM SHAKESPEARE

Along with the bride who walked down the aisle in her beautiful
white gown thinking thoughts of a wonderful life to be, you,
the bridegroom, shared those moments and thoughts. Perhaps
you wore tie and tails or a suit with a carnation in your lapel.
You stood before your minister or rabbi or priest shining and
proud and yes, perhaps a bit nervous. But your nervousness
was quickly allayed when you took your bride's hand and made
your vows. As the years went on you started plans and dreams,
probably children. You turned to her when you were hurting.
Perhaps co-workers had been less than kind. You might have
lost a job or a business. She was there for you. Your wife traveled
with you on that dream vacation or perhaps sadly you never got
to take it.

It is unlikely from the time you married and through all the
byways that make up the curving path of life you ever thought
you would be left without her. Left as half a couple. No, you
believed somehow the two of you would live out your years
together and it would be an endless marriage.

How different is your new reality!

As you stood over her coffin you were dazed, and wondered

if any of this was real. Could there be any sense in such a heart-rending situation? What would become of you? How would you manage all alone?

One man who became a widower after his wife had been ill a short time said his first reaction was a wish to punch the doctor. "He was talking about my wife. We had been married thirty-two years. Sure, we had our ups and downs, our good times and bad, but she was my *wife*, the person I relied on to be there. Suddenly this man was standing at her hospital bed, shaking his head and telling me that the person I had relied on wasn't there anymore. I know the statistics. I know that women outlive men. That's what I always expected to have happen in my life. But that's not the way it worked. She died first. I didn't know what to do."

His candor was refreshing. There are many times in a life when we make certain assumptions. It is part of our cultural conditioning. Men simply assume that their wives will be there until the end. Insurance actuary tables confirm this assumption. When his wife died he was not only bereft of his partner, he was also bereft because somehow the system had gone awry.

One man said during the time of his wife's wake he could not stand the "dithering fuss made over him by everyone including his children.

"They seemed to baby me as they do their own children. I'm certainly not one of their kids yet I didn't want to turn them away so I just let it go on."

This man found after some months that he had erred. It would have been far better, according to him, had he simply called a halt to a pattern he had no desire to see furthered. He did not enjoy being "babied" because it made him realize all the more strongly just how vulnerable his position was.

"My kids never treated me that way before and this sudden turnabout was no help at all."

He ultimately sat down with his family and did express himself, did share with them how he felt about what they were doing. He said at first they were offended. They seemed to think he was telling them not to involve him in their lives. But slowly, patiently, he made them understand the role reversal was weakening him rather than strengthening him.

"Now we all know one another better and can help one another when the time is right. But what a price. My wife is dead!"

He said until he sat down with his children he never realized how often his wife had served as an intermediary between him and his offspring. None of them had developed the habit of communicating directly with one another because the mother and wife had acted as a sorting machine. Because of this he and his family had to learn how to have direct contact with one another.

Often the wife has been the communciations link to the world at large. How cut off the widower may then feel at her death.

Very often widowers suffer from the reverse of the most pressing problems confronted by widows. While widows are hurt because they feel abandoned by society and frequently claim the world is paired off, two by two, with no room for a single woman, this is rarely the case with a widower. Instead, men often have to fight their way through the crowds of women who flock to their side at the time of their greatest pain.

One widower, an extremely acute observer of behavior, insists widows and others who came to his wife's funeral seemed to be sizing him up for future attention even at that early moment. Other men have said they experienced the same sensation.

Things are not easy for a widower. He needs to deal with learning self-sufficiency and many other things in this new plateau of his life. He needs also to deal with his sexuality. This, as it is for widows, is a real and important issue. Men, like women, feel the need to be touched, to be held and cared for. Unless they begin dating quite soon, they feel equally the emptiness of that unused pillow lying next to them.

There are many areas in which widowers experience the same response and pain as widows. Much may depend upon the role he played as a husband. Sometimes widowers feel the same sense of uselessness that widows feel when they have nursed a mate for a long time.

One man for many years had cared for a wife who suffered

from a chronic illness. Because he was retired, taking care of her had become the sole function in which he felt useful. When she died he was not faced with the plight of many of the "hamburger set." He was fully able to cook and clean for himself. But still the anguish that besets everyone who mourns a special person also affected him.

"When I would get ready to leave the apartment it took me a long time to not automatically reach for her walker or look around for it. I would get to the car and instinctively walk to the passenger side to open her door."

Many other widowers experience the same things. They forget briefly what has occurred and open a restaurant door and stand aside to let their wives enter first.

Frequently widowers are faced with day-to-day problems and decisions that at their vulnerable time take on great potential for pain. One man said his wife's presence seemed to override everything he touched or did. "She seemed to be looking over my shoulder as I did the laundry and washed the dishes." He said although she died nearly a year ago he still thinks in terms of wanting her to approve of how he does household chores.

"I felt strange," he said, "when I went into the paint store and picked out a color for the kitchen that needed painting. My wife always chose the colors and here I was making a decision in her area. Her sphere. I kept wondering if she would approve."

He said his first inclination was just to cover the walls with the same color that was on there but he decided to make a different choice because he knew he was taking a first step toward establishing his new status in life. Although he was not comfortable, his inner sense of survival convinced him it was necessary.

When his children came to visit after he had repainted the room they were surprised. "They looked at one another and I think they saw that their mother was truly dead and things would not be the same for them or for me. They might not have liked it at first but I think I did them a favor. At least I hope so!"

Up until that painting time the pattern had been their constant reminder that mother had always done things thus and so. They wanted no change, but ultimately change would come to them anyway. He merely moved it along a bit more assertively.

The lesson to be learned here is, when is help no longer helpful? Probably when the person being aided does not feel he is moving forward as a result of the help.

While many widowers have the "advantage" of still needing to carry on their jobs, they pay a heavy toll for this luxury. They pay for it in their deprivation of a time to mourn. They go to work and their employers are not certain about what they may appropriately demand by way of a work load from a newly bereaved man. The man, attempting to duck the pain he is feeling, throws himself into his work and often does not come up for air. By the time he gets home he is so tired he falls into bed and awakens just in time to start another day. On the surface this might seem like a lifesaving technique for a widower. But he must allow himself some time in which to grieve because pain of that sort will not stay buried and frequently will raise its ugly head sometime in the future.

Often fellow workers have done all the "right things" by sending a card filled with signatures, perhaps sending flowers and sometimes even attending a visitation time with their spouses. But when the widower returns to the office or the job, he finds, oftentimes, he is greeted by a group of people who appear to walk and talk gingerly around him. It is very rare indeed for a co-worker to ask a widower how he is feeling and really *mean* it. It is more rare still for the widower to respond honestly. An honest answer can run the entire gamut on any given day from managing well to being overwhelmed with emotion. Yet to share the pain at the office does not seem to be quite what is expected or desired in the work situation. That work situation is also carried over into lunchtime. In his own way the widower often finds himself isolated in a crowd.

One man said his company had an annual family picnic to which all families were invited. Each was assigned food to bring for the day-long event.

"When they passed around the slips of paper they just walked right past me. When I asked what my assignment was, Joe, my buddy, looked surprised. He said they didn't think I would be attending—after all it was a family function—and if I did I certainly would not be bringing anything!

"What did he think? Just because my wife was dead didn't mean I had lost my humanity. I sure wanted to go to that picnic but I suddenly didn't feel welcome anymore."

Sadly, he did not attend and found himself raging inwardly all that day and by the time the picnic day came along he was barely speaking to his co-workers.

"They would walk around me kind of softly and give each other knowing looks that I felt like pasting them in the mouth for! They never even asked why I was so angry. They just assumed it was because I was grieving."

Of course in the cool light of reason this man should have told his fellow employees just what he was feeling. Since none of us are mind readers this responsibility has to rest with the person experiencing the pain or anger.

As in many other phases of coping with the death of a special person, how you are treated can frequently be determined by *you:*

• When the assignment slips were passed around the man could have said he wasn't certain he could attend but would appreciate being included in the preparation plans.

• He could have added that he would like to be included in or at least asked to any future company events.

It would benefit him to know the choice is his. If you are forthright about your feelings your chances of being understood are greater. This can help you to avoid the pitfall of feeling even further removed.

One of the more difficult problems a widower faces is the inability to share feelings intimately with a friend. Certainly men have a fair share of bowling buddies and co-club members and bridge partners. But close and intimate friendships between males is rare. There is a standing joke that when two men have not seen one another for twenty years and feel a genuine fondness for one another they must first punch each other on the shoulder playfully before giving themselves permission to hug!

Rather a sad commentary on how most men interact with one another. This makes it all the more difficult for a man to have a close and intimate discussion with another man about his emotions, his anger and guilt, after his wife has died. When asked how he is doing, the widower himself is more than likely to respond with an innocuous, "Well, it's rough, you know." How inadequately he is describing his feelings! Does he cry? Does he resent her death? Does he feel there were times he could have been a better husband? She a better wife? He is sharing none of this with his friend because he has not been conditioned to do so. "It's rough" is a poor substitute for describing emotions that are painful and intense.

Life has been compared to licking honey off a thorn. Nowhere is this more evident than when a man experiences the intense pain of having his wife die. He has tasted the honey most of the time; he has come to accept its presence as his due. Then, when faced with the prospect of a new, unfamiliar life, he begins to see only the thorn. He is convinced there can never be joy again. But unless you absolutely and utterly give yourself to bitterness and despair you can find meaning and happiness once again. It may not be the same kind but there is hope for anyone who is mourning the death of a wife. Whether or not you choose to remarry is not the issue. You must choose to rebuild your life first and then make an intelligent decision about whether you wish to have another wife.

You cannot avoid the fact that you are outnumbered by women. You may in fact turn out to be one of the men referred to as "casserole kings." These are men who are deluged with casseroles and any other "goody" an unmarried woman might think of to entice you. If you appreciate these gestures, fine. If you do not, however, and most men do not, then a firm handling of the situation is required.

• Thank the woman who is on your doorstep. Say you appreciate her thoughtfulness but you are well able to provide for your own meals. If the food is given in a *returnable* dish and you are not interested in maintaining the contact by all means ask her to come in and wait just a moment while you transfer the food into a container of your own.

• For your own comfort, learn to cook. You might soon tire of having to eat out, especially if you live in an extremely hot or cold climate. If necessary, take a cooking class.

• If you know other unmarried men, ask them to join you and make this a night out for all of you.

• Try not to begin dating women before you are ready. You will certainly experience some nervousness when you do begin, and if you feel ready at least you will feel more comfortable with your decision to date.

• Don't allow yourself to be "mothered" by well-meaning female family members. Too much mothering may feed into a sense of helplessness. You have lost so much with the death of your wife, don't lose your status as a functioning, thinking, adult male.

• Remember, help is no longer beneficial when the mourner feels imposed upon. If you feel resistant to aid that is being offered examine your feelings. It is possible to tell someone nicely to step back a bit, without losing the relationship. If you say nothing you will harbor ill feelings and ultimately push the friend or relative away. By explaining your need to start doing a bit more deciding about things yourself, you are being honest and assertive—both qualities to be admired.

For Children

Do ye hear the children weeping, O my brothers?
—ELIZABETH BARRETT BROWNING

Perhaps one of the most difficult tasks any youngster can undergo is that of trying to make some sense out of the death of a parent. So many questions go unexplained. So many feelings are ignored. Frequently children are merely offered platitudes when they deserve the same respect for their pain as any adult deserves and expects.

Without question the child whose parent dies will be altered for all time. That does not mean the child must become an inadequate adult or a nonachieving youngster. Nevertheless, the child's life will always be colored by the death.

One man whose mother died of a heart ailment when he was in his early teens describes the impact of a parent's early demise.

"No matter how I tried to understand and work things through I always came down to the bottom line that she could have lived had she chosen to. The doctors talked with me, my Dad talked with me and it made no real difference. I felt abandoned. Mothers are not supposed to leave their children by up and dying on them! Especially when those kids still play Little League ball and go to Cub Scout meetings where everyone else's mother sits and watches!

"Sometimes I hate her for dying and other times I understand she didn't choose to die. But the bottom line is she died when I still needed a mother."

He was so hurt by this, he said, before he would agree to marry his wife he insisted she have a complete physical examination to make certain his children would never have to face the pain and aloneness he endured.

Ironically, although his experience was painful, he apparently received more help from other adults than most young people get. At least he was in a situation where attempts to answer his questions were made. That is not the general rule.

In most homes when a parent dies virtually no attention is given to the children. Instead they walk around looking for someone with whom to speak. If they are talked to at all, they generally hear clichés or, worse, statements that are simply untrue. "Mommy is away for a while." "Mommy is in the hospital now." In fact, with the best of intentions Mommy is placed anywhere but where she really is and that is dead.

With all the love and care in the world the surviving parent generally simply cannot muster the energy to speak to the children. Instead, immersed in his own pain and bewilderment, he allows them and their needs to be ignored. What most children express when they reach adulthood is that they really lost both parents during that time.

Frequently, these children must deal with a parent who is simply too tired or too uninterested to become involved in their schooling. No one asks whether homework is being done. Unless such youngsters have great inner strength or some friend of the family to whom they can turn, they are like kegs of dynamite waiting for the match. They, too, often turn to negative aspects of their personalities in a bid for attention. Sadly, only then does their parent see or hear them.

Here are some areas in which to act when a child is hurting.

• Call the school the day before your child plans to return and ask the teacher or homeroom counselor to meet the returning student outside the classroom and offer private condolences.

Then, if the youngster is willing, the teacher might ask if he would agree to having his classmates offer a moment of silence in memory of the dead person. If this is done in younger grades make certain the time is limited to a few moments as children who feel tension may begin to giggle out of nervousness. Further, the teacher may ask one of the class leaders to help the returning student catch up on his work. This contact with the "popular" student may help the youngster reintegrate with his fellow students more quickly.

• There are support groups for young people whose parents have died. If children are willing to attend it may help immensely to have an arena in which to discuss the problems they are trying to cope with and cope with alone.

• Hire a high school student to come in after school and do homework with your child. If you cannot offer your companionship, try to find someone to help fill the void.

• Force yourself to spend a set amount of time really listening even if that time period is only half an hour after school or before bedtime. You brought these children into the world and you have a responsibility to them.

A woman once asked how she could explain the death of his father to her child when she did not understand it herself. Her therapist gave her a simple rule of thumb: "Don't reply. Hug. When you're ready the replies will come."

Sometimes young people are not even given the dignity of a decent explanation of what transpired. How did their parent die? Was everything possible done? Was the youngster himself responsible because he didn't keep his room clean? What about God in all of this? What does it feel like to die? Who will provide for him now? Who will take care of him? The questions are endless. They run as long and as deep as a child's imagination, and that can be boundless.

Young children cannot take in all the ramifications of the death of a parent at one time. One young woman whose husband was a police officer killed in the line of duty said she explained to her son again and again that his father was dead. The boy, about seven, seemed to be listening intently. When she was all through he looked at her and said, "When's Dad coming home so we can have dinner?"

According to many in the mental health community this is not an unusual situation. Children have their own limits as to what they will internalize at any given time. It works almost like food. They can only absorb so much at a time and then they are filled up and can take in nothing else for the moment. Therefore, when explaining to a child it is important to keep the situation simple. Tell enough for understanding and if the child is not satisfied allow him the opportunity to ask questions. These may not necessarily occur at the time you first sit down with him. Hours may go by or even days before more is asked. Then, as before, keep your answers simple and do not fabricate when you do not know. Honesty is the easiest and by far the most helpful approach when a youngster asks questions.

As they attempt to grope forward, children need guidance. Unfortunately, if you are a surviving spouse, offering guidance may simply be too difficult at first. The risk is that early patterns may prove lasting. This is a time when early counseling may be necessary. Contact a clergyman, funeral director, school counselor or professional mental health person whose *specialty* is dealing with survivors. Many communities have services available on a sliding financial scale. Meet as a family unit in order to learn how to function as one!

Very often, the adults around a youngster whose parent has just died do not understand the depth of emotional feeling the child is experiencing. Sometimes the child may be merely playing and looking supremely uninterested in all the emotion and tumult around him. Unfortunately this attitude is taken literally by far too many adults, and they do not address the child's emotional needs. While it is important not to push more information on a youngster than he wishes to have at any given time it is equally important to recognize the child is hurting even if he is at play. Sometimes giving the child a hug can be enough for the moment. At other times talking about the tragedy and validating how the child is hurting may be helpful. At least he then feels there is a willing and listening ear for him. A hug always offers warmth and to a youngster it can offer a steadying hand in a reeling world.

Remembering the child and showing concern can also be the role of a close family friend. A child generally trusts such a friend and he or she can offer real support by showing tenderness and offering a caring heart.

Although a French proverb says a father is simply a banker provided by nature, fathers make much wider and deeper contributions than those from their wallets. They are often the ultimate symbol of security for children. This surprises many people. After all, in most traditional homes the father is gone most of the day and spends very little time at home. Yet he may still be the bulwark of the establishment. When all else fails and all avenues lead to dead ends, children often turn to their fathers.

What happens when that father dies and the children are still at home? In most cases the household continues to run because the mother is there to prepare the meals and the like. Insurance has often provided a blanket of financial security. But the cornerstone is missing and that is very difficult for offspring of any age to come to terms with.

"When my dad died it was like a shot out of a gun," said one teenaged man. "He went to work one day and they called us from there. He had a heart attack and he was dead. Can you imagine, my dad was dead! I didn't believe it. I kept thinking such stupid things. Who is going to help put the dock out at our summer place this year? That was the first thing I thought about. I wasn't going to let my mind deal with that moment. That day. I was just going to look down the road because that moment was too painful."

This sense of not wishing to deal with the moment is often expressed by surviving sons and daughters.

There are, of course, families in which the father's death is more than an emotional hardship. Many sons and daughters find their whole lives have changed owing to their father's death. Often, youngsters feel they can no longer continue with their educations despite student loans and Social Security benefits.

While these benefits will aid a bereaved son or daughter they do not provide revenue for the family. While we hear of many self-made people who grew out of this morass into financially secure men and women, there are far more who threw in the towel and merely worked at jobs instead of building careers. Sometimes hard choices must be made. Education may have to be dropped or deferred. Some young people work through the day and attend classes in night school. Since Social Security currently stops at age eighteen, it often becomes mandatory for a mother to take a job if she wishes to help her child complete his education.

Kipling, in his "Mother of Mine" said,

> If I were hanged on the highest hill,
> Mother o' mine, O mother o' mine!
> I know whose love would follow me still,
> Mother o' mine, O mother mine!

That is far and wide the traditional view people have of mothers: the nurturer, the forgiver, the one who bandages the knee and rocks the cradle.

How does a youngster feel when he is told of his mother's death? The great stabilizer of his life is gone. How could she do this to me? What happens to me now?

One of the most troublesome phrases offered by well-meaning people who do not know quite what to say is, "Now you must take care of your mother" to a boy or "Now you are Daddy's little helper" to a girl. What a great responsibility to place upon a youngster! How difficult to visualize filling Dad's or Mom's shoes when you are eight or ten or fifteen. How unjust. Certainly there will have to be adjustments in how the family operates. Work and meals and after-school activities all need to be thought about and reworked. But they need rethinking as a family unit and not by outsiders who place the child in the role of an almost-spouse.

One woman whose husband died after only a few days of

illness has had great difficulty with her sixteen-year-old son.

"It's not that he's bad or gets in trouble with other kids. He just thinks he's the head of this household now. I was always a passive wife and let my husband run things. He ran the business. He ran this home. We both wanted it that way. Now he's dead and I feel out of my depth and yet I don't want any sixteen-year-old laying down rules about how I should live my life!"

Another woman has a daughter who is fourteen. This girl was very close with her father, who died of cancer. It seems that whatever the widow chooses to do comes under the fourteen-year-old's scrutiny. "Dad wouldn't have liked that." Or "Dad would like you to do thus or so." The widow, who has a highly developed sense of humor, said she feels as if she is living with a hall monitor who is laying down rules established by the school principal!

Many men who are widowed have commented on how critical their children are of female friends. They maintain this applies to children of both sexes. "But what can I expect after my brother told my daughter she was in charge of the house now? There is no reason she shouldn't feel she has a say in my adult life, at least according to her."

Boys are frequently told by well-intentioned callers that they are now the man of the house when a father dies. Or, if the mother has died, they are encouraged to become Dad's buddy, to help Dad get over this rough time. It seems to be completely forgotten that this is a youngster who has very little control over how his parent will respond. In order to be a buddy you need to have a buddy. Parents immersed in their own pain are rarely that.

There are, however, exceptions. One young woman knew she was dying of cancer and as she felt her death drawing closer she consciously began withdrawing from her son and encouraging her husband and son to become closer, more equal partners. Father made the decisions. Father and son cleaned house together and helped Mother. When a difficult problem arose for her son she would suggest he call Father at work even though he had a thriving medical practice. Although it was horribly painful for her to make the decision to withdraw, she regarded it as an ultimate act of love. She wanted to die knowing things were in place for her son and for her husband. She died feeling she had achieved that goal.

Her husband, in the aftermath of that tragedy, believes his wife acted appropriately and with great regard for her survivors. Not all people would agree. Many would say, perhaps, that whatever time she had remaining should have been intense quality time. Not everyone acts the same under the same circumstances. There are choices to be made and people must do as they think best at such an emotional time.

Sometimes when parents die young their children are left with values about parenting that are different from society's. One woman whose mother died early wanted nothing more out of life than to marry young and begin a family immediately. "I want to put the odds in their favor. If I marry young the chances I will live at least past their teens are great. I want them to grow up with an intact household."

Of course, there will be those who say they plan never to have children. After all, they can die and leave their children with all the so-well-remembered pain. It is important for anyone who thinks in terms of having a family and who has experienced the death of a young parent to get some counseling or attend a support group in which others with the same experience will share their perspectives.

When you love someone, there is never enough time. If there has been a close and loving relationship, surviving children, whether forty or sixty years of age, will still mourn the death of a parent. They, too, hurt. With the death of their parent goes a part of their own history. This is a time when many tender memories are shared or recalled. Despite all the current writings about how older people are "warehoused" by society there are any number of loving and giving relationships with older parents that are not condescending but rather meaningful to both parties. Mothers and daughters who always spoke by telephone daily had a special bonding. Regardless of the daughter's age, she will miss that daily contact.

Although she was in her middle-thirties when it occurred,

one woman recalled how quickly she chose to deny her mother's death. "My mother just could not be dead. It wasn't happening. Here I was pregnant with our first child and it was something Mom wanted so badly—to be a grandmother—and then she was just dead. Suddenly. I kept looking down at my fat belly and feeling so confused. Why? Why *then?*"

She said her mind would get distracted during those first days and she would forget momentarily. Then there would be another onslaught of the hurt she felt. How could her mother be dead? These things just didn't happen when someone was pregnant with a first grandchild.

Another woman, married more than thirty years and the mother of four children, said when her mother died she found the enormity of it unbearable. An introspective person, she said she believes there is a sense in all of us that somehow we are our parent's children. There is still a haven for us regardless of how long we have been married and how far along we have gotten in our lives. "It came as a shock to learn my mother still held such a strong place in my world. After all, we weren't even living in the same city. It was strange to feel orphaned at almost fifty years of age. I could almost imagine what a kid had to feel when that experience happened to me. I just couldn't believe any of it. That my mother was dead. I guess that I had a sense of mothers being forever. Maybe we all do. When that moment comes and someone tells you your mother or father is dead there is no way you can possibly believe it. How can something that is forever suddenly be terminated?"

There are many sons and daughters who have expressed much the same thought. The feeling that parents were immortal was always with them. They never gave a thought to their parents' death. Ironically, this did not apply only to teenagers. Very often older people with grown children of their own would know intellectually their parents would die. Yet, when the event actually occurred they were shattered with disbelief.

From working on batting practice with a youngster to sharing a business with an older son, many fathers develop close and loving relationships with sons. It is important not to assume that a fifty-year-old man is not hurting just because his father was seventy when he died. Each relationship is individual, indeed even between siblings and parent.

If there has been difficulty between parent and child it can make the finality of death even more painful. People feel there will always be time in which to put affairs in order. In reality, that is not the case. If things have not been put in order, children experience a pain that may last years after the death despite the fact that the parent was old.

It has been said that the problem with old age is that there is not much future in it! If all parents and children could remember that when they interact, perhaps there would be less of the guilt-ridden grief so many people face when their parents have died.

If you wish to give comfort to another adult whose parent has died, it is important to know the degree of closeness. Ideally, condolences should be tailored to the situation, but you don't always know the case. Err on the side of assuming the best possible relationship rather than otherwise.

If your children are younger, sit down with them and go through these steps.

• Ask them to draw a picture about what they have been feeling since their parent died.
• When they are through, ask them to describe the picture to you.
• Ask what they remember about their dead parent. Using a sheet of paper, make notes about what they are saying and date the paper.
• Offer to take them for a ride or walk in order to end the topic when you feel you have all had as much as you can handle.

If your children are teenaged, sit down with them after a meal and not during it.

• Tell them you wish to share some of what you are feeling, and share it. If it includes being angry with your dead spouse share that anger.

• Ask them what they are feeling. Ask each child separately by name. Are they frightened? Are they lonely? What do they miss the most?

• Offer them the opportunity to put this on paper. Tell them you wish to put it away in order to have them review it some day.

• Ask them each to share a good memory and then a bad memory of the dead parent to enable them to develop a sense of balance.

WHILE HAVING THESE DISCUSSIONS WITH YOUR CHILDREN MAKE CERTAIN YOUR TELEPHONE IS OFF THE HOOK OR TURNED OFF. THIS IS NOT A TIME FOR INTERRUPTIONS OF ANY TYPE.

For Siblings

The crest and crowning of all good,
Life's final star, is Brotherhood.
— EDWIN MARKHAM

One of the platitudes that frequently plagues young people is that experience is the best teacher. In fact, experience is the worst teacher—it gives the test before presenting the lesson!

Often when young people are confronted with the death of a sister or brother they are thrust into the middle of a tragic and ugly reality without any real experience or education about how they are to conduct themselves. Frequently the logical people to whom they should turn, their parents, are so devastated that they are of no help. In fact, many young people have described their parents as negative forces when a sibling dies. Many issues arise when a sister or brother dies that are never considered beforehand and rarely addressed afterward.

Far too often we treat our children in a childlike manner. We tend not to validate their feelings as we should. We often approach the consoling of a child with the mental attitude of, "He's just a kid, and what do kids know?"

In truth kids know a great deal. They know when they are hurting and when things are not being done to help ease that hurt. Often we carry into our dealings with children the attitude that because they are young they do not have profound feelings.

Many youngsters who had to deal with great pain by themselves because of this attitude have spoken of just how deep their feelings were at the time their sibling or special person died.

While we do not have the right to try to measure the intensity of one person's pain against another's, it is important if we wish to help our children to know that they, too, are hurting.

When an infant is stillborn after nine months of discussion with a young child about the new sister or brother, explanations are difficult. The same applies if the baby died after living only a few days. It is rare that a living child actually sees the dead stillborn. Therefore, there is always the level of fantasy that plagues those young survivors. Somehow the living sister or brother cannot get a mental image of the dead child and there is a sense of emptiness in the youngster. He cannot understand, frequently, why his mother and father are so despondent, so distressed. After all, they did not really know the baby. Why the fuss? Unfortunately, few parents take the time really to explain, on whatever level the living child is able to understand, the death of nine months of hopes and wishes and plans. Most youngsters are told, while the mother is still pregnant, how much fun it will be to have a baby. They are promised permission to hold and play with the infant. They frequently help set up the new nursery. Therefore, there is a sense of expectancy about having the baby come home from the hospital.

Can a child of four or younger understand just why the parents are so pained? Possibly not, but an attempt to explain should be made. The living sister or brother, regardless of age, must be considered a full-fledged member of the family. Information must be scaled down, but it must be given.

One woman now in her fifties still remembers what it felt like not to be informed about her sister's death. She was six years old when the infant died of a lung complication. She recalls vividly people crying and her home continually full of strangers who sat with her parents. She remembers not being able to get near her mother or father because the crowd around them was so large. Although she describes herself as a highly verbal six-year-old, she simply could not make her presence heard or felt.

She wandered aimlessly around the apartment trying to find a spot for herself, trying to find someone to speak with.

"This went on for days and days. Finally I cornered one relative who happened to be a clergyman and I asked where my sister was. Why was everyone so upset? He told me God wanted her but before he could continue he was called to sit with my mother. I never got a further explanation.

"When the house finally quieted down I thought I would have a chance to be with my mother and father. But that was never to be. From that day, the day everyone left, until my parents died I was never able to get close to them again. I felt removed, pushed aside. No matter how hard I tried I couldn't break into their trancelike state.

"People do grow up and learn to manage with whatever life doles out to them but when my sister died I lost a sibling and a mother and a father. Her death became almost more important than my life."

This woman has gone forward with her life and built a flourishing career and a happy marriage with four active, thriving children. But there is still a place in her heart, she says, that weeps with the anguish of being abandoned at the age of six.

Although there are no monsters in this sad tale, in its own way it is a horror story; one fraught with anguish and misunderstanding and the displacement of the living for the dead.

What makes this story particularly poignant is the fact that it is not unique. It is instead a fairly common one, only varying in degree. Living children are often ignored. It is the rare child indeed whose pain is acknowledged by a parent or relative. The children are only noticed if they go outside and ride a bicycle or play loudly in the middle of the floor. Children need a break from all that pain, and they need someone to share it with.

One young man whose sister died said he resented it bitterly when he was chastised for bringing out his trucks. He was told he showed no respect for the dreadful circumstance that had occurred. This man, although young, was forceful. He told everyone in a loud voice that no one was showing *him* any respect because they were not talking with him and they were telling him to leave his parents alone. He remembers well confronting his weeping mother and challenging her because she was ignoring him.

"I told her I mattered, too. I needed her attention. I didn't want a bunch of strangers making my peanut butter and jelly sandwich because she was the only one who knew just how much jelly to put on!"

He said in retrospect the sandwich statement was foolish but somehow it got his mother's attention. Although she was still immersed in her pain she did get up from her couch at lunchtime and see to his sandwich. It was a small victory but he at least felt noticed!

Many children taught from an early age to believe in Santa Claus and the tooth fairy carry this mysticism into their thinking about death. They begin to believe they are omnipotent and have control by wishing for certain things. They are convinced that their wishes are being heard. If the wish is not granted, they feel, frequently, that the fault is in themselves. Somehow they were not good enough: a very hard and bitter thing to accept with a whole lifetime spread out before them.

Many youngsters who have had to deal with the problem of vying for a parent's time have felt resentment. Others have felt anger because a sister or brother carried tales to the parents. Although these are perfectly reasonable emotions when the sibling is healthy, they take on completely different overtones when that sister or brother dies. The most negative thought they ever had gets blown out of proportion until the surviving child believes completely that he was to blame for the tragedy.

One woman whose brother died when they were both young recalls vividly just this feeling.

"My brother was sick. He had cancer. I tried to be as patient as I could with him, as kind. But deep down in my heart I resented the time my parents spent with him at the hospital. Their whole lives revolved around whether or not he needed oxygen on a given day. I would come home with an excellent report card and they would give it only a cursory glance. Certainly now that I am an adult I can understand that report cards are not as momentous as having a dying child. But I sure didn't understand it when I was a kid.

"There were many times I wished my brother would just die so I could have my parents back. Then when he finally did die I felt responsible. I certainly couldn't turn to my parents and tell them I had wished him dead. They would never have understood. This became a dark secret that I kept buried in me until years later I discussed it in therapy."

Wishing someone dead certainly does not sound like a kindly attitude, but when a youngster feels his position has been totally usurped, when he is convinced that communication with his parents is blocked, he frequently reverts to this wishful thinking. To his lifelong pain and suffering, he adds the idea that somehow he was responsible. Cancer did not kill that woman's brother. She did. Or so she perceived it. This is a feeling that can be shared within a group or, if necessary, with a private therapist, because the emotion is fairly common and yet remains one of life's best-kept secrets.

Some things that may be done to help do *not* require stores of energy a parent simply does not have. Someone close at hand, perhaps a clergyman or a funeral director, should remind the parents that attention must be paid to the living child or children. Certainly it is impossible to expect a vast amount of attention, but some is necessary. If children have always shared a bedroom it is a basic act of human kindness to ask the child if he wishes to remain in that room. Possibly switching the furniture around and placing beds at different angles may be of help. Perhaps removing the bed of the dead child could ease some of the pain of the surviving child. These are things that need discussing and need explaining. Children need to be remembered; they need to be asked what they feel.

Most important is the restructuring of the family. All too often, when there has been an illness, children are left to fend for themselves. This pattern grows even stronger after a death. One mother of teenagers, when shown the family disintegration, was alarmed. A divorced mother, she was merely using the home as a place to hang her hat. Ultimately, after counseling, she told her children they would from here on in share three meals a week. She allowed their input by asking which nights would work best for them. Not only did she regain a hold on her family, her children had the benefit of structure and with it the wonderful blanket of security it so often accompanies.

Mental health specialists have derived a rule of thumb that may be helpful in learning how to communicate with youngsters about the death of a sibling, or about any death. They believe a child of five knows death is final. A child of six becomes quite emotional. A child of seven is curious and apt to ask many questions, and a child of eight is able to understand the information and cope on a higher level than one might expect.

As children become older, they can be made a productive part of the dying process in a terminal illness, providing thought is given to their understanding and limitations. When a child wishes to help his dying brother or sister, it can become a beautiful experience. Tasks may be assigned such as checking of intravenous fluid levels, keeping track of visiting times, preparing meals. If a sibling is given such opportunities while his brother or sister is dying he will be able to hold onto his memory of assisting and hug it tightly when he becomes a mourner. By being allowed to help he is being given something to put into his emotional bank for the day after the death when he feels the bank is empty.

As these survivors become older still, there are problems that may arise and should be guarded against. One young man had pulled off the road to change a flat tire and was hit and killed by a drunk driver who swerved into him. His sister, aged twenty-two, had always lived at home with her parents; she received the call from the police. She accompanied her parents to the funeral home where they were asked to make selections and decisions about the type of funeral they wished for their son. In each case the mother would turn to this sheltered child and say, "Angela, you decide."

In sharing this experience, Angela was bitter.

"All my life they treated me like a kid. When I wanted to go away to school they insisted a daughter belonged at home. I even had time deadlines when I went on dates at twenty-two. Suddenly when it was time for me to be their child they turned me into the adult of the family. I made the decisions they wanted to the best of my ability. The funeral director was a big help.

He kept trying to involve my mother and father but they just wouldn't listen. The two of us made all the decisions but I am bitter as hell. I needed to be parented *then,* not when I was going out on a date!"

This role reversal is a serious but not uncommon problem. When a child dies, more often than not, the parents themselves wish to revert to being children, to those glorious days when life did not hurt so much. Yet, from Angela's perspective, such withdrawal was a great injustice.

On the other hand there are some adult children who actively wish to take on the role of parent at such a time. If this is a mutually agreed-upon decision, then well and good, but a parent should not feel his role has been usurped nor should an adult child feel pushed into manhood when parents have tried to keep him young.

It is very difficult in a close family to deal with happy times when a sister or brother has died. Many a Thanksgiving meal or a Christmas celebration is marred by the knowledge that the sibling will never again be a part of the festivities. Often this places extra burdens on surviving children. They frequently have to assume the role of more than one person to help fill the void. Frequently this is a silent, unspoken family expectation. If Betty always brought potato salad and Betty is dead, now it becomes Annette's turn to bring that salad along with her own offering. When she walks through the door carrying the two items, more often than not, especially early on, the sight of the potato salad is like a knife wound in the family's heart.

Would it not be wiser to do away with the potato salad and substitute another dish? This in no way means denying Betty lived, it merely means those still alive must go on and discover new means of coping.

Very often siblings suffer from "survivor's guilt." Why him and not me? To feel this is normal. To wonder why is normal, yet because it is rarely discussed it becomes a hidden item and as in all mourning emotions the deeper an issue is buried the more difficult it is to mend. At the recently erected memorial to the soldiers dead and missing from the Viet Nam conflict, in the nation's capital, a colonel was snapping pictures of the names etched into the marble of that memorial wall. Every soldier who died or has not been accounted for has his name engraved there. The colonel had tears in his eyes. When condolences were offered to him he said, "I am with the Green Berets and I toughed out a lot of situations over there. My brother, he was just a kid who decided to follow in my footsteps. He was killed a day after he landed; a sniper got him. He was young and had everything going for him. He shouldn't have died like that. I've lived and experienced. He never had a chance." When the colonel realized he had been crying he surreptitiously wiped his eyes and walked away, camera in hand.

"Why him and not me?" is a recurrent theme through the lives of most surviving siblings. It is of course a question that cannot be answered satisfactorily. The best anyone can really suggest is that there are no answers, because that is the truth.

Surviving sisters and brothers frequently get caught up in the trap of feeling they must now live for two. This is even more the case when dealing with twins. In a group setting this becomes a major issue and one that needs airing and re-airing until it has been brought home to the survivor that no one can do more than live the best life he or she possibly can. To live for two is in its most literal sense carrying around a dead weight. It will slow down the survivor because the load is backbreaking.

There is certainly room for sadness and feeling alone and lonely. There is room to question why not me. These are legitimate issues that need exploring. But they must not become a life's work or the sibling who survives is not fully alive. When that occurs there have been two deaths.

As a parent, take a few moments to really think about your dealings with surviving children. Ask yourself:

- Have I acknowledged their pain?
- Have I spoken individually with each child to know what he is thinking?
- Have I, even in little things, forced myself to attempt to be a parent?

- Have all disciplinary rules been removed from our home? Is there any structure whatever?
- Do I assume because my youngsters seem to be back in their routines that they are not hurting?
- Do I acknowledge that when they joke it is no different than when I do? Even in the midst of enormous tragedy people *do* smile. So do kids.

For Friends

When the rest of the world steps out your true friends step in. —ANONYMOUS

Perhaps one of the most overlooked groups of people who mourn deeply when a special person dies are friends. It has been said that a true friend will see you through when others see that you are through. What a sense of loss it is to know that the person you respect and love has died. While often you felt duty-bound to call your sister or brother or mother there was never a sense of duty about calling your friend. She was special to you in a hundred ways. You could share your intimate emotions with her and know they would not be looked upon with disdain. You could admit you had made a fool of yourself in a situation without being told that you always were a fool, even as a child. You often could look at one another and know that you had each taken in what a third person had said and was attempting to do.

Sometimes in long-term relationships there may be a sense of inseparability, a sense that identities have become intertwined. If the friendship has gone on long enough there may be the involvement of your children and hers. In fact, this person who was once a stranger had become an integral part of your life.

Now, with your friend's death you are truly bereaved.

Men, although less frequently, also develop close and lasting friendships. They regard these friends as far more than golf or bowling buddies. They are intimate companions. The people they feel free to share their innermost thoughts with. Sometimes men who wished to preserve macho images before wives and girlfriends would know they could turn to their old friend and share their fears about work and love and life in general.

You may have found that your old friend was the person with whom you could laugh with the greatest sense of freedom because that friend would understand the origin of your humor. In many cases, he was there when you went on your first date and made such a fool of yourself that you barely could talk about it with him and certainly would not share your embarrassment with anyone else. As you grew older you found yourselves able to recall those early moments with camaraderie and the certainty that there was a spirit of good will between you.

What a devastating loss to know that all that history you shared is now gone and, you fear, irreplaceable. You are truly bereaved.

When a special person dies there is a great void in which friends of any category find themselves. Family members frequently assume that friends who make condolence visits are there to comfort them. The reality is often the reverse. A close and dear friend is not a comforter. A close and dear friend is a mourner and a mourner of the first significance. Yet rarely are friends given their due. Rarely is a special friendship acknowledged. Even in eulogies, mention is made of friends in a more general rather than a specific way. Family members tend to decide that to single out a special friend might offend another. Yet that special friend should be recognized by the family and those who wish to offer condolences should accept this person as a mourner.

One woman died not long ago of cancer. During her final illness her children stopped to see her as often as their busy lives allowed. Her husband continued with his work and saw her after hours. But her two closest friends made her final months their life's career. They cooked for her and shopped for her. They alternated visiting so she never felt alone.

"If she said she needed some time to think about what was happening she knew I would leave her bedroom and be there for her in her living room. She never knew isolation and I thank God for it," said one of them.

"Then she died and it was an excruciatingly painful death. That was when the kids were together all the time and her husband stopped work. Suddenly after she was dead there was time! Well, they seemed to turn to me and Joanne for support and guidance. We did the best we could but who was there for *us*? Who could we turn to and say we were devastated by her death? Who was there for us?"

People who were not intimate with the family also wished to make condolence calls. When they came to the home they would not turn to the husband or children. They would turn to the dead woman's friends and ask, "How is everyone doing?"

"No one, but no one, recognized our pain and our grief. No one perceived us as mourners and that made us furious aside from all the other emotions we felt."

In a similar case, a corporate executive, a busy man himself, recalled, "You know, a lot of his 'buddies' would come and say things that were well-meaning but trite. They would lean over his bed and sometimes even talk around him as if he were already dead. They would leave and that was when we had our time to talk. My wife used to get annoyed because I always went to the hospital before coming home but we knew he was dying and the time spent was important to him as well as to me. Both of us needed to walk through this thing together as much as a well and a sick person can do such a thing.

"Sometimes we would just sit there and not talk at all. Both of us were thinking of when we were younger. Sometimes he would talk about what he was feeling about dying. About all the things he wouldn't have a chance to do. At first I used to turn away so he wouldn't see my tears. Then I decided, what the hell. I love this man. He's been a good and loyal friend all these years. Let him see my tears and know he will be missed and mourned."

The man said once when his friend saw him crying he, too, burst into tears. No words were exchanged but if the friend was able to pinpoint one special moment that superseded all other moments in their thirty-year relationship it was that time when they wept together.

"It might sound funny to say this, but we formed a bond when we shared our tears that even his death will never sever."

Despite this intimacy and commitment this close and dear friend shared the fate of most friends after the death. All the focus, all the condolences, went to the family. Never was a word of comfort offered to this man who had been such an important part of his friend's life. No one ever addressed his loneliness. No one ever asked if he felt anger or pain or bereavement. Those who came to call only asked how the family was doing or where to hang their coats.

Friends hurt too. They know pain. When their special friend dies, they have a past that can never be recaptured with any other human being. A close friendship such as this cannot be replaced. This does not mean there will never again be a good and loyal friend, a close friend. But a part of old history and the specialness of that particular friendship is gone for all time. Yet no one recognizes these mourners.

Then there is another type of friend, the one for whom there has not yet been an appropriate modern-day label. In an older era the friend might have been called a paramour. If you have loved a woman and shared much of your life with her and yet not married her, your status at the time of her death is sharply in question. You might well have to contend with a disapproving family who hated your living arrangements and still regard you as an interloper. Yet the dead woman's life was wrapped around yours in the most intimate and loving manner. How do you claim your place in the mourning process when such a tug-of-war exists? You are indeed a mourner but a mourner with no status.

Women caught in the same complex situation have often felt the brunt of family disapproval when the man they lived with died. One woman who steadfastly has denied the accusation is believed to have broken up her friend's home. How do you feel when his children and former wife, for whom he may not have cared, and his parents, turn their backs on you and do not welcome you into the family mourning room?

The problem becomes even more difficult when the special friend is of the opposite sex and there is a divorced or still legally married spouse. Regardless of how long the relationship continued, no matter how gentle and loving and caring it was, the relationship is still regarded as illicit by most of society and the man or woman who has lived with the now dead person is at best ignored and at worst vilified.

"I knew they hated me. There was never any question of that," said one woman. "But, my God, I never understood the magnitude of that hatred until John died.

"I knew all this because his older son came to my office one day. I guess he saw how distraught I had been at the funeral. We went for a cup of coffee and that was when I learned the facts of life. John is dead. I can't berate him. No apology to his family would mean anything. But he was very special to me. I loved him and he loved me. But I have to mourn alone. I can only share brief little episodes with the few friends we made mutually. My family was furious because I moved into an apartment with him before being married to him and certainly could never understand the depth of my pain."

Does this same difficulty also not come into play with former spouses? How difficult to wish to comfort your mutual children when they are made full parties in the mourning process and your mere presence exacerbates already high emotion and pain wihin the grieving family. Perhaps even though your spouse is now dead and you had the most bitter of divorces there is still a place within you that recalls the days when you were in love and planned a future together. This, indeed, is a most difficult position and one that is not uncommon.

If lovers and former spouses are not welcome in the family room they still do have a place at the funeral. A good suggestion is to attend the services only and to sit in an unobtrusive place.

Friends who are younger also frequently find themselves mourning alone. Despite all the caring and loving in the world, parents are not always able to understand the magnitude of pain that a young person may feel when a friend dies.

One young man whose friend died when they were both in the fourth grade received every kind and loving attention his parents had to offer. As the years went on they were certain the young man had "gotten over" his friend's death. However, as a senior high school project the boy was asked to write a short paper about a significant happening in his life. That short paper turned out to be a forty-page treatise on the life and times of his dead friend. The teacher was overwhelmed with the magnitude of what her young student had written and must be feeling. She contacted the boy's parents who were surprised and appalled at how much emotion still remained.

"We were certain we had done everything possible to help him when his friend died. Yet obviously more needed to be done."

One young woman had a friend who died more than fifteen years ago when they were both ten years of age. To this day she has never fully shared with her family the magnitude of what that death meant to her. She said when she feels low and worried she can still conjure up her friend and see him as he would be today, no longer a youngster but a person also in his mid-twenties. She said she sometimes has conversations with him and it helps her see problems through to a conclusion.

Does she mourn him? Not exactly. It is not an ongoing emotion but rather one that lies dormant and comes to the fore when she needs to feel she has a special friend. When asked why she never shared this with her parents she said they simply would not understand and perhaps might make light of something very important to her.

We all know friends are important. They help balance out a life and give us someone with whom to share intimacies and things that amuse us. But in the final analysis, although we have lived with our friends, have worried with them and laughed with them, there is still one aspect of friendship that has not yet fully been accepted by society. That is that friends do grieve. They hurt. They mourn.

They should be considered.

If you have endured the painful experience of having a friend die you might well consider what you wish your position to be with the family. Ask yourself:

- Do I wish to remain in close contact?
- Can I still share my own wishes and aspirations with these people?
- Can I stay in contact with my dead friend's children and be helpful to them?
- Can they be helpful to me?
- Will I feel better if I am able to "do things for the family"? Does doing things make me feel closer to my dead friend?
- Can I help myself more by remaining involved with the family or by gently removing myself?
- Have I remembered to grieve or have I gotten caught up in "caretaking"?

The Road
to Healing

Just as important as identifying who can be a mourner—and as we have seen that encompasses nearly everyone—is to understand some of the pathways mourners will face on their journey toward healing. The road will be tortuous and filled with fear and pain. Yet near journey's end there may be a new beginning; a fresh path. A path filled with promise and hope, two emotions mourners were certain they would never again feel.

In discussing sorrow, denial, anger, guilt, powerlessness and depression, the most important lesson you as a mourner will learn is *you are not alone.* The most important lesson you as a helping person will learn is how not to allow someone in mourning to feel isolated. If knowledge is power, then understanding is the motor that transforms that power into action. Use your understanding well, for if you do you will lend this world a touch of grace.

Pathways Through Sorrow

I walked a mile with Sorrow and ne'er a word said she;
But, oh, the things I learned from her
When Sorrow walked with me.
—ROBERT BROWNING

There was once a great actress who put on her brightest red dress and made up her face to perfection the day after her husband was buried. People seeing her as she shopped were scandalized. She came across an old friend who chastised her for her unseemly dress and conduct.

"Oh, but you should have seen me yesterday," exclaimed the actress. "Then you would have known what true sorrow is!"

This story has several morals to be drawn and raises several questions. How long does true sorrow last? Do we have the right to judge the actions of anyone who has experienced the death of a special person?

What exactly is sorrow?

Sorrow is what we feel. It is that inner sadness we carry with us as we go about our daily lives. Sorrow hurts not sharply but like a dull thudding that has no beginning and no end. Sorrow is an emotion.

Funeral director Thomas Lynch has broken down the process for us so we may better understand what we feel after the death of a special person. He has defined commonly used terms in order to help us realize what we are experiencing.

He defines bereavement as a period of time in our life following the death. He maintains that the length of time says nothing about the quality or duration of emotion but only signifies a date within a personal history. Bereavement is what we feel separate from sorrow yet a part of sorrow.

Many people have described the feeling as a part of the body being severed—an arm, a leg. Severed without anesthetic.

One father whose son died in a car accident said, "I remember when the police came to tell us. I remember well. It was as if someone had come along and punched me in the stomach. I felt airless."

He described it as many emotions combined into one.

A mother whose child died of Sudden Infant Death Syndrome, sometimes referred to as crib death, described it differently.

"There was a sense that a part of me was missing and would always remain missing. In some ways I felt the same when I gave birth to her. Here she had been within me for nine months, kicking and moving and being a *presence* even though I could not see her. Then I gave birth to her and there was a sense of terrible, painful separation. It was as if something that had been a part of me for so long was now gone.

"When my baby died I felt with even greater intensity that sense of a part of me being gone. Only this time there is no compensation, no holding and cuddling. Only that emptiness."

Emptiness is a word frequently used by the bereaved. Yet it is not descriptive enough. It does not describe the bottomless pit that many feel they have fallen into.

One woman, a widow in her mid-fifties, recalls vividly when her husband died, although six years have elapsed. "He had cancer. We had been told he was terminal. There was no hope. We both knew that. Yet when the end came it was beyond being a shock.

"Up until that point I was still someone's wife. We held each other's hands and hurt together. Then he closed his eyes. I knew for him the pain was over. I suppose I was glad for him, but I am not certain because my pain was still continuing. Only now I would not have his warm hand to hold onto. When he died I guess I was different than many people. I had no problem believing it had actually happened. But I did have a problem knowing that from that moment, that instant when he shut his eyes, anything I did would be done alone. I could no longer do for him. Only myself. Somehow it didn't seem enough or even worth the effort."

One young woman, seventeen years of age, recalls when her father died of a heart attack.

"I was called into the principal's office and no one would really look at me. It was an odd time because I was in the middle of a biology test. The principal's secretary refused to answer me when I asked what was wrong. Why had I been called there. All she said was my uncle would be there in a few minutes.

"I'm not stupid now and I wasn't then. I begged her to tell me if someone was sick, if there was anything I should be doing. All she would say is that I should sit quietly until my uncle came. I finally pushed past her and opened the principal's door. There he sat behind his big wooden desk. When he saw me it was like the secretary all over again. He couldn't look at me. I got so angry that I pounded on his desk. I could feel myself shaking. Finally, he got up and tried to put his arm around me."

"Your father died half an hour ago and your uncle is on his way."

"I'm sure he was saying it kindly but I felt a blind rage. My uncle. What difference did it make? There I was being asked to stay quietly in his office and my father was dead. Couldn't anyone understand?

"When my uncle finally got there I started screaming at him. I told him I hated everyone and I meant it. I hated them. Daddy was dead. Dead. No one seemed to know what that word meant but me. No one understood!"

In many ways the young woman was not far off the mark because understanding what death means, its impact upon someone else's life, is very individualized, very personal. Others around her could understand what the father's death meant to them but only she could know the full implications of what that death meant to her.

There is an old adage that cautions, "My truth is not your truth." How apt that adage is in our dealings with the death of a special person. How difficult and wrong to say "I know how you feel" when in reality this is not possible. You may commiserate but you cannot know, because each of us is unique and our relationships with others are equally unique.

The daughter's reaction to her father's death was similar in many ways to how a sister or brother feels when a sibling dies. There is a sense that no one can fully comprehend the magnitude of the death and its impact upon the surviving children. Very often there is a real rivalry between children for parental attention, toys, whatever may seem intriguing. This rivalry is considered a normal part of the growing-up-within-a-family process. It only becomes a real difficulty when a sister or brother dies. Then the feelings of guilt, discomfort and doubt set in.

Always at the back of the mind lurks the question of "why him and not me?" Also, it is not uncommon for sisters and brothers, when they are quarreling, to think: if he or she was dead none of this would be going on. I would get all the attention. She would not have tattled. The toys would be mine. Probably no child exists who did not at some time have such thoughts. What happens then when a brother dies? How does the surviving child come to understand that being angry and wishing someone dead does not make them die? All too often, at the moment of impact, that time when the surviving child is first told, the thoughts fleeting through his mind will dwell on, "It somehow must have been my fault. I was selfish. I wanted everything for myself. I must be to blame."

If more adults would understand this and recognize that this type of reasoning can destroy the child and then the man, perhaps more attention would be paid to surviving youngsters at the moment of impact.

Those of us who have already experienced the death of a special person have already acted correctly or incorrectly, adequately or inadequately. We have no way of undoing what we did, but we do have a certain amount of clout remaining. By learning where we should have acted differently we can help those around us when their moments of crisis occur. And for all people there are such moments. Whether they come earlier or later does not really matter. No single individual will go through life unscathed by death. Life just does not work that way.

George Santayana once observed that "one's friends are that part of the human race with which one can be human." How true that statement is. How comfortable to be able to let your hair down and share confidently, knowing your words will remain confidential.

Not long ago, a beautiful Chicago artist died very suddenly. Swarms of family and friends gathered after her burial. There was an assumption on the part of her friends, some lifelong, that their function was to somehow ease the pain for her family. Although everyone did indeed try, there was also, according to one friend, an additional reason for their being together.

"I came from Texas because I needed to be where she was last. I am trying to be helpful to her family but I am also feeling great pain. We went all through school, starting at the elementary level, together. When I received the call, my first thoughts were flashbacks to how we were when we were kids. I tried to picture what it would have been like walking to school without her and I felt as if no one would have been at my side. Funny, I didn't think of her as an adult friend but rather as a child friend. The pain of that was excruciating."

The impact of a death upon a friend should never be overlooked. Frequently the contact is even greater than that of parents and children or sisters and brothers. Friends suffer the same sense of severing as does a family member.

The burden upon grandparents is also very great. The sense of bearing a double responsibility is always present. One grandmother, upon being told her granddaughter had been killed in an automobile accident, recalls vividly how she felt at the moment of impact.

"I look back upon it now and cringe at my own behavior. I cannot believe I could have reduced myself to such childlike actions. I got the call and simply slid to the floor.

"It would have been bad enough to have fallen to the floor. But I actually lay there like a child and kicked and screamed

and pounded my fists. I was no help to anyone! I feel so ashamed
even recollecting this and it has been years since it happened.
Almost ten. But I can still remember how I felt. Then of course
my son and daughter-in-law became very angry with me. They
had their own pain and I not only was not helping them I was
adding to their burden."

As the grandmother shared her story her eyes welled with
tears. They probably were there for many reasons. After all,
her granddaughter was dead, her children were deprived. She
had "let them down" in her own eyes and maybe in theirs.

These instant gut reactions people have vary as all responses
will vary, but there is one common trait. Few people can ever
forget that initial moment when they were told. That moment
is locked into a time warp that remains present forever.

Funeral director Lynch defines mourning as a process of recovery and adjustment to the death of a special person. Mourning is the method by which the powerful emotion is slowly and
painfully brought under control. It is the day-by-day living with
our pain.

There is a biblical passage that reads: "Blessed are they that
mourn for they shall be comforted." It must seem strange indeed
to see mourning described in a positive rather than a negative
light. Generally, when we conjure up a mental image of the
word we see people crying, slumped over in pain.

We rarely think of mourning as a process of recovery! But
indeed that is what it really is. You may hurt. No, you *will* hurt.
But without the process of mourning there can be no recovery.
Any surgical patient will attest to the fact that before he was
healed and felt well he endured varying degrees of pain. No
patient can avoid that process. No bereaved person who has
endured the death of a special person can avoid the process
either.

Many people have shared their mourning techniques. You
have probably been given much advice about how to help yourself through this arduous time. Probably the best aid you can
offer yourself is to learn to roll with the punches. Give yourself
permission to have bad days without being panicked because
you are backsliding. Equally, give yourself permission to have

good days without being guilt-ridden because you can still have moments of pleasure.

We are not taught how to mourn nor should we be. Each of us is an individual. But certain things are imperative. To know you will survive and that you have a right to survive probably ranks first in importance. If you can come to grips with that you will have eased your resistance to bringing this powerful emotion under control. It is not productive to question whether you should have been the survivor. The question you must ask yourself, in order to be kind to yourself, is where do you go from there? The fact of the matter is that you are the survivor.

One man, shortly after his wife died, decided to take a long-planned trip alone although the two had originally wanted to go together. He went to the western part of the United States to canoe and white-water raft. His trip lasted nearly three weeks. Fortunately for him, he was with a tour group and did not have to wander about alone.

"Only the nights were bad, when everyone went to their own rooms. This was a couples trip and that part was kind of difficult," he said. "But all in all I had a great time."

Great time indeed. He was whistling as he unlocked his front door and began bringing in his gear after the trip. Suddenly, he said, he looked about him and it was as if a thunderbolt had clapped him on the head. Jean, his wife, was dead. Then the thunderbolt hit him in the stomach and the pain grew worse. He found himself on his knees rocking back and forth with dry, wrenching sobs coming uncontrollably from deep within him.

"Sure I had a great time on the trip. But no one told me to expect it to hurt so when I got home."

He had given himself a much-needed and deserved break. The only problem was that no one had warned him of the pain he would feel when he came home to his empty house. Not everyone has as intense a reaction. But for many, returning home, going through that door following a time of pleasure, may be difficult. You may do a loved one a real service by explaining this.

One woman whose husband died of cancer describes her mourning period as one of "disappointment."

"I kept expecting people to come to me and do for me and take me places but no one did. Not my children. Not my family. I was alone."

When questioned further the woman revealed that her children did come to visit and help as did her family. However, when faced with a seemingly bottomless well of fear and pain, far too many people begin to realize that no matter how much is done, it will never be enough. There is such a deep chasm that all the sands of the Sahara cannot fill it and make it level.

There is a great temptation, when mourning, to begin looking for replacement people. You may feel the best way to help yourself is to find someone who will act as a stand-in. That is not fair to you or the person you select. There can be no replacement people. You may find others with fine qualities: some sympathetic men and women to whom you may go with problems, others with whom you may socialize. But it is not reasonable to expect anyone else to fill all the roles the special person did. People are individuals and that is most important to remember when mourning.

No one has the right to tell you how you should be acting and reacting. Since it is very common to try to make things all better for others, sometimes we overstep and begin to offer advice and insist, for instance, that the mourner "get out more." "Begin to visit friends." "Play cards." All these things are fine if the mourner is ready. But well-meaning people may actually add pressure and be counterproductive if you still need time to be at home and not push yourself.

Since mourning is the day-by-day living with pain, be kind to yourself. If you find you cannot see further than one day ahead, do not chastise yourself. Be pleased and proud that you have made some dent on a given day. That is all you have a right to expect of yourself. Beyond that, you are adding an expectation that cannot realistically be met. The danger is that you may begin to feel you have failed "again." Not only were you not able to keep the person you loved alive, now you can't even plan how you will feel an hour from now! What a sense of deprivation this brings with it. How impotent not to be able to plan even the simplest thing. But what a relief to know that these feelings are a normal part of the mourning process and yes, you are all right.

A particularly difficult case is that of the bereaved twin. A twenty-four-year-old woman whose twin sister died in an automobile accident felt herself gearing up terribly as her birthday drew nearer.

"I planned to get away. I just didn't want to be home at our birthday time. Naturally we always spent it together. We were not the kind of twins who fought for separate identity; we loved our twinness. I decided to take a cruise because it was something we had never done together and I had never done in my life," the surviving sister said.

"Well, I got on the boat. It was nine months since she had died, and it really felt okay. But then our birthday date came and I just could not bear it. I learned there was no escape. I would never again have a normal, happy birthday because half of it was my sister's and she was dead. The trip was ruined for me and I stopped at the next port and flew home. Now I just don't know what to do, how to help myself because part of myself is just dead. That's it. Dead."

There is no question that mourning for this woman takes on a different perspective; she was a twin who took joy in her twinness. Still, reality must be faced. Although she perhaps attempted to take control a little early by going on the cruise, she is still alive, and like countless others with situations that are somewhat different, she must find ways to go on with her life even though her initial try was a setback.

Sometimes this requires the courage of doing the same difficult thing more than once so you are desensitized to the pain after a while.

• In the beginning, however, there must be the commitment to life. Without that all efforts will fail.

• Perhaps in grieving it is more important than in any other endeavor to internalize the saying, "If at first you don't succeed, try, try again."

It is important to know this because in grieving many early steps will fail but they must still be taken in order to have some experience upon which to build.

Perhaps making a pact that on their birthday this twin will go to the cemetery in the morning and then to a restaurant later in the day would be helpful. That way she is acknowledging the dead as well as the living. She has given herself permission to live with her pain rather than die of it.

Bereavement, mourning and grief are the three problems death entails. Grief is the response to any loss or separation, real or imagined, actual or symbolic, of any emotionally significant person, object or situation which is perceived to be of an irredeemable or permanent nature, according to funeral director Lynch.

Grief is always more than sorrow. It is the rawness you feel at the center of your being. That rawness often includes fear and loneliness and dread of the obstacles you will now face as you try to find a new way of living. This rawness goes deep to the core of us all when a special person has died. Frequently you will find yourself experiencing physical pain caused by this rawness, and unless you are forewarned that pain may panic you. But learn to expect it. Know it will happen. When you feel this pain handle it just as you would the pain caused by an abrasion. Pamper it. Take care of it. Be gentle with it.

One woman who worked for many years before it was fashionable for women to hold jobs was aghast at how intensely she hurt when her father died. The woman had never married and her parents played a greater role in her adult life than parents do for most of us as we grow older.

"I felt paralyzed," she said. "I never expected to feel such hurt as I saw him lying there. After all, I am a grown woman. An executive. I'm no longer Daddy's little girl. Yet my reaction was truly just that! It shocked me."

She proceeded to explain how she dealt with her pain. "I did the only thing I knew; I threw myself into my work. I demanded appropriate behavior of myself and felt I could battle my way up just as I had done throughout my career. Well, it just didn't work. I finally sat back and took stock. The rawness was still there. Only now I was thoroughly exhausted along with it. The problem was I had never been in the habit of pampering myself, of being kind to myself. All I knew was how to drive, drive, drive my way upward.

"Well, it just didn't work when my father died. I finally went into counseling and was taught that even high-powered executives should be nice to themselves. I took a little time off from work, began to let myself cry, visited the cemetery often and slowly but surely the rawness began to diminish. It took a long time for it to go away but at least the pain wasn't hindering me any longer."

It has been three years since her father's death and she feels confident that things are on their way to being controlled.

One of the real problems in coping with grief is the anxiety it produces. It is not uncommon, after a special person has died, to feel that you are in limbo. You had someone whom you loved greatly. Now that person is dead. What are you going to do with all that love? You are sitting with a mass of emotion swirling about you and you suddenly have no place for the mass to land.

It is a bit like the anxiety you may have before giving a party: "Suppose nobody comes?" There you, the griever, find yourself. All the goodies baked, the room decorated, and no one with whom to share! That is what an unspent mass of emotion is like. Perhaps just having that mental picture may be of value.

Now you have this delicious food, this lovely room and you are alone. How do you proceed? What might ease the pain? Perhaps the greatest thing you can do to help yourself is not to lose sight of just how attractive a setting you have created. That others could not share in it is very sad indeed. But you did all you could.

The same applies to how you might ease the pain you feel after the death of a loved one. You established the best possible relationship with the person who died. Now you are left with the empty shell of memory. It is very sad that this is the case, but try to remember you did all you could to make the person's life decent and good by simply being yourself, a decent and good individual.

If you can accept that idea you can eventually form new

relationships without fear, because you will remember you are a good person who is capable of bringing your good qualities into someone else's life. But that is for later and not for the early days. Now you must recognize the loss.

Many people experience physical sensations aside from rawness when someone they love has died. There is a sense of someone sneaking behind you and slamming two books together that is caused by an adrenalin run. Many people find themselves gasping for air as if in panic that all the air would soon be taken up and none left for them.

These and a multitude of other physical symptoms are common and are things you may expect to occur. Perhaps you may derive some comfort in knowing this.

There is another ironic problem you may confront. You may find yourself unable to conjure up your special person's face and body. You may only be able to draw a shadowy image, blurred features, while you frantically try to recall the way your special person really looked. Some mourners have the opposite problem: "I see him wherever I walk. Wherever I go," is not an uncommon statement. Perhaps you do not wish to let the dead person go. Perhaps you feel a presence that is very strong around you. Many people have expressed this sensation. Most often if that is the case you feel a level of comfort. Although you cannot touch the dead person you are experiencing his company just less than tangibly.

Many people, especially in the early days, hope to see an image of their special person when they sleep. Those who do so generally regard themselves as fortunate and feel varying levels of frustration at having awakened while experiencing a sort of "contact" with their dead person.

Although that image can offer warmth in a world that has grown deadly cold, there are times of intense sorrow when it is almost impossible not to find some way of blaming yourself. People magnify trivial incidents in order to accomplish this self-blame. Often their need for an answer to "why" is nearly insurmountable. Perhaps there is a sense of "if it's my fault at least there is a reason he died." The need for that reason can be near frenzy for some.

Self-blame is magnified a thousandfold when a special person has died of suicide. Very often that self-blame is cruel as well as unjust.

If your loved one has died of suicide frequently you will find yourself reaching for some way in which you could be held responsible. You may be berating yourself with questions like these:

- Did I not do enough?
- Did I not give enough?
- Was *I* simply not enough?

To help balance some of this destructive self-blame, help yourself by using some new language. There is a tendency to say someone "committed suicide." The sense that someone acted out their anger and pain in the most aggressive and hurtful way is our image of suicide. There is also the sense that someone got the last word without allowing you to make the situation better or even to explain it from your point of view. All too often loving survivors feel inadequate and helpless and view the suicide as an act of viciousness from which they had no protection.

When you decide to help yourself it might be useful to begin with a new vocabulary for suicide. Begin to think he "died *of* suicide." In this context, suicide becomes a death like cancer or heart failure, for in reality there are some people who simply cannot live despite the finest ministering we may offer. If you are able to make this transition in your own mind you may find you will become kinder to yourself and less punitive. As you ease up on yourself you may allow some logic to enter your thinking and with that logic may come some peace.

Remember, it may all begin with this new terminology.

This perception of suicide originated with Monsignor John Trese, who works extensively with survivors suffering a loved one's death by suicide. He says that after hearing a multitude of stories involving those who took their own lives his view, which had always been traditional, has altered. His new concept is that suicides are not necessarily indictments; they are not necessarily proof of mistreatment by those who surrounded the dead person. He believes firmly that some people simply *cannot* live. Things are just too painful.

Not long ago, a young woman attending a high-pressure university in the Midwest died of suicide. She was found hanging in her room by her roommates. A year afterward they are still in shock.

"What could we have done for her that we didn't? She didn't leave a note. She didn't tell us anything except that she was doing badly in one of her classes. How could we have known?"

The answer, of course, is they could not have known unless she chose to share her inner pain with them. This was not the case. Instead, she went quietly about her business, going deeper and deeper inward, and ultimately she ended her life.

How helpful it would be if her roommates could look at her death not from their vantage point but from hers. Not from the standpoint that somehow they were unable to help her but rather that she was unable to live.

Since suicide is not an acceptable form of dying in our society we all too frequently try to find self-blame and often self-blame is unjust. If you are the survivor of a suicide perhaps to know that person simply could not live will ease some of your hurt.

Another difficulty in coping with grief lies in observing your behavior and not liking what you see.

One mother whose thirteen-year-old son died of leukemia shared her experience with this difficulty. "Although Jamie had been sick for years, I had always managed at least to show some interest in what my other two kids were doing. But after he died I seemed to change. I was no longer a loving and warm mother. Sure, I took care of their physical needs. I didn't cook a lot and would order food sent in, but I did take care of their physical needs. It's the emotional side of me that seemed to freeze. I couldn't give them any warmth. I didn't even want them hugging me. It used to make me feel guilty because I was unable to return any warmth to them."

The mother eventually went for counseling and discovered that her response was not unique. Rather it was one that many people feel when a special person has died.

She found through therapy that it was possible to reawaken love and affection for her surviving children. She began by making it a point to hold each of her children's hands once a day. With this she gradually lost some of her coldness. From hand-holding a small kiss on the cheek became part of the ritual. Once this had become comfortable she included a hug.

The children responded well to any positive overtures, for they, too, were hurting. Ultimately the mother found her responses had become genuine rather than a therapeutic exercise.

One widower said he found it impossible not to feel irritated at things people did. He maintained those around him only succeeded in annoying him when they tried to show concern.

"I remember wishing that they'd just all go away and leave me alone. Everything everyone did seemed to bother me. Nothing was right. I finally blew up at both my daughters for fussing one day and we cleared the air. I just didn't like being pampered is what I told them."

The widower added, however, "You know, they were really surprised. They assured me they were treating me no differently than they ever had. This was how they always were and I had always encouraged them to treat me like that.

"Believe me, that was some revelation."

The widower was genuinely surprised. He had not realized his response had changed. He assumed the change had come from those around him.

One high school girl found herself with an entirely different problem. "I knew it could not be that I suddenly got stupid when my mother died, but my grades went down. I met with the school psychologist and he told me that was fairly common. But what really drove me up a wall was suddenly not being able to find my papers. Nothing was in place any longer. I used to be one of those finicky people whose records and tapes were arranged alphabetically. I had different dividers for every class and every section. After Mom died, all that seemed to stop. My life seemed to become cluttered. I couldn't find the energy to keep things in place. It took quite a while to straighten out this problem. I need to be orderly and now I'm so glad it's beginning to happen again. What a relief!"

The sense of things being out of place is not an uncommon difficulty. You may be feeling that things are just too hard. If that is the case, learn to be kind to yourself. Use as much organization as will keep you comfortable but not so much that the organizing itself becomes oppressive. If you do the best you can it will simply have to suffice until you are ready to climb another rung of the ladder out of your pain and begin living through your mourning.

Bereavement, mourning and grief are each painful emotions. Sometimes our desire to recover makes us expect more of ourselves than is realistic. As part of the Anglo-Saxon ethic, which in many cases has become our American way of doing things, we have the traditional stiff-upper-lip method of handling emotions. We shy away from displaying any intense feelings. They frighten us. Yet by ducking these feelings we are harming ourselves.

It is most important to remember tears are natural. They came into our lives at birth. Try not to fear them. Teach your friends not to be afraid for you if you are weeping. THE TEARS ARE MERELY EMOTION TURNED LIQUID. Let them worry for you if you are *not* crying. If you are sitting overly cheerful with your heart in tiny puzzle pieces within you, is there not more to fear than an honest and open expression of your pain?

There are those who fear that once they begin to cry they will never stop. You may have had that fear. But you know the truth. The tears do dry up. The well empties itself for a while and once again you are able to go about your business even if you cannot go about it to your complete satisfaction. There will be another bout of tears down the road, because they are normal and healthy for you. If allowed to remain unreleased, they can slowly turn to poison within you and harm you.

In the early days of your mourning, simply to survive day to day can be enough. But know that further down the road there is room to better your life. With enough time, by rolling with the punches and crying when it feels right to you, you will once again not only find happiness, but find that you can create it.

Along with giving yourself permission to *feel* your mood of the moment, whatever it may be, here are some other things that might be of value in helping yourself deal with your pain and sorrow.

• In the Jewish faith there is a mourning ritual in which a bereaved person says a certain prayer, called kaddish, either at a temple or at home at the same time daily. It brings about a certain discipline and routine that is often helpful. People of all beliefs may translate this idea into their own lives. Set aside a grieving time for yourself. Make it the same time daily. Sit in the same chair in the same room. Give yourself half an hour in which to think about the dead person, look at pictures or videotapes or old letters. Take a prayer book or a book of poetry and read it. But know, regardless of how you wish to spend your grieving time, that it is something you must give yourself daily. When you are through with that half hour get out of your chair and do something active—take a walk, perhaps scrub clean a room and then get back to your normal routine. When you promise yourself this half hour daily you are giving yourself permission to spend the rest of your day productively, because you know there will be a moment to pause for a bit and remember and reflect upon your loss.

• If the pain becomes very great, perhaps facing it directly might be helpful. Go to the cemetery, or plan to.

• If people around you wish to help, tell them it is far kinder not to offer advice about what you should be doing. Instead, ask for their involvement. "Don't tell me I should be getting out more, please help me by inviting me out," you might say.

• Ask a friend to select a place that is quiet and relaxing for an outing. Too much frenetic activity can further strain your already tense nerves. A good first time out may be a visit to a friend's home. This may be especially helpful if finances are a problem.

• If asked to become involved in a card game or other activity requiring concentration when you are having an attention-span problem, do not simply say no. Ask that you be invited again some time in the future when you can be more focused.

• When you're ready to engage in some group activity, offer to bring some refreshments even if they are just potato chips and a dip. By making yourself involved in the activity you will feel more a part of things and also make yourself a more welcome guest.

Pathways Through Denial

I'm not afraid to die, I just don't want to be there
when it happens! —WOODY ALLEN

Two famous Broadway producers were pallbearers at the funeral of the great escape artist Harry Houdini. As they lifted the beautiful and heavy casket to their shoulders, one of them whispered to the other, "Suppose he isn't there!"

In large measure that is what denial is really about. The feeling we have that none of this is happening. That our special person is really not in the casket, not dead, and we will wake up and find it was all a bad dream.

But, sadly, truth does win eventually.

A widow who now acts as a speaker for groups of newly bereaved women shared her experience when she was first told that her husband had died. "I remember so well that initial time. I stood in the emergency room and shook with fear. My legs felt like they couldn't support me and yet I couldn't sit down. I had been called at work because he had been in a construction accident. I rushed to the hospital and I was all alone. I never even thought to call anyone to come with me. They wouldn't let me see him because they were working on him.

"When someone finally came out to tell me he had died I looked at them stupidly. What was being said simply did not register. My healthy, strong husband had kissed me goodbye, taken his lunch bucket and whistled as he walked through the door. A few hours later he was dead."

She said in looking back over that time the magnitude of what she had been told was simply too much for her mind to comprehend. "I couldn't take it all in. I just kept screaming, 'No! This is not happening!' "

You, after having experienced the dreadful sensation of having been "told," know full well the enormity of this widow's experience. You have been in her shoes when a special person in your life has died, no matter what your relationship was. You know the sense of unreality that overtakes us when a special person has died.

That sense of unreality is generally referred to as *denial*.

According to funeral director Patrick Lynch, denial has been defined as our conditioned response to the news of a death. One of the first things you probably said was "No, I don't believe it."

This happens long before you have come to any understanding about the finality of death. It is your instinctive protection against this terrible knowledge. At first that sense of protection can be helpful but if denial is allowed to persist it may hamper your normal, necessary encounter with grief and mourning.

Since all people are different no two will share the identical experience of denial, or the identical timing. One father whose ten-year-old daughter died in a playground accident said, "I always seemed to have a sense that none of this was happening. Sure I went through the motions of taking care of things that needed doing, but I never felt as if it were *me* doing those things."

He added that, to this day, he does not know exactly when reality set in. "Suddenly it was there and it was bad. I know it was some time after the funeral. I thought I was in bad shape when I didn't feel like me, it hurt like hell. But I didn't know what hurt meant until I began to believe that all of this was really happening."

One bereavement counselor described that first shock as having almost the effect of anesthesia.

"Sometimes it can help in those first days following a death.

Especially when funeral arrangements must be made and so many decisions are thrown at you," she said.

There is a story about an old coat that was dirty and worn. The coat feared its end had come when its owner purchased a beautiful new coat cut in the latest of styles. Although the owner did not know the coat had feelings—he viewed it as an inanimate object—it was indeed very verbal. One day the new coat looked over in the closet and noticed the old one looked entirely different. "What happened to you?" he inquired. "You actually look wearable."

"Well," the old coat said, "first they brought me to a laundry. They took sticks and paddles and beat the dust and sand and mud out of me. I happened to see a mirror and felt good about how I looked. It was worth the pain to become clean again.

"As I was admiring myself and thinking how handsome a coat I had once again become, they grabbed me and threw me into hot water and then warm water. Then they washed me again and rinsed me. My, how it hurt when they wrung me out! Then they pressed me. What an ordeal."

The new coat, hearing all this, commiserated.

"But then I got another glimpse of myself in the mirror and saw myself as you see me now. I had been transformed. Once again I was something to behold.

"It was then I realized that before anything can be elevated it first has to suffer!"

How true that statement is when you have experienced the death of someone special in your life. Although there is no perfect time frame, no one moment in which you will begin to feel certain emotions, you cannot truly consider yourself on the road to healing until you do feel them.

Sometimes when denial works as an anesthetic, it affects your ability to do things. You might not be able to act as, in retrospect, you would have liked. Your decision process may not have been intact.

There have been many people who, weeks, months, or even years later, have wished they had done things differently at the time of their special person's death, but denial made them unable to act. One young woman whose sister died of cancer regretted for years not speaking up and telling her family she wished to place a doll in the coffin. "I was in such shock I simply felt I had to swim with the tide. That whatever others did was the 'right' thing. I felt I had no will of my own. What was so weird is that I was always the tough kid in the family, the one with the big mouth. But when it mattered most, I suddenly couldn't face up to what had happened and I just didn't want to interfere."

She has talked with her parents about this, and they, too, feel certain regrets. "We know she is angry with us, but there was nothing we could do for her at that time, nothing we could offer. We needed all the help we could get and had nothing to spare for anyone else."

Although this statement might make the parents sound uncaring, that is far from the truth. They are caring people. Like their daughter they felt young and vulnerable, and all they could manage was to swim with the tide.

It might have been helpful if a funeral director had suggested placing objects in the coffin that were meaningful. People include hymnals, private letters and poetry. Sometimes a young child might wish to draw a picture to put in the pocket of the special person who died. Above all, it would have been helpful to know you had choices, but since you were stunned, these regrets must be put aside. You must not chastise yourself because you were numb and in pain and not thinking clearly.

If this regret is pulling at you or at your children, make it a point to go to the cemetery and bring flowers to the grave. That is something you still *can* do.

Many funeral directors find it useful to visit the family in their own home. One director said he makes it a point to do so because frequently families do not include youngsters in the planning of the funeral. He said when he sits down and begins to ask youngsters if they have any ideas about what they would like to see done, the families are often amazed. Yet they should not be. If a child was fond of Grandma and she is dead, that child may well wish to place in the coffin a picture or a toy that was meaningful to the two of them.

He says his home visits serve another function too. By going to the house and dealing with the children as well as the adults he is setting a tone which he hopes they will follow. He is in effect reminding adults that the children and their feelings matter also. He believes this to be one of his most valuable services.

A group of men sat around a table discussing denial recently. They had been widowed anywhere from several months to three years. The scene was a support group meeting. One of the men at the table said, "You know what was strange? My wife and I always went shopping for my clothes. I didn't buy a shirt without her for forty years. When we had somewhere to go I always asked her what to wear. Was it dressy? Could I get away without a tie? Well, then she died. She had a cerebral hemorrhage. I kept feeling none of this was really happening, especially when I had to go into her closet and pick what she would wear at her funeral. She wasn't there to tell me. *I* had to decide. I just kept feeling this was not real."

When we started talking about selecting his late wife's dress it seemed all the other men at the table had similar experiences.

"I guess I was lucky because my daughter came and decided for me. I couldn't have figured it out by myself, you know. The whole thing seemed unreal and the idea of *me* choosing for her or even my daughter choosing for her seemed like a fantasy. As recently as she was able, she was still shopping with my daughter and advising *her* about what to wear. Now the tables were turned and we had to figure things out for ourselves. Well, we just were not used to making those kinds of decisions. And here we were, forced into it."

Another man, of the Orthodox Jewish faith, said he was grateful that he was not faced with that particular issue. "We bury in linen or cotton shrouds and do not concern ourselves with clothing. The only decision I had to make was what material I wanted used. Even deciding about that seemed unreal. How could I be deciding about my wife's shroud when she should have outlived me by at least five years?"

A man of about sixty-five or so with a thick thatch of white hair still had a somewhat puzzled look upon his face.

"In all the years we were married, my wife took on the duties of social secretary. She made the plans and did the inviting.

Most of all, she did the telephoning. She died at home of cancer and the strangest thing was after calling the doctor whose number was written above the telephone, I knew I had to make a lot of calls and let people know. My kids, her sister, my brother. Well, I didn't even know where the telephone directory was! Our personal directory, I mean. I just never bothered with those things and I never learned about them. Then, while I was still not believing my wife was dead I had to go scurrying around looking for a phone book so I could call people. I never even knew what to say. I just couldn't bring my mind to accept that this was now my job and I had to do it."

The feeling of denial is indeed an odd sensation. In some ways, it is a calming force. One that helps lessen the harsh pain of death. With denial there can be an almost tranquilizing effect upon the mourner—a sort of natural buffering. While we have all probably experienced denial to some extent it is necessary to go past that point in order to rebuild our lives.

One young woman, nineteen and in college, says she misses her mother now more than at any point in her life. "I feel like these are the years we should have been sharing. These are the times. I would like her to know my new friends. My new world. But I'll never forget the horror I felt when they told me she had died. I knew she was sick and dying slowly. We all knew that. But when my dad called us out in the hospital room and told us I screamed and shouted at him. I kept telling him he was lying. This could not be happening. She would get out of that bed and be there for me. She wouldn't ever have left me like that. She's not dead, I kept saying. No matter what anyone told me I wouldn't listen to anything. I kept shutting my ears and screaming 'she's not dead!' "

"When I asked to see her they wouldn't let me. I was sixteen and they should have. Maybe then I would have believed them. But I just kept on screaming for days that she wasn't dead. Even at the funeral home. I would look at her and think it was someone wearing a mask; my mother did not look like that. When people offered me their condolences, I kept telling them she was not dead."

The young woman finally, slowly began accepting the truth

as the weeks went by. She ultimately wound up in therapy where the psychologist dealt with her sympathetically yet firmly. While he acknowledged her pain he suggested that she begin a new dialogue with her father; one that was more positive and less angry. He also helped her realize how important close girl-friends could be, especially if they were sympathetic and would allow her to talk out her pain. Then he suggested she become active in a support group which offered her a forum in which to share her pain and loneliness and anger without being judged.

Sometimes parents of married children who die face an entirely different type of denial. One woman whose son died and left a widow and three young daughters has not come to terms with her position as a bereaved parent. While the son was alive the daughter-in-law could deal with a strong woman who was her husband's mother. But now the younger woman has remarried and there is great conflict between the two women.

"I don't think of her as my former daughter-in-law; she is my daughter-in-law, the mother of my granddaughters. I always felt free to come and go in that home. After all, I paid for it and practically furnished it. If I wanted to talk to my son or the kids I just stopped over or called when I wanted to. Now that she's remarried she's trying to change everything. She wants me to stop calling so often. She wants me to let her know before I come over. She wants me to talk to her first before buying things for my grandkids. That's plain foolish. Just because my son is dead I don't plan to make any changes. I will not be pushed aside!"

The saddest part of all this is that in her zeal not to be left out this woman is forcing her own way there. A newly married woman certainly has the right to pick and choose who will visit and when. The bereaved mother simply will not come to terms with change because that would mean acknowledging her son is really and truly dead.

Unless this woman does this and soon, she will find her former daughter-in-law has pulled away completely and, worse, taken the children with her.

Then there are people who insist they felt none of this denial.

One grandmother who had raised her grandson from his younger years said never for a moment had she experienced anything of the sort.

"Believe me," she said, "I knew he was dead. No question about it. It was booze that got him. I was sure I had taught him better than that. But no, he got behind the wheel of his car after leaving a party and plowed into a tree. I believed it, all right. Then I had to go through the business of burying him. Me, burying my own grandchild. Had he not been such a fool he would have been burying me. But that's not how life goes all the time, is it?"

She said because the boy was orphaned at a young age, all the responsibility fell on her shoulders. Although she had two sisters, she was the eldest and the one who always did the deciding.

"I was always the one who took charge. I am the eldest. I saw no reason to change the way things always were at a time like that. My boy was dead. I raised him and it was up to me to bury him."

She explained hastily that offers of help from her sisters had come forth immediately. Others had been willing to try to ease her burdens. But since she viewed them as *her* burdens she refused all assistance.

"I come from an old world way of thinking. Things were not always as easy as they seem now. Nowadays there seems to be an authority or adviser for everything. That's just not how it was in my day. We were taught more self-reliance."

Whether or not that is the case, this grandmother was convinced her perception was correct. But does "toughing something out" make us stronger or better?

Those who have experienced such hurt would agree they could have done well without such pain. Many people have experienced the sense of being pounded and pummeled and wrung dry before they have been able to go forward, but there is almost a euphoria when the pain eases. If you have been beset with any of the woes denial brings into focus, know you may find relief within the structure of the support group. One of the things you will learn from sharing the experiences of so many others is that the pain does abate.

Whether or not you begin by denying and then work your way through the varying stages, the pain does ease. You will not always feel you are walking with a gaping wound inside of you.

For many, the first step in addressing denial is the funeral.

There are those who insist they recall very little of the event, especially their own part in it. Others say making the arrangements and viewing the body brought back the sense of reality.

"My God, how I hated reality then," said one distraught father. "I didn't want to look at my beautiful daughter lying there so still. I wanted none of this to have happened. But it did."

Many funeral directors throughout the country have discussed this question of denial and still have not been able to decide whether it is helpful to try to break into it.

"I have had people come to me who have absolutely no touch with reality whatsoever. They are sitting there hearing me explain what needs attending to in order to bury their mother or father or child or parent, but they are not hearing. Very often the same question has to be repeated over and over again. Sometimes, although I finally do receive an answer, I am still not certain they have taken in the question," said one director.

"After all, how much can be expected from someone who has just had all the wind knocked out of them? How does anyone think and make clear decisions when a child has been murdered, for example? I hope I never have to know myself."

Another director said families who come to make selections often walk around dazed as they go from casket to casket. They have no real comprehension of what they are seeing.

"That is why it is helpful to bring along a friend or relative; someone whose judgment you trust. All too often there is a real regret later for things that might have been done and were not. Also, some people regret what was done and wish they could make changes. But as we all know it is simply too late."

The director said it has always struck him as tragic to have to make great decisions at a time when one is not capable of even thinking or making the smallest decision.

There are people, however, who find the planning of the funeral to be the thing that pulls them away from denial. Many families work carefully to plan hymns and music. There are people who go to the funeral home fully prepared to discuss prices, and which services they will be needing. Sometimes these people do not even begin to feel a sense of denial until sometime after the funeral.

As in any other aspect of dealing with emotion there are no set rules, no predetermined right or wrong feelings.

Sometimes when there has been time to plan, people are able to infuse much of their own personal expressions into the funeral. One woman whose husband died of cancer had felt troubled about having visitation at the funeral home.

"Here my husband had worked hard to provide us with a huge home and all the room in the world. I decided to go back a generation and have the visitation in our home. When he died we had three teenaged children. By having all the visiting at home I believe my kids got better back-up than they would have received in the funeral home."

She said her home was constantly filled with people, young and older. There was a sense that teenagers could come to the house in blue jeans as they had always done and mingle with her children more freely.

A variation of this idea was used by a woman whose husband died a lingering death. While the body was displayed at the funeral home, the funeral director told the friends who stopped there that the family was receiving callers at their home. He suggested they go and pay their respects at the house. This woman also said she felt it helped her children to become reintegrated with their friends.

"Frankly, it also helped me. Many people came to my home and that is where we wanted them. We had none of this what to do with the "off hours" problem. I recommend this to all mourners if it is at all possible."

The concept of having the home act as the setting for mourning is not unique. It can serve an important function for many. That function is to have friends and relatives gather around in the most natural setting. This can even be done when a family decides upon cremation. If that is their option, they should still have their time to share with their support system.

The concept of the gathering of the clan, the coming together of the support system is very much a part of the Jewish ritual following a funeral. Although Jewish people bury their dead quickly, generally within a day following the death, there is a seven-day period of mourning, dating from the time of death, in which people are expected to visit the bereaved family in their home. The bereaved family does not have to concern itself with meals or "what to do with themselves." They know that directly from the cemetery they will go home and be encompassed by many loving friends, relatives and neighbors.

Contrast this with the numerous families who leave the cemetery and are dropped off at home by the director or drive their own car and walk into an empty house. They sit and look at one another and wonder what to do next.

In a civilized world no one should be alone at a time like that. There should always be some support. No one should have to be concerned with what to do about dinner. Yet, hundreds of thousands of people sustain the death of a special person, the funeral, the burial and are confronted with just such a scene. What an act of goodness to know that it is important to be there after the funeral as well as before. Being there after is often being there when denial begins to subside and reality starts to enter.

People who are mourning need all the support they can get at such a time. Often, just a visit for half an hour by different caring people can act as a ray of sun in the hard cold world in which people grieve.

Many directors work hard at trying to establish just such support groups for the community at large. These funeral directors are part of an ever-growing network of caring people who feel it necessary to extend their services beyond the burial.

In Ohio, for example, the state-wide funeral director organization has made a concentrated effort to help those who are grieving to organize into groups and meet one another for support and comfort. The organization and individual directors support these groups financially by bringing in speakers and having regional lunches and meetings. Frequently directors make a practice of attending these meetings just with the idea of bringing someone along whom they feel is in need.

Some funeral homes around the country are employing full-time grief counselors whose function it is to call upon the family weeks or months after the burial. They offer concrete guidance and suggestions at a time when people have generally gone beyond denial and are more receptive and able to retain information than they were at the time of the funeral itself.

One Midwestern grief counselor has met with great success in her home visits. She has become more sure that very little valuable counsel really penetrates when the death occurs. It takes some months before reality obtrudes and "how it will be" is faced, she explained.

The counselor, whose services are without fee to the client but are figured into the cost of the funeral, said, "One man with whom we spent a lot of time during the funeral arrangements kept assuring us he had everything under control. Everything was in place. We had no need to be concerned. He sounded very convincing. Yet when I went to his home some months later just to chat a bit and see how things were going, all his wife's clothes were still in the closet. He had not yet gone beyond heating frozen dinners. He had not even learned to operate the coffee pot and was still running to a corner store and carrying home Styrofoam cups of coffee!"

She said when she finished her visit they agreed it was time for him to hire a housekeeper to come in, at least for a few days, to teach him how to operate his appliances and to begin the task of removing his wife's possessions.

Funeral directors also set the tone for society when a child is stillborn or dies shortly after birth. They believe that the parents of such a child will heal more easily if both of them take an active part in deciding about the infant's burial. This relatively new concept frequently means visitng the mother who is still in the hospital and making arrangements with the couple in that setting.

Many parents have written to say they found this particularly helpful. "When a baby dies at birth you somehow don't quite know what you are. After all, that child did not live. You didn't get to know it. You only had all your wishes and hopes poured into this being you never knew. I had a terrible time understanding our position as a couple," one woman wrote.

She went on to explain that the funeral director helped clarify their position. He stressed that they were mourners. He told them they were indeed bereaved parents and suggested naming the baby. His philosophy was the child was not an "it." This is quite in contrast with how things were done half a century ago when such infants were buried in unmarked graves, places the mother would never have known how to visit should she have felt the need.

There is a point at which it is essential to stop and face our own tragedy. No two people find that point at the same moment, of course, but somewhere along the path through denial that time does come. Although it sounds minor to those who have not endured great personal loss, dealing with the dead person's belongings does indeed require a high level of bravery. It is an act of courage to acknowledge that, yes, this dreaded event did occur, but now I must go on. You who have had to do so know full well the resources and courage you had to call upon.

You know it is not an easy task to do away with the belongings of a loved one. First of all, you cherish them, right down to the worn pair of slippers you always threatened to throw out. Suddenly instead of being an affront they have become cherished reminders. This may be true of a son's torn T-shirt or a mother's apron you always hated. When that person was alive it was okay to criticize these things, but how different when the owner of that shirt dies. Suddenly things take on an entire new aspect: they become dear heirlooms rather than junk, and you want to keep them.

There are, however, people who have gone beyond keeping some special mementos. They are the people who have turned thier homes into mausoleums. When a rumpled bed the husband slept in is still rumpled three years after his death; his half-smoked pipe still sits in the ashtray; his closet is still packed with his belongings, you know the survivor has not yet dealt with the reality that must be confronted.

Although no one can establish a timetable for another mourner, there is such a thing as *reasonable*. After a reasonable amount of time no dead child's half-eaten sandwich should sit in a bedroom, as is the case in some homes. There comes a moment when cleanups and changes are necessary, necessary for your own well-being. You are in effect telling yourself it is time to know he is dead. Time to go a little further along the path toward healing.

Not everyone is capable of doing their own cleanup; for some people the pain is simply too great. There is nothing wrong with asking for help. This is surely an area in which you may safely call upon all those friends and acquaintances who are eagerly trying to find some useful role for themselves in your tragedy. Ask them to pack things away. Offer to let them keep something if it would be meaningful to them. You will be met with a generally willing acceptance in your request for help.

One woman whose child died could not bear to remove the signs of the child's existence. Instead, she called in a cleaning woman who was not intimately involved with the family. She told the woman where all her child's possessions were and asked that they be packed and removed while she spent the afternoon away. Although the cleaning woman might have felt a bit squeamish, her feelings could not possibly have been as deep as those of the mother. When the mother returned home that evening she found the room cleaned, the closet empty and the toy box removed. Although she cried, for here again was a symbol of her loss, it was far less painful than her having to deal with the procedure itself.

One daughter, on the other hand, said she felt great therapeutic value in disposing of her mother's belongings. "I cried at every Mother's Day gift I came across," she said, "but when I was through and felt so spent, the sensation was strange. I felt then and not before that I had truly come to grips with her death. It hurt. But I knew the fantasies that she was not really dead were behind me. In an odd way there was relief."

While in the early moments and days perhaps flashes of denial serve as blessed anesthetic for souls who are in pain, after a time the anesthetic must begin to wear off and allow the true human being who has survived to reemerge, to begin to function and act, especially to act in one's own interest. There is no virtue in two deaths and one burial. You who are alive must live!

To begin that process:

- Know you have a right to live.
- If someone you love is dying, prepare yourself to ask the doctor to allow you to see your special person in the hospital after the death. That is the beginning of coming to terms with finality.
- Viewing the body at a funeral is harsh but also another step in reentering the world of reality. After the viewing whenever you begin to think, "This didn't happen, I don't believe it," you will have the image of that viewing to help remind you that it did.
- While it is not necessary to rush to do so immediately after the funeral, it is important, after a reasonable length of time, to remove your special person's clothing. If you cannot do so, ask a trusted relative or friend to take care of it for you. Places like the Salvation Army and Goodwill Industries can always use personal items. When you remove the loved one's clothing you have begun to understand and know your new reality.
- Rather than allowing pictures of your special person to remain everywhere you look within your home, designate one special place and hang a grouping of pictures or one large portrait. You are honoring your dead person but allowing yourself some breathing space.
- Begin going out slowly. When in a restaurant do not allow yourself to be seated near the kitchen because you are alone. Insist on a good table. Reaffirm that because you are a widow or widower does not lessen your "personhood." You matter!
- Find a good support group where people are willing to discuss openly their problems and successes. Listen and participate.

Pathways Through Anger

He who will not reason is a bigot; he who cannot is a fool; and he who dares not is a slave. We must not become slaves to anger. —ANONYMOUS

In living through your mourning, you, the survivor, have frequently felt about your special person, why could he not have had even five or ten more years of life? Why was I left to deal with all this pain? Why could he not have lived to be older?

There are many moments during the mourning process where this sort of questioning changes dramatically from the rather benign "why" to far more virulent feelings of rage over the injustice of this event. This anger, this sense of unfairness, this frustration at your own lack of control, is common. Few survivors have not experienced it in one form or another.

Anger is an emotional response of no specified intensity aroused by what is considered unjust, mean or shameful.

How well survivors know this feeling!

One woman whose son died said she always walked around with a sense of anger. "There were days I was just a little angry and other times I would be in such a rage that I saw pink that blotted out any other object from my vision. I hated that time because I never knew what I would feel like from hour to hour. It was very difficult for me in those days."

She said she now feels almost fortunate because with time her anger has reached a level that is low and manageable.

"My goal for myself is to stop asking 'why.' Then I won't get incensed and churn up all this anger. I am trying to lower its level and as time has passed it seems to be working."

In general, when attempting to cope with anger, survivors grope for an answer to "why"—why this person, why now, why not me? When you begin asking "why," the logical thing is to expect an answer. Since you do not generally hear a loud booming voice responding, you begin to dredge and dredge until you come up with your own answer to "why." Frequently that answer will hit on one or more of five targets.

- The doctor
- The clergyman
- The funeral director
- The person who died
- God

You may have others you wish to blame but in general these five individuals are targets for most of our anger after a death.

Expressing anger toward the doctor after a special person has died of illness is not really illogical, although most of the time it is unfair.

This massive communication gap that seems to exist between survivors and the attending physician must be broken down with modern techniques and education.

Countless times families have shared their frustration, which ultimately becomes anger at the doctor. The seeds of anger are often planted early on during the illness.

One couple whose nineteen-year-old daughter died of hepatitis feels great animosity toward the doctor.

"He's a bastard. He kept telling me things would be better. He was so casual about all of this that I believed him. He'd walk into her room at the hospital. She'd be lying there all hooked up with tubes and he'd give her a cheery 'hello' and pat her on the shoulder and that would be the end of it! That's medical care for you. Then after she died, we tried our damnedest to sit down with the man and ask him why she died. What went wrong? Well, he wouldn't even come to the phone. His nurse wouldn't even set an office appointment. All we got from him is a dead daughter."

This was the child's father in all his rage.

The mother on the other hand said much the same but in a quieter tone of voice. "He really didn't communicate with us at all, you know. She was our daughter and we certainly had a right to know what was happening. But he never seemed to work or do anything when we saw him in the hospital room. Then later, like my husband says, he was just unavailable. I wonder if he has a daughter. I wonder how *he* would like to be treated. But because he's a doctor people would handle him differently, I'm sure."

To this couple it truly does appear that the doctor did nothing, and many people feel the way they do, that the doctor generally walks into the patient's room, takes her hand, says a cheerful greeting and asks how she is feeling. Many patients insist he is not really listening to the answer! Then he reaches for the chart at the foot of the bed, reads it and walks away.

What needs to be understood is that the doctor *is* working when he looks at those charts. The numbers and comments do mean something to him. He then goes to the nursing station and makes judgments on how best to handle the patient, what to add or alter in response to changes, or lack of changes, in the chart.

Most often, surviving families do not look at this aspect of the doctor's treatment. They only think of it in its most superficial light. He came in. He stayed a moment. He left.

One woman who has been widowed a year also speaks with great anger about her husband's physician.

"He never told me anything," she said of the doctor. "He would walk into my husband's room and nod at me like I was just slightly more than a piece of furniture. Then he'd look at the chart for a moment and that would be that. Well, let me tell you, I needed more. Much more. I needed some explanations about what was happening. My husband had cancer; we knew that. But I needed to know more. I wanted to know just what they were doing with him and why.

"As a matter of fact, I know I wouldn't be this angry today had I been made a part of the team. After all, next to my husband I am the person most affected by his death. Yet no one felt it was important enough to sit me down as many times as I needed and talk with me! If the doctor had taken a few minutes each time he saw me and told me what was going on I would not be so bitter. He would have also been preparing me had he done that."

The woman, who stands erect in a way that tells the observer that correct posture was a part of a refined upbringing, added, "I have my dignity, you know. It is not ladylike to run down the hall chasing someone. Yet that is what my contact with the doctor was. If I didn't chase him down the corridor there would have been no exchange whatsoever!"

Doctors frequently will be more communicative with the adult children of a dying patient than with the spouse.

One daughter said there were times when she felt her mother's doctor was sharing too much. "I didn't understand his medical jargon and I would try to get him to explain in simple English but he would just go on and on almost as if I was his colleague. Yet when Dad would come along he simplified his answers. I don't know if I should feel flattered or offended for my father. With all the explaining we still did not communicate. But I guess he did his best. I'm not really angry at the doctor, I guess, but I do feel a sense of oh, frustration because I didn't understand."

When she was through explaining she put on a somewhat whimsical smile. "Does it really matter, though? Mom is still dead, isn't she?"

There are children, teenagers and younger, who feel completely removed from all the proceedings surrounding a parent's final illness. Many of them rage inwardly, many outwardly, but few do not rage at all. Often their anger is directed at the doctor "who should have been able to save her." Rarely is a surviving younger child given the dignity of a medical explanation by the

doctor or by any family member. Younger people feel the injustice of this keenly. They wish above all to know just what has
transpired and why. Are they wrong in expecting this? Is it
unreasonable to want information about the event that will change
their lives for all time? Shouldn't a daughter know that her
father is terminally ill and that she should expect changes in his
behavior and in her life? Shouldn't she know this in order to
better plan her time to spend more of the remaining days with
him?

One teenaged young woman said exactly that. "If anyone had
told me, really shared with me just what was going on, I wouldn't
have slept out so much. I would have talked with Dad more and
found out what he expected me to do with my life. Instead, I
spent stupid hours at sleep-over parties and never had long
conversations that I should have had. I used to leave the house
because I was sick and tired of the sick-room atmosphere. It
made me angry. It made me feel different than my friends. Had
anyone told me he was going to die, well, the heck with it. I
would have stayed home more.

"One day I was at the hospital and saw the doctor. I walked
out of Dad's room with him and asked what was happening.
The answer I got was stupid. He's coming along as expected!
What the hell does that mean? Why didn't he tell me Dad was
dying? I had a right to know! My mother was in such a stew she
would have botched up any explanations anyhow. The doctor
should have told me. I'll never forgive him."

There is another dynamic that comes into play here. This
daughter, faced with the death of one parent, may not be eager
to place blame upon the mother. Wasn't it the mother's responsibility more than the doctor's to keep her child informed
so the daughter could make proper decisions about how to spend
her time? It is easier to be angry at a stranger but it is sometimes
an unjustified anger.

Another overlooked group of people are the surviving sisters
and brothers of the person who died.

"Jim was my brother and we were very close. I don't think
we even fought as kids," said one man now in his forties. "But
when I was told by my sister-in-law that he was dying of cancer

I was shocked. I immediately got on the phone and called his doctor. His nurse wouldn't even put me through, for God's sake. She told me the doctor had talked to Jim's wife and any information I needed could come from her.

"Jim's wife! She was so befuddled by it all that she was practically babbling and I couldn't get any straight information out of her."

How helpful it would have been had the doctor called a family meeting—even had he charged for his time. He could have invited all concerned to meet with him in order to explain the illness and answer any questions. How much anger could have been avoided.

In fact, this doctor found himself the brunt of rage in an awkward situation according to the bereaved brother.

"I'm not real proud of this, but after Jim died I ran into the doctor at a show and I called him every filthy name in the book because to this day I don't know what happened to my brother. I know he had cancer and he died. Well, that's just not enough. I wanted to know about his treatment. Should he have been seen by another doctor? Well, when I wanted questions answered by my brother's doctor, he was out to lunch."

It would be helpful to this man to attempt to separate his anger; to explore the real reason for it and perhaps even to come to know there was no culpable party. Sometimes people just die.

Those in the medical profession do need to know much more about dealing with families. Most doctors maintain they were taught almost nothing about talking to survivors. It is not uncommon for residents to be ordered to tell the family about a loved one's death. These young people, like their seniors, lack training. They also lack experience.

Since death is so much a part of medicine this lack of knowledge may seem inexplicable and heartless to a suffering relative. Furthermore, when a family is handled ineptly it can retard the healing process for them. People have a right to know how a special person died, and why a special person died; they need to be assured that effort was put into trying to save that person. Without this knowledge too much is left unanswered. A grieving person does not need to grope with more questions. Just trying to deal with the large issue of "why did this happen" is more than enough. If a doctor can be helpful in answering some part of why, it should be his moral responsibility to do so.

This is an issue that does need exploring. How can a doctor best help an entire family, thereby diffusing the anger that might otherwise come to rest upon him? Frequently different people within that family unit have different questions. They feel frustrated because the spokesperson, generally the spouse, may forget to ask a question that someone else in the group feels is pertinent. Or there are times the doctor will answer in medical terms rather than lay language and the spouse is too embarrassed at what seems to him to be his own ignorance to ask what the doctor means.

In general, survivors cannot take in a great deal of information at the moment of impact. What they need is privacy— a room where they will not be disturbed, a doctor who can touch an arm or hold a hand and offer a sincere and honest "I am sorry."

Setting aside a time for family conferences with the doctor cannot be recommended enough. One family member should ask the doctor or his nurse that the doctor be available at a given time, for perhaps half an hour, and say that the family will pay for his time. Many people would willingly pay the fee, take the time from work, just to have the opportunity to have their questions answered, even after the death.

This arrangement would not only help the bereaved family to have an idea of what was occurring and to hear it first hand, it would save them misplaced anger at the doctor. All too often when a frightened relative is trying to explain that a special person is dying and why, the story gets confused, tangled, because the teller may not understand and emotions might get in the way.

Another source of anger survivors feel is that when the person has died not only were they not given enough caring attention at the time of impact, they were not given a place to deal with the impact. That is indeed a serious problem.

One woman, whose life-long best friend died, speaks with great fury about how events transpired.

"We all knew she was dying, of course. Cancer. We were there, me and the family. A resident called her husband out into the hall away from us all and told him she died! Can you imagine that, in a hallway. That is wrong, wrong, wrong. I wanted to know some things. Did she regain consciousness? Did she say anything? Things like that. But I never had a chance to ask. Never at all and I am angry. Damn angry at that doctor's insensitivity."

Of course a hospital corridor is not the place for any important communication. Some hospitals around the country are now establishing grieving rooms. Some are located near emergency rooms, others near surgical floors, and some hospitals have them on all floors. How much more appropriate to take a family to such a room, allow them the dignity of remaining together and giving them an opportunity to cry and vent their emotions in an appropriate setting rather than asking them to hear important news in a hospital corridor where one is asked to refrain from crying and screaming because other ill patients must not be disturbed. Shouldn't all hospitals have this type of setting in order to enable the doctor to help family members cope with the enormity of death?

There is a need for new dynamics in the doctor–survivor relationship in order to prevent bitter feelings. That need if met can prevent bitter feelings after the special person dies.

Dr. William Jones of Oakland University in Michigan, a pioneer in bereavement counseling, said this lack of healthy communication between doctor and family is one reason for lawsuits after a death.

"In most cases litigation may go on for as long as four years. During that time survivors are still living through the life-and-death impact. That is also true during the trial. In my view litigation will probably prolong adjustment to the new situation. Suing does not coincide with nurturing."

Since doctors are human beings, they will have, like all of us, varying strengths and weaknesses. Some doctors simply cannot deal with a newly bereaved family. Their medical training has been deficient in this area. They feel a personal sense of failure at having been unable to save the special person; they do not feel they have the right words to offer comfort.

These real and human responses must be acknowledged because all too often the anger we have toward the doctor may well be because he cannot handle dealing with death.

One family's son died in a city unfamiliar to them. They did not have the comfort of his cardiologist, whom they knew quite well. Although they had met their son's surgeon, who is world renowned, at least three or four times, it was a resident who told them their son was dead. To the mother, it made no difference who gave the information. They were strangers in a strange city. The father, though, was offended that the surgeon did not personally tell them. This surgeon, however, did take the time a week later to write to the family to offer condolences and to invite the parents to ask any questions they deemed important. The letter was thorough enough that no further contact was necessary.

This surgeon is a man who only gets "the tough ones." Doctors from around the world do not send easily mended heart problems to him. Bearing in mind that he, too, like you, is human, how many times can he don his greens and go into surgery only to have to come out and tell a family he was sorry their child or spouse or sister had died? How often can he do this before it begins to jeopardize his ability to go into surgery with the best mental attitude? No patient deserves less. A kind, caring letter can indeed serve to buffer both the survivor and the doctor, and to allow each to get on with his life.

The responsibility to share such painful news then falls on another person and it is difficult. Such a person needs training and a proper private setting in which to do his sad job. Since little training is offered in medical school, perhaps sitting down with the hospital social worker would be of value. One such group is the men and women who are pediatric oncology social workers. They become fully integrated with the dying child and his family during the illness, often knowing the people involved more intimately than the doctor. Part of their professional doctrine is to be there as a support to the family when the child dies. They make certain they know the family beforehand so that newly grieving people need not contend with unfamiliar faces at a time of such pain.

Since it is difficult to separate anger when there is so much pain spilling over onto it, it would be helpful on a calm day to write a checklist asking yourself what you are really angry about.

- How did the doctor offend you?
- How did he treat your special person?
- Why was he the doctor of choice? Did you help select him?
- How did you feel about him when you first met him?
- Did you perceive him as being kindly? Caring?
- Did his attitude change? When?

When answered honestly, these questions may help you see more clearly that perhaps the doctor is not the nemesis you have been thinking him to be, but rather a convenient focal point for your anguish.

Albert Camus once said, "We turn to God only to obtain the impossible." When someone has suffered the death of a special person that statement becomes abundantly true. Since most people attempt to communicate with God through those they perceive to be his messengers—ministers, priests, rabbis and preachers— these individuals are often on the firing line when it comes to dealing with the impossible.

Frequently when a special person dies and the anger is very great the clergyman will bear the brunt of the unhappiness. Although in many cases it is grossly unfair, survivors will turn on these people of God with great venom, emotionally and some- times even physically.

Since most believers consider their clergy to be God's mes- sengers, it is completely logical at a time of great pain to turn to that person for answers. Unfortunately, ministers are mortal and cannot always give answers that will satisfy or appease some- one who is grieving. There are very serious communication difficulties that frequently arise.

One woman who lives in Alabama had an experience that should be shared with all who mourn as it points out the fallibility of trying to give answers verbally when a hug or a touch might have done the job.

Her son, an only child, died while he was in his twenties. The mother, who is divorced and transplanted from Texas, did what she felt was logical. When her son was pronounced dead at the scene of a motorcycle accident she turned to the one person upon whom she felt she could count, her minister. She went to his office and wept her heart out. Then she turned to him and in a simple, probably childlike way asked him, "Why? Why my son?"

"Perhaps this was God's way of telling you to be a better person," was the reply.

The woman has not been back inside a church since. What a tragedy. Of all times when she needed religion, needed to feel there is indeed someone to turn to, she found herself being guilt-tripped, being blamed. The very man who should have offered solace offered insult. And what an insult that was!

You may have experienced some discomfort with a member of the clergy at a time like this. It is not uncommon. In fact many clerics know there are often very limited people within their ranks. If you have had a negative experience, perhaps drop the cleric a line and suggest how he or she might better have handled your situation. A letter of this sort will probably help you both, and may help others who turn to this clergy-person later.

• Begin by accenting the positive. If he was helpful with children, say so. Was there an elderly person whom he remembered to comfort? Did he suggest anything unique that made the funeral or mourning period easier? Was his biblical selection of value? Tell him.

• Try to enlist him as an ally. Let him know you hope to help others.

Since so little is taught in theological seminaries about death, that information can be invaluable to a caring, open-minded cleric.

Or if you are active in a church, ask the minister to invite several bereaved people whom he trusts and knows well. Tell him you wish to share your experience as the recipient of his ministering.

Begin by telling him what was helpful:

- The eulogy
- His presence
- His suggestions
- His obvious sadness

It might be equally helpful to all in the congregation to discuss what did *not* work for you. Try to do this without displaying anger, as your message will be better received if it does not sound like an accusation.

If he lacks the capacity to care and learn you do indeed have a right to your frustration. Bear in mind, though, the minister is not God. Do not give up on Him.

FIND ANOTHER CHURCH.

Petty slights and injustices can take hold within you when a special person has died. One woman, a widow of nearly a decade, still holds her rabbi in great contempt. She is angry because he did not mention her children from a prior marriage when he gave the eulogy for her husband.

"After all, my husband raised them, too. They are people and he should not have ignored them like he did. All he talked about were the children from that other marriage, his natural children. I haven't set foot in his synagogue since then and I never will!"

In hearing her tell the story, you may feel that she has taken a triviality and allowed it to be built into a major offense. Once again, she has placed the mantle of infallibility upon another human being. Since all of us err, there is a certain injustice to her dismissal.

The larger issue, of course, is the fact that she is angry because her husband died. She most probably needed something on which to focus her anger. Most people seem to feel this same need.

Begin to separate legitimate anger from an inner rage at your ill fortune by asking yourself these questions:

• Do you honestly believe you or your special person were abused emotionally?
• Did an authority figure let you down by showing he was normal, fallible? If such a person displayed indifference or insensitivity, you have every right to your anger. If that person was unable to ease your hurt or make you feel all better, that is unreasonable. No one can take away the pain of such a dreadful loss. Only you can work at it by yourself, in a group, with a therapist. Only time and effort are your allies.

Use them!

Bear in mind that angry people are not easy to be with. Despite the best intentions, the people who make up your support system may wear down unless you display control at some point. If you do not, you will simply be too exhausting to be around for any length of time.

Sometimes the need to find someone or something to blame takes on strange proportions. One man, recently widowed, "groused" (that was his word) because the minister was not dressed in a black suit. It seems the minister, who had known the family for many years, was paged at the airport after returning from a trip and was told to go to the church immediately for the funeral. Believing his presence to be more important than his attire, he arrived at the church wearing a gray pin-striped suit. Although the widower found the eulogy flawless, he was nevertheless angry because the minister "didn't show the proper respect."

How do you define proper respect? Is it in the deed, the word, the clothing? Certainly this is individual, but had the widower not needed a focal point for his anger would a gray pin-striped suit have become an issue so divisive between two men who had known one another for many years? Is this not yet another example of the need to identify why a mourner is angry?

For many surviving children, especially those below the age of twenty, there appears to be little comfort offered from any quarter. Parents, relatives, friends, all are wrapped up in their own grief. Young people question only their own place in the new order. Where will they fit? Is college still possible? How will their lives be altered?

These questions are frequently asked of a clergyman because the clergyman appears to be the only person even remotely interested in listening. If these children and their ministers could only learn the honesty of sharing that not all life's questions can be answered, a greater sense of ease could perhaps be achieved. Instead, young people turn to clergy with the sense that they will receive godlike advice. The clergyman is placed in the position of not wishing to fail the young person and does not disabuse him of the notion that a cleric is godlike.

One seventeen-year-old whose mother had just died left a session with her priest incensed. "He was so patronizing to me. He's known me since I was a kid and maybe that's the problem. But, damn it, you can't stay a kid when your mom has died. That's when the line changes. He didn't understand me when I told him I wasn't there for platitudes. He just kept on quoting from scriptures that he felt would help. I needed him to tell me how in the world I was going to make it without Mom. I didn't need biblical references! I don't know, maybe I need to speak to a younger priest or something."

How do you answer someone who feels patronized during a crisis? As a listener, as a survivor, should not great compassion be shown for a motherless child filled with fear of the future? Certainly the priest could not have set out to do the young woman less than justice or offer her less than his best counsel but the communication gap between what was needed and what was given is very wide indeed. Perhaps a younger priest, or just another priest, would have made a difference. Few clergymen are equally attuned to every age's problems. Try someone else, but don't give up.

One woman whose brother had been killed while in the Army tried to explain to a clergyman that she felt responsible.

"I had told him to enlist. After our folks got divorced there didn't seem to be any other way for him to get a college education or learn a trade. I heard the television ads and suggested he give it a try. After all, they promise career training. Well, he took my advice and was shipped overseas and killed in Viet Nam.

"When I tried to explain to our minister just how much I was to blame for all of this he just seemed to shrug me aside as if what I said had no relevance. No one else was listening. I expected him to. He wasn't being fair."

Fairness. Since you, as a survivor, know so well there is no such thing as fairness, it is perhaps unjust to expect this of our religious leaders. You are angry. You need a focal point for that anger and clergypeople are well aware of this. Yet, they all too often are vilified because there is no one else upon whom to focus your anger. When that occurs, everyone loses.

One minister in Ohio summed it up well. "When people ask me 'why,' I no longer attempt to even answer that question. They are really not hearing me, anyway. That 'why' to me simply means the person needs some real human warmth and feedback. I make it a point to put my arms around the person and tell him how truly sorry I am—and to be a good listener. If I don't have all the answers, I don't pretend I do. Instead, I say, we'll just have to do the best we can as situations come up."

This minister demonstrates he wishes to stand in as a helper and does not wish your anger as a survivor to focus upon him. He believes he has accomplished this to a large degree with his approach.

There is the additional problem of the eulogy when a special person dies. It is rare that all people immediately involved walk away satisfied that their own special part in the dead person's life has been acknowledged. People will sit through a funeral and wait to be recalled and hope that whatever part they played in the dead person's life is discussed. Owing to solely practical matters, rarely is everyone given the recognition he or she needs. Time does not permit, and people overwrought with grief *do* forget to share with the minister certain things that perhaps should have been included in the service. There are some avenues of recourse, even if there will never be another eulogy. You could help compile the newspaper notice, and help yourself and others to receive acknowledgment. Or you could put together a book of remembrance for the family, something that will let them know how important their special person was.

One woman traveled hundreds of miles to attend the funeral of a close friend. When she got to the funeral home, the clergyman, after being introduced, noted how glad he was to see her. "You can really help this family a great deal. You can see how griefstricken they really are!" The friend was very distressed for she had traveled to be a mourner, not to be a part of the support system.

"I should have been in there with these people I've known all my life, yet somehow I was not made to feel a part of the proceedings. We were very close and suddenly our relationship was diminished. Even the clergyman did not understand."

Perhaps this is the essence of the problem: somehow clerics are supposed to know all and understand all. *Even* the clergyman did not understand.

When you experience such negative situations it is important to speak up, not to keep silent, not to assume "that's the way it has to be." Although you may not effect change for yourself, your voice may help another friend further along the line who feels shut out. In the long run there may be some satisfaction in this knowledge for you. To be effective:

• Let the cleric know your displeasure.
• Tell the funeral director you felt slighted because you wished to remain in the family room—especially if the family wanted you there.
• Explain up front that you are a mourner, whatever your relationship.

Perhaps if enough people share their experiences with clergy and others in authority, they will understand and ultimately do what they really wish to do: that is *help*.

But when someone special has died you experience such a sense of deprivation that feelings become overly sensitive and almost anyone is fair game when you lash out.

The clergyman has a difficult task attempting to bring some order into the lives of those who survive the death of a special person. It is a most difficult task and all too often leaves the clergyman frustrated as well. He knows he is only able to help to a limited degree. Many clergymen and women have commented on the dreadful sense of inadequacy they feel, especially when the death has been tragic or sudden. Perhaps if you remember that these people, despite years spent studying theology, are not more than human at the bottom line, you may develop a more tolerant attitude toward behavior and things that were said or perhaps left unsaid when your special person died. Perhaps by understanding the difficulties and limitations of these clergymen you could diminish your level of anger. Certainly, without understanding, this simply cannot occur.

If your feelings are stronger, examine them. Are you really angry at the clergyman's action or words or are you angry at and frustrated by the death of your special person? Once you understand the true cause of your anger, you can lower its level and continue with your life.

Socrates once remarked, "To fear death, gentlemen, is nothing other than to think oneself wise when one is not; for it is to think one knows what one does not know. No man knows whether death may not even turn out to be the greatest of blessings for a human being; and yet people fear it as if they knew for certain that it is the greatest of evils."

Because we so fear death, we become angry as we become mourners. Our angry attention often becomes focused on those professionals whose work is exclusively with death—funeral directors.

As a survivor you felt yourself becoming increasingly angry. All too frequently funeral directors become the bad guys when your special person has died. You may have looked at this person and thought to yourself, "My husband is dead and he is making money off my tragedy." This is certainly not unique, but rather the norm among mourners. There may have been great suspicion when you first had to deal with the funeral director. If he made any suggestion at all, you may have interpreted it to mean he was looking out for more money. It is unfortunate that so many people have this negative view of funeral directors. In such a crisis, how can you make appropriate decisions when you do not have a modicum of trust in the person there to guide you?

Current national legislation makes it mandatory for all funeral directors to issue an itemized statement of every charge that is made. At the time of the death of a special person, few people are attuned to just how much each item costs, nor do they care, but for many it matters later. Many directors recommend you bring along a close friend or relative to lend some clarity to the decision-making process.

Generally, funeral directors are stuck in the middle of conflicts.

One widow, quite angry with her funeral director, said: "My sons went along and made all the arrangements. They never consulted me. They spent my insurance money and came back to tell me how it would be! Why didn't the director ask if there was a widow? How did he dare make the arrangements without checking with me? After all, he was my husband. It was up to him to see *I* was represented."

It is always easier for us to blame an outsider than a son or daughter who has usurped authority. We do not have to *live* with the director but we do with our families. Often people do not wish to bring such displeasure back home; it seems easier to leave it at the funeral home.

Widowers in particular often feel such rage at the death of their wife that they come into the funeral home prepared to do battle: anyone or anything may prove to be the focal point of that anger. Working at calming down such a man is difficult indeed. He generally is not hearing well because he is in shock. He is also having great difficulty paying attention to detail. Funeral directors have said this is indeed a problem that requires infinite patience. Questions are frequently asked over and over again, yet when the widower leaves the director's office he will return to his family saying nobody wanted his opinion.

Nothing could be further from the truth according to most directors. They, indeed, want input. After all it is your special person who is being buried and you should make the decisions.

Since few people are assertive when they are hurting, the burden of responsibility rests with the director. He should offer to come to the hospital if there is a stillbirth, to the house for other deaths, when it is possible. Selections may always be made later. Since people are more comfortable in their own surroundings, a dialogue of what they truly wish to be included in the funeral may be easier at home. The director must ask pertinent questions: Are there other children? Sisters? Brothers? Close friends? He should suggest that a mourner be accompanied by a close friend or relative when making decisions about the burial or cremation. He should help in the selection of the burial outfit—or at least make the offer.

One director whose community is comprised of many elderly people frequently drives the widow to a local department store if she wishes his help to purchase a new outfit for her dead husband.

If people do not have a clergyman, the director should suggest one who delivers eulogies that are sympathetic.

If the mourners do not wish a cleric, and a family member or friend is to give the eulogy, the director might help that person with guidelines. Such guidelines should include the following:

- A chronological history of the person who died
- His most special characteristics
- Some anecdotes gleaned from *more than one mourner* that describe the type of person he was
- Possibly some parable about the dead person and his dealings with those left behind

While the inner anger at the death and our loss takes work to lessen, it is possible to help alleviate external anger. Ask a friend or relative whom you trust to help guide you through this morass. If he sees you are going in a direction he feels you will regret later—perhaps you are not telling a director or clergyman what you really wish done but are instead sharing that information only with your friend—he may be able to help you avoid anger that serves no purpose other than to make you raw and even more distraught.

One young woman now in her mid-twenties said she had felt completely ignored and was furious during the entire sad process of her brother's death until the director came to her home. "He actually took the time to talk with me and ask what would be meaningful to me. Well, my brother and I shared a lot of record albums and I wanted our favorite one—the one we always fought over—in the coffin with him. My parents would never have asked me what I wanted and if it hadn't been for the director I would have been angry with myself for years probably. But that's how it goes. Other people in my home may yell about being overcharged and everything else but he was sure my friend that day!"

All professionals have their specific problems, and funeral directors are no different. They are in a business where they *never* see happiness. Instead they are confronted with every negative in the human spectrum of emotions. Perhaps to know this might help the perspective. While it is easy to be filled with hatred and anger when a special person dies it is not helpful to let that anger fester. To know funeral directors are also feeling people with lives and problems of their own might help improve your perception at a difficult time.

Many times friends come along to help make funeral arrangements. They are genearlly welcomed by the director because he knows the degree of confusion a mourner experiences. But there are times when friends do step over the line in the zeal to protect. If you have had the experience of accompanying a family member you know that feeling well. You wish to do all you can to aid your friend but sometimes that aid is *too much*. There is a point where you must step back and let the bereaved person make his or her own decision. If you do not, there can be great regret later.

Most people find their protectiveness comes to the fore over the issue of how much to spend. You, the survivor, have a sense that you wish to do all that is possible for your special person as this is the final act you will perform for him. Certainly that is to be commended. On the other hand, there is a level of self-protection you must employ. No ethical funeral director ever tries to encourage a survivor to spend more than he is able. Friends often enter the situation with a degree of suspicion and a fear you will be overcharged. This fear is easily transmitted to you, the mourner, and often wrong decisions are made for that reason.

One bereaved father went into the funeral home surrounded by his brother and two close friends. All were so suspicious of each cost that they came away having arranged a very Spartan funeral. When the child's mother came to the funeral home to see her young son she was enraged. "We have the money, after all. He's never going to go to college. Why should a cheap funeral be his final earthly happening?"

The father, who was telling this experience, said he merely mumbled that he didn't want to get "taken" by the director. This answer, he said, never satisfied his wife.

Funeral directors have worked assiduously to upgrade their profession. In at least one state they are required to get a certain number of education hours each year in order to stay abreast of current mental health thinking. The hope is that this type of program will make directors better able to handle each situation as it arises. Because each death is an individual matter after all.

Cicero once said if you have no basis for an argument, abuse the plaintiff. If you are unable to justify the death, to answer the inevitable "why" your special person has died, you frequently find yourself inexplicably angry at the dead person. You are, in effect, abusing the plaintiff.

You have probably been extremely angry at the dead person. You have felt like shouting and screaming at him for causing you so much pain. Know you are not alone—that is most important. You are experiencing an emotion that is extremely common. One mother used to wait until everyone had left the house for the day and then she would rant and rage at her dead daughter. She would scream at her for leaving and leaving such agony behind her. She feared sharing her feelings with anyone because she believed it was nearly sacrilege to be so angry. After all, have we not all been raised to "not speak ill of the dead"? Yet this mother found herself screaming at her child who died in an accident, through no wish of her own. Illogical? Perhaps. But certainly not uncommon.

Sometimes there are emotions that simply must run their course. There is no magic that will erase this type of anger. The most helpful thing to know and hold onto is the certainty that you are not alone. Nearly all mourners have been angry at a dead loved one during some period of grief. Know you are in the majority. Do not add a feeling of isolation to your other pains.

One woman finds herself in a rage during all major holiday seasons. She feels neglected and abandoned. "Now if I want to go to a picnic, I have to rely on others. I'm not a free agent anymore. When my husband was alive he drove me everywhere. How could he have done this to me?" She asks the question of all who will listen and of course no one can reply for there is no rational answer.

One widower said he and his wife always promised to be together but she broke her promise and he is angry. Now, thrust into a strange new world where his orderly routine no longer exists, he feels abandoned. With that feeling comes great anger. Great rage. A sense of rejection.

Surviving children who are not yet settled into their own adult lives suffer terribly from anger. There is a sense in many of them that "If my dad had really loved me he would still be alive." No amount of explaining and discussing seems to dispel this idea when the young person has come to believe it. It takes years and often therapy or perhaps a strong support group before a surviving child can really understand that the parent had no wish to die.

Surviving sisters and brothers also feel angry and abandoned. One young man, just before his wedding, felt a surge of anger overtake him. His brother had been dead for ten years. "But when I walked down that aisle my brother, not my friend, should have been my best man. My brother should have proposed the first toast." Certainly there is no logic to this concept. When someone dies involuntarily, how can they be faulted and raged at? Yet this is frequently exactly what we do.

One woman had a friend who was very close to her. The friend developed cancer and died within six months of the diagnosis. "Now I have no one to talk with. No one to share with. How could she have done this to me?"

When a grandchild dies there is a sense of great deprivation and accompanying anger. The grandparents feel cheated, and who can question the validity of that emotion? "We moved to Florida and bought a condominium with an extra bedroom so our grandson could come down over the school vacations. He was our only one. We planned this for our retirement. Then he was hit by a drunk driver and killed. Now we have nothing," said the grandfather, his eyes welling with tears. "Nothing. How could he have done this to us? He knew we loved him so! How could he have died?" He pounded one fist into his open palm. Surely there was no point then of reminding him that his own daughter and her husband were still alive and could visit. He would not have taken it in. Only time, sometimes a lot of it, seems to ease the anger. Yet to be told that when you are in the middle of your rage is offensive and often makes you even more angry.

There is, of course, an entirely different set of emotions that is brought into play when a special person dies of suicide. There are differing schools of thought about this entire issue. Generally people call it "committing suicide," thereby suggesting that it is a voluntary act over which the dead person had full control. Certainly any right-thinking parent, widow, widower, child, brother or friend would be enraged to think their special person electively abandoned them. It is an affront. It says to these people they were not good enough to help—not capable enough. It says they were insensitive. It invariably makes them feel they should have known and above all they should have been able to prevent it. That is what most people think of someone committing suicide. Since these people are made to feel not good enough, unworthy, unhelpful, unfeeling, is it any wonder there is much anger when someone commits suicide?

For many years now families have labored under this yoke. In some religions a suicide is not even buried in the tended part of the cemetery: grass and weeds are allowed to grow wild. There is shame. There is guilt. It is not good enough that the family feels their own special added burden because of this kind of death, it seems society is frequently bent upon heaping even more pain on those who already suffer so greatly.

One mother who is a nurse experienced the suicide of her only daughter. She kept reiterating that she worked with sick people all the time, how was it that she was unable to see how much trouble her daughter was in? After her self-recrimination she began to cry. "How could she have done that? What could have been so terrible in her life that this was even possible? Why didn't she come to me? Sometimes I hate her."

How much more gentle to think her daughter *died of* suicide. Many people in the mental health community believe there are some who simply cannot live. They suffer internally so much that being alive is like having a cancer of the soul. To understand this and come to accept it has helped many people. This is new thinking, a new perspective. Some people simply cannot live.

One woman whose husband died of suicide bore him great rage. Because he was a fairly prominent man, many people knew the cause of his death. She felt shame. She said she would walk down the street feeling people were looking at her and viewing her as an inadequate person. But when the concept of his dying *of* suicide was presented to her she seemed to straighten up and stand just a little taller. The iron band of self-accusation had been lifted. In time she came to fully accept the idea that her husband, like many others, simply could not live.

One widower whose wife died of suicide when she was just forty years of age always made it a point to tell anyone he dated just how she died. It was as if he felt a moral obligation to cast himself in the role of a merciless man who should be dated with caution.

"After all, if I had been a more understanding husband she would still be alive today," he explained one day while sitting with a group of other survivors of suicide.

One of the group members took issue with this statement.

"She died of suicide because she could not live. You could not have taken away her hurt anymore than you could have cured any other fatal illness!"

The widower paused for a moment and slowly told the group members he would have to begin thinking along those lines if he wished to save his sanity. "It's my only hope. I can't go on like this. Blaming myself. Maybe she really couldn't live. Maybe."

With that maybe came an intonation of hope this man had not had before.

All young people have a sense of omnipotence. They believe they can control events depending on their behavior. This is even the case when parents divorce. When a special person, parent, brother or friend dies of suicide, young people are convinced they are responsible. Since they hate carrying that burden, and of course it is an illogical one, they become angry with the special person who died. One young man said of his father, "I hate him for killing himself. He should have been here to advise me as I was growing up. He should have been here when business and school decisions had to be made. How the hell could he have done this to me?"

Then, after a pause he added, "Why didn't I see what was wrong with him? Why couldn't I help him?"

Again, how much more helpful it would have been for this young man to have been told his father died of suicide. Does it not have the power to bring about a change in perception?

One woman is very angry because her father killed himself. She has four children all close in age. "They should have had a grandfather. They were cheated. If he hadn't committed suicide our family would be whole. I hate him!"

There is an old saying that hell hath no fury like a woman scorned. There is perhaps one worse fury and that is the fury of a mother who believes her child did not get a fair shake. Ask any mother who has broken up a playground fight between her child and "that little monster" and you will know true fury. How much deeper then if the mother feels their own father deprived her children of something that should have been their birthright? That is why it is so important to reexamine our societal attitudes about suicide. As long as we believe it is a voluntary act committed by a rational person rather than an act committed by someone in dreadful pain that he believes to be irreversible, generation after generation will go on feeling the pangs of a guilt that should not be theirs to carry. The anger and the rage expended by survivors could be better employed at working through their mourning and grief.

Voltaire once said "To believe in God is impossible, not to believe in him is absurd."

Of the many angers you might feel when a special person has died, one of the most difficult to deal with and yet one of the most ordinary is the anger you feel toward God. Many people who were deeply religious, or thought they were, have turned away when a child dies. "If there was really a God, how could this have happened?" is a fairly common response.

People who have been active churchgoers for years have labored with their anger at such a time. When there is no one left to blame and no one with whom to find fault and yet the desperate need to do so lies within you, frequently you will latch onto God as the culprit.

This is true of the whole spectrum of important loss. The problem with focusing your anger on God is that it prevents you from getting help from your belief in God. It is easier to feel there is a plan, a reason for the death of your special person. If you feel anger toward God it becomes impossible to accept this concept. If you were raised with the Ten Commandments, and you begin berating God, you will eventually begin to feel a guilt that is unjust toward yourself. Your burden becomes even greater when you feel you have blasphemed. Yet to feel this anger is very common: people at funerals scream to the high heavens about their rage with God.

If a parent feels all those who should have done their job in order to save their son did so properly, who is left to blame? This sense of flailing your arms about at something invisible that does not give you an audible response is devastating. Just at the time you are most in need, to deprive yourself of anything that may offer comfort is sad indeed.

"My husband was only sick for a week. No one even knew he had a bad heart," said one woman. "There can be no good God if my husband is dead. I am expecting our first baby. How can there be a God if such a thing can happen?"

You may well have heard such statements or indeed, you may have made them. In the final analysis, there is very little that can be said during the height of someone's anger to ease the rage. Sometimes just offering a friendly ear may eventually help the rage subside.

One widower who was left with two young children said his rage toward God was enormous. "Here I am and my children are motherless. How do I begin to raise them? How could there be a God who would allow children to be raised without a mother?"

Again, platitudes don't resolve anything. It is better to be a good listener and offer a hug than to argue a case that cannot be won.

Children whose parents have died often have difficulty when they are sent to Sunday school to learn about God and religion. It takes a special kind of minister or clergyman to recognize that these bereft youngsters need to discuss their anger with God. They often feel He is a vengeful God. They often feel any prayer is hypocritical, and they experience great discomfort in offering it. There are no really solid answers, according to most clergypeople. The most comforting thing probably is honesty. We do not know how God works or why He works. That is a concept most people can accept.

One young man stopped believing in God after his sister died.

At first his family fought him when he vilified God. They fought him when he stood alone and would not attend church. Finally, after seeking counsel with a therapist, they stopped becoming entangled in the issue. The sister has been dead for seven years now and he, on his own, has decided that perhaps he will attend Mass during the coming Christmas. Some things cannot be done by force or insistence. They must flow naturally. In much the same manner, things may subside naturally if left alone. Anger toward God, in many cases, is one of those things.

In general, there are so many angers you feel when a special person dies. You have such an overriding sense of injustice that nearly anything can be turned to anger when you are mourning. Nearly anyone can be the victim of that anger, its focal point. You may benefit immensely by knowing that. You are not alone. No emotion you feel, regardless of how negative, is so terrible that it can't be shared. There can be great comfort in knowing that you are not isolated. Others have felt as you do. Others have had to come to terms with their rage.

Bear in mind, there is no point in attempting to interject logic when a mourner is in such a period of anger unless you, as part of the support system, have been through the experience. If you know someone who mourned a similar death, and has come to grips, at least partially, with his anger, you might want to introduce them.

If you know no such person the clergy or funeral directors can be helpful as resource people. They are the ones who know the mourners.

It is always a surprise to see the instant rapport established by fellow mourners. How comforting to hear, "I remember when I felt as you are now feeling."

By lending an ear you are doing a great deal of good. Sometimes anger is like an infected sore that must ooze until it is cleansed. If you have been a fellow mourner it would be helpful to tell someone who is angry that verbalizing what they are feeling can ultimately result in cleansing. However, some discretion must be used. A mourner must not rage continuously in any given situation. He must exercise some control over where, when and how long. It is possible to do this. If the mourner fails to impose controls over himself, a friend might gently remind him he has gone on long enough for the people he is with at that given time. They may even establish a prearranged signal.

With the beginning of this discipline may come a longer-ranged discipline that will enable the mourner to be more comfortable to be with. In other words, a caring person may actively help someone who is grieving to keep his support system—the system that may well serve as his mainstay during his time of mourning.

When feeling intense anger a mourner may ask himself some pithy questions that require real thought.

• What do you think about when the waves of anger are set in motion?
• Are you angry because you are lonely?
• Are you angry because your life has changed so radically?
• Are you angry because you lost the ability to keep your special person alive?
• Is it easier to be angry with the doctor, funeral director or clergyman than the ill fortune that is intangible and cannot be seen?

When you have completed your checklist read it over and pull it out whenever you sense rage building within you. If you think there are some things that need to be discussed with a particular professional with whom you dealt write a letter and let him know. Be specific. Use the checklists outlined earlier in this chapter (pp. 115–121). Tell him he must learn better skills for families or there will be many more angry survivors. Since no one likes to feel they have mishandled a situation, seeing your words on paper may have real impact. In any event you will have the assurance that you acted in a forthright manner by letting him know your displeasure.

• Finally, if you are angry because you wish you had done things differently at the funeral, use the first birthday after your special person's death and perhaps invite close people to your home.
• Play his favorite songs on the record player.
• Read his favorite passages of books or poetry aloud to those who are gathered.
• Ask everyone to say a few words about him. Ask them to share their favorite memories—and perhaps even their most unpleasant.

A year later it may be easier for you to remember the things you wish to share because some time has elapsed since he died.

MOST IMPORTANT OF ALL, STOP ASKING WHY HE DIED. THE ANSWER IS NEVER WHAT YOU HOPE WILL SATISFY YOU. LET GO OF THE WHY AND BEGIN TO HOLD ON TO LIFE. THAT IS INDEED LIVING THROUGH MOURNING.

Pathways Through Guilt

Of all sad words of tongue or pen the most
destructive are: "If only I had."
—ANONYMOUS

Once a trio of young men who lived in the Bible Belt were caught
red-handed breaking the sabbath. Guilt-ridden for their sins yet
fearful of the punishment they were likely to receive, they were
taken before the stern preacher the next day. They shook with
fear as he asked for an explanation of their behavior.

The first young man, feeling great guilt, said, "Sir, I was
absentminded and forgot that yesterday was the sabbath."

"That could be," replied the preacher. "You are forgiven."

Also very upset, the second young man said he too was absentminded. "I forgot that I was not allowed to gamble on the
sabbath."

"Well, that could also be," said the preacher. "You are forgiven."

Finally, the preacher turned to the young man in whose home
these events occurred. "Well, what is your excuse? I suppose
you were absentminded, too!"

"I sure was, sir," said the lad, a known troublemaker and the
instigator of the card game.

"What did *you* forget?" inquired the preacher.

"I forgot to pull the shades down!" replied the boy.

This little story illustrates well how people perceive themselves when feeling guilty. The first two boys simply forgot and did not knowingly commit a wrong. The third boy knew full well he was breaking the sabbath and therefore knowingly did commit a wrong.

These same principles may be applied when a special person dies and you are feeling somehow responsible. Ask yourself whether or not you in fact *did* bring about his death. That is a simple yes or no question and it is unlikely that yes is the answer. If you did not bring about his death, then you are abusing yourself and holding yourself responsible for something which is totally beyond your control: you did not hold the power of life or death; his death was not a function of your being.

Guilt has been divided into two categories by the National Funeral Directors, according to bereavement counselor Marilyn Gilbert. She says, "Frequently survivors recall things that could have been done and that is common. It is realistic and has an honest base in *fact*. Unrealistic guilt stems from situations that were uncontrollable. That type of guilt is irrational and must be discussed with a professional. Unresolved guilt, whether normal or neurotic, can be harmful either physically or emotionally."

Webster defines guilt as the act or state of having done a wrong or committed an offense; culpability, legal or ethical. This is not to be confused with the sense of wishing that things had been different. People often wish they had done more, said something different, behaved more kindly. These latter feelings are common and almost universal in the grief process. You feel guilty in thought but you are not guilty in fact.

Mourners frequently completely overlook reality as they frantically search for a meaning to the tragedy. Why did this happen? How? Somehow it must have been my fault. These are common thoughts. Try to remember those nagging moments of guilt will overtake you, and when they do you are not alone. You share these emotions with most of the bereaved populace.

You may have intense feelings that you should have done

more, you should have called another doctor, you were sometimes mean or hostile to your special person, you should have recognized that person's medical symptoms.

All of these and a host of other destructive thoughts find ways of working into your inner self at the time you are most vulnerable. There are even those who welcome the pain these sensations cause, for rather than having nothing to focus on, you can at least "luxuriate" in blaming yourself.

Dr. Philip Muskin, a psychiatrist at Columbia University, says, "The wellspring of guilt runs deep. Sometimes there is an unconscious sense of triumph that is momentary at having outlived the special person."

According to Dr. Muskin, bereavement as well as life are comprised of millions of moments, some happy and others painful. He said those who deal with long-term illnesses tend to go more gently into grieving: "There are fewer loose ends, often self-forgiveness and a more positive self-judgment. Also, there are those who strongly believe in an afterlife that offers them comfort."

He said frequently people feel guilty because they are experiencing a sense of deprivation and feel guilty over wanting pleasure. For many survivors, sexuality is a source of great distress because they feel they should not pursue pleasure. Often when a child has died one or the other surviving parent will reject sex. Surviving siblings and children and friends may also reject sex for the same reason.

"But," says Dr. Muskin, "sexuality is normal. The desire for pleasure is normal. People are entitled to sexuality and intimacy."

All too often bereaved people feel that to give in to such normal, healthy impulses is against society's rules, not what is done. Yet to share that intimacy can offer some pleasure and relief from our pain. "It is really a catch-22 situation," said Dr. Muskin.

Perhaps the greatest gift a friend, a counselor or a member of a support group may offer is that of giving someone who is grieving "permission" to enjoy something of his life. To assure him that he is not unfeeling if he experiences or desires pleasure.

One young man was driving his car and ran a red light. His three-year-old son, who was not buckled into his safety seat, died in the collision with a car crossing the intersection. The man has suffered immense pangs of guilt. "How could I have run that light? Why didn't I buckle my son in his seat?" These and many other things have run through his mind, adding greatly to an already overwrought sense of pain. This man feels like a murderer, but he was negligent. He is also a victim: a victim of his own negligence, but it goes without saying he will bear the burden of this the rest of his life. Despite any forgiveness his church or family might offer it will never be good enough. He will go to the end of his days feeling he killed his child unless strong mental health intervention is called into play.

Dr. William Jones, a "significant loss" pioneer of Oakland University, says when a bereaved person is finally willing to listen, "intent is the issue. Did others find you guilty? Did you want to kill your child? It is very sad that people are looking for self-blame when they are already hurting so badly."

This man who does not perceive himself as a victim but rather as a murderer is dealing with a double tragedy. A murderer is someone who has deliberately committed a culpable legal offense. Does this in any way describe the father who drove a car in which his child was accidentally killed? Certainly not. Yet to convince the young father of this truth would be a hard task indeed. He has so incorporated his own culpability into his mourning that he seems unable even to attempt to separate the two. Yet in that separation could lie his salvation and his sanity.

Guilt is nearly universal to those who have suffered the death of a special person. When a child dies as a result of stillbirth there is enormous guilt generally upon the part of both parents. Frequently media information becomes a conveyor of guilt, and can cause great suffering. The question of whether or not smoking marijuana harms a fetus; the effect of the use of harder drugs: "Was my baby premature because I smoked cigarettes? Is that why she died?" "Was it that drink?" These and many other such questions torment young parents groping for a reason for the death of their perfectly innocent child.

One woman whose nine-year-old was dying of cancer cried

bitterly in a hospital waiting room. Between sobs she said, "I used to get in back seats with guys a lot. I felt guilty, sure, like God was watching me, but I thought, 'What the hell?' Now I know what the hell! God waited and my baby is dying. He never even had a chance. He is paying for my sins."

This mother was in a situation where a hospital social worker or psychiatric nurse could well have offered her some ease. She said the social worker did come around but she had no wish to share her guilt with anyone. It is only to be hoped that someone somewhere will be able to speak with her. Perhaps her clergy-man, if she will only open herself to sharing.

She had a further problem in that she was divorced and not in contact with the child's father, who had left the state without a forwarding address and had ceased sending child support.

"I hope he feels guilty too when he hears. But he says the boy isn't his! Well he is, I swear it. Oh, my God, what can I do?"

Although the listener can do little to ease the guilt and the distraught feelings the woman sits and heaps upon herself there is one thing that can be done: hold her hand, put an arm around her shoulder. Touching. She probably would not hear mur-murings of sympathy but she certainly would understand the sensation of human warmth. Sometimes that is the best you can offer. It may not seem like enough but it is frequently more helpful than the platitudes that spring so readily to your lips, statements that can be misinterpreted by a distraught person.

While you may be helpful by listening sympathetically it is nearly pointless, especially in early days, to argue with the prem-ise of magical thinking—the sense that one's thoughts and un-related actions can bring about such a catastrophe. Acknowledge the mourner's pain and perhaps as time elapses you will be able to interject some reasonable questions.

- Is God after all such a cruel God that your son paid for *your* sins with *his* life?
- Is this the God you've worshipped?

When people become intimate in support groups this issue does surface. Hearing others express similar self-blame may help to ease some of your own pain. If you are still overwhelmed by such pain after a period of time—say four to six months—it might be a good idea to enter into private counseling.

Widows too have very deep and special problems. Many women have bemoaned the slowness of the ambulance's arrival. "I know he would have been alive if I had called sooner," said one woman. "I just didn't believe he was really having a heart attack. He could talk. All he said was his chest hurt. I almost drove him in my car but a neighbor said an ambulance would get him to the hospital faster. Well, it might have had it gotten to my house quickly enough! He died on the way. I probably should have driven him." Somehow this woman was determined to find a way of casting blame upon herself. It was almost a need to give reason to the suddenness of his death.

Another widow tells the story of her husband, an athletic man in his forties, who collapsed and was near death en route to the hospital. She rode in the ambulance with him and asked only that they take him to the closest one. She was assured that that was what was always done. As she rode with the siren blaring she was consumed with doubt and guilt and questioning. They had argued earlier in the day. An intelligent woman, she knew as she rode and watched frantic life-support measures that she would have to live with that last morning always.

When the ambulance arrived at the hospital her husband was quickly transferred inside where doctors worked over him frantically but to no avail; he was dead. As she waited in the emergency room she telephoned her married son, whose first response was anger: "Why didn't you take him to the hospital that specializes in cardiac care? Why is he there?"

The woman, already overwrought with anxiety and guilt over their morning quarrel, cut her son off: "I was the one on the spot, not you. Whatever decision was made I had to make alone. Don't you dare lay that guilt on me. I simply will not accept it!" She went on to shout at him and ask how he dared challenge her decision. "You weren't married to him. I was."

The son grew silent over the telephone and finally when he could find his voice he said he was coming right over. "Thank you," was all the mother said as she hung up.

While she waited her mind went back to what she had said to her son and she recognized the truth of her words. Since that time so early in her mourning, despite being in shock during part of that time, she has never allowed false feelings of guilt to overtake what was real and solid, and that was her marriage.

"Had I known he was going to die, I would have avoided that quarrel. But no one knows when these things will happen. I have to think that we had a normal, healthy marriage. One that was important to both of us, as was our life together. I cannot allow myself to dwell on the negatives. We all have them in our marriages. That's the thing to remember."

There are many women who complain about how they "no longer have a moment to themselves." Their newly retired husbands, unprepared for retirement, have no hobbies, no interests. These women can no longer meet with friends for lunch because they feel so guilty about leaving their husbands home alone. Sometimes they become irritated when they cannot scrub down their homes as they once did because their husbands want to be on the go.

As these women become widows, they feel terribly guilty. If you are such a widow, try to remember that what you were feeling was normal. After all, your life pattern was interrupted. You may be feeling you "begrudged him what years he had to live." How unfairly you treat yourself with such thinking!

One woman said, "All I wanted to do was go with my friends. I deserve to be a widow. I didn't appreciate him enough." Such thinking is not uncommon. It is needless and frequently creates a major stumbling block toward healing, but it is not uncommon. It is a real emotion felt by many other widows.

Sometimes just to know there are others who have felt as you feel can be helpful. There can be great comfort in the fact that your feelings, which seem to be running amok, are in fact felt by hundreds of thousands of others in your circumstances.

There are younger widows with small children who feel great guilt because their marriage had not yet stabilized. "We never really had a chance. We got married and had a baby two years later. I never had the time to go to work and feel good about myself. I used to resent his taking off every day and leaving me behind. We fought about my going back to work but he wouldn't hear of it. He would say 'a baby needs his mother' and I guess he was right. Now I'll never have the chance to grow with him and tell him I love him and share the baby with him. It's just all over. Done."

Her husband had left for work and been killed by a drunk driver who never even saw the red light he ran.

Another young widow feels very guilty because she had never come to terms with her husband's family. "I see them now and they try to be so helpful. He used to tell me how unhappy it made him because we didn't get along. He used to say they were such nice people. Now that he's dead I see the truth of what he was saying. They are good people. They love my children. They are kind. They even try to encourage me to date. That may sound strange but they really do. I'm just not ready, but when I am I know they'll support me. I wish he could have lived to see all this unity. God, that hurts me!"

Perhaps one of the easiest things to forget when a husband or wife dies is THERE IS ANGER IN ALL LOVING RELA-TIONSHIPS. Many mourners find themselves perplexed by this. Through much of their lives men, in particular, have been too busy to really explore the emotions that seem to lie dormant within them. Now, suddenly, they are alone and the person with whom they should have shared those emotions, their spouse, is dead.

One widower said, "My wife used to bitch a lot about being left home alone because I worked so many hours. I used to get annoyed and shrug off what she said. Well, let me tell you, now *I* am the one that's alone and I finally understand what she was talking about. All those empty hours she spent. I should have found another job. I wasn't fair."

It's possible you have felt much like this recently bereaved widower. You may feel you should have made a big change. Perhaps the truth is that you should indeed have done so, but your reality is that you didn't. In your desperation to find a reason to blame yourself, not having switched jobs may sound as good as any other cause for self-blame. But is it? Was your role as provider important to you, your wife, your family? Perhaps this was the best you could do with your life. It is possible that somewhere down the road you will come to feel some comfort in knowing the truth of this. If you find it, be a friend and share how you came to your truth with another widower or a support group. You may be doing an immense kindness, for many men have great difficulty in sharing emotions.

One widower in a second marriage completely severed all ties with his late wife's children. He wanted nothing to do with any of them.

"What bugs me is they seem so surprised. They were rotten kids. They gave her endless grief. I had to stand by at the sidelines and watch her slowly being eaten up by those kids. Well, I don't have to do that any longer. Guilty? Sure, I feel guilty. I should have kicked those kids the hell out years ago. Then we could have had a life. Look at her. She's dead. Her first husband was a bastard. I loved her but I didn't help her. I should have been tougher. Yet I'd try and she would start crying. She was always afraid of losing her children. I should have helped her. I should have run interference for her with those kids. Now it's too late. She's dead."

You may know people whose sentiments echo those of this man. You may be such a widower. You may feel the futility of guilt for what you should have done, or thought you should have done. In a calm moment you might ask yourself whether your wife would have appreciated you chasing those children, bad as they might be, away.

In an honest moment when you are not feeling consumed with the guilt about what you should have done, you might even acknowledge to yourself that the truth is she would have been furious. Possibly rather than strengthening your marriage by this action you would have weakened it. But if your grief is new, it may well be too early to really sort through your feelings on this matter. Everyone who has experienced a death generally feels some guilt. Now that you are beginning to explore your emotions, tuck that knowledge away. You are not unique. You are not a freak. You are a grieving, hurting person trying to make sense out of a sometimes senseless world.

When you are feeling the pangs of separation because your

spouse has died and you were unfaithful during your marriage, that is generally a burden you carry alone. It is not easy to cry out your pain and shame when people come to offer condolences. Many who have been unfaithful maintain they always loved their spouse, an extramarital fling had nothing to do with their spouse. They are probably telling the truth. The difficulty they face is in finding someone with whom they can share this innermost guilty secret. Whom can they turn to? Family? Children? Clergy? Probably not.

If you know such a person and are a friend you may perhaps be most helpful by listening nonjudgmentally to the outpourings. Regardless of your moral or personal views, when a person is in mourning is no time for a lecture on how he mistreated his wife and broke his wedding vows.

One man told a friend he never quite understood what made him unfaithful. "It might just be a character flaw," he said. A group of friends who knew his background well merely sat during visitation and listened. They watched as he knelt at the open coffin and cried and begged his dead wife for forgiveness. No one uttered a word. When the priest entered the room, the man suddenly dried his eyes and extended his hand. When the priest asked how he was doing, the widower said, "Fine. Just fine."

Standard man talk. Meaningless. Emotionless. Unchallenged most of the time. With an answer that belies no feeling how could the priest possibly have offered even the slightest degree of help?

If you are a friend attempting to offer support and comfort to mourners experiencing guilt it is most important to be at the funeral home and available during the long periods of time that will follow. Stop in to visit or at least telephone. Invite the mourner to take a walk, or have a bit of food together. Provide a shoulder to lean on. An arm around the waist. A hand to hold. You have much to offer with these gestures. You may feel that there is something profound you should be saying or doing. Yet, truth to tell, being there is probably all you can do to be helpful. That and reaffirm how much the mourner means in your life. Remind the griefstricken person of his worth to you.

There is, of course, the added anguish of watching someone

you care for tearing himself apart because a wife or husband or child was a suicide. The guilt such people feel is immeasurable. The dead person, according to how the mourner feels, has proven the mourner's inadequacy. How much more intense is that sensation of "I should have done more?" "Why wasn't I there?" "What could have been wrong with me?" "I was so insensitive."

Again, it is helpful to know that some people simply cannot live. Because suicide is nearly always guilt-producing in survivors it is important to think of the special person as having died of suicide rather than committing it.

One man, a brilliant professional, spent an entire life of torment inside himself. Despite growing success in business he felt more and more tortured all the time. He had attempted to take his life several times but had been prevented by police intervention. When he finally succeeded he left a note that was not vituperative. His widow insists there was no hostility in him. "It took me years to come to terms with it but he really couldn't live. It was like having cancer for which there is no pain killer. All the morphine in the world couldn't have stopped the hurting within him. I didn't understand this until after I went through years of therapy. Now I do and I mourn for what he lost and for what he might have been."

The widow learned in therapy to separate her own discomfort—the sense that she could always heap more blame upon herself—from her thinking about why her husband had to die.

One woman who frequently chastised herself at the suicide support group meetings she attended was interrupted by a facilitator who thundered, "How dare you place yourself so high? You are not God. You cannot control human life." The woman was so startled she stopped bemoaning her tragedy and began to listen as the facilitator started discussing legitimate self-blame as opposed to illegitimate self-blame. As time went by she began to heal. Although it is impossible to say for certain, she may well have begun to heal when she was challenged, when she was forced to stop and listen to herself.

You may be friendly with the parent, husband or wife of a suicide. And you may find that there is little that will comfort your friend at the time of impact. But perhaps further along the way you might share this concept that the person did not "commit" (a legal term) suicide, but rather died of it. The change in these few words has helped many people to reexamine their feelings toward their own special loved one who died of suicide and their feelings toward themselves. There is probably no person for whom support is more important than the person dealing with a death by suicide. You may be called upon to be a good listener. You will hear the survivor attempt to justify his interactions with the dead person when there is no need for such an exercise. Be a patient listener and do not cut off the conversation. You may be one of the few allowed on the inside. If you do enter that part of the mourning process you will hurt, there is no question of that. But your hurt will seem secondary to you compared to the pain your friend is suffering. He will likely be racked with guilt and at the beginning that guilt may seem impossible to overcome.

It is important to remember that despite this hurried world the healing of guilt simply cannot be speeded up. It is a process that requires time. Know this and do not try to push your friend too quickly through the guilt he must face alone. With proper support and perhaps a support group or therapy he will probably find a time somewhere down the road where he is ready to let go of his guilt and accept the sickness of his special person. You, functioning as a sounding board, may well help further that process.

One young man said he will probably never be able to come to terms with his feelings about his younger brother. "I probably will go to my own death feeling guilty about the way I treated him. He was just such a little wimp. I used to be ashamed of him. He acted jerky and people would tease me because that dumb kid was my brother. I remember how I used to feel when that happened. Angry because he was an odd kid. Then one day he was riding his bike down the side of a street. His chain came off and he fell off the bike and landed right under the wheels of an oncoming car. He died instantly. I should have defended him. Maybe if I had been nicer he wouldn't have been so jerky. I never even gave him a chance. Now it can't be undone, ever. I hate to even think about it, because of how I acted. I'm really sorry he's dead. Maybe if I had given him a chance he would have been a sharper kid."

How often these sentiments are expressed by a surviving sister or brother. Children suffer terribly when faced with a sibling's death. There is anger in all loving relationships. This is certainly true between many children who fight for position within the family for attention, for independence.

How many older children have seethed in the silence of the night because they are no longer the only child? How many have wished a brother or sister dead? How many children have had to deal with the problems created by having an ill sister or brother and seeing all the parental energy diverted to that one child? The wrong one from their point of view. What horror a child must feel when that sister or brother dies. What a nightmare to undergo. Generally the problem is compounded by a desperate, often bewildering silence on the part of the sibling.

"What was I going to do," said one young woman, "go up to my hysterical parents and tell them I used to wish Katy dead?"

The problem is real and deep. How does a child handle such a burden without adult intervention? Few children indeed could tell a parent what this young woman expressed to a therapist. Sometimes it is a matter of timing. Certainly at the time of the funeral the parents frequently can pay little attention to their surviving children. This is a major difficulty and one that causes many problems in the years that follow. Even if their parents did manage to display great attentiveness, few young people could even consider sharing such a "dreadful" secret. And many surviving siblings are scarred for life precisely because they did not share.

Sometimes it is imperative that others intervene. A newly bereaved parent is not the best listener or adviser. They have a hard enough time just holding their own world together. Many people with newly dead children are not effective parents to those who survive.

Situations involving young siblings are fraught with the potential of lifelong distress. Perhaps the best possible course for such people is to join a support group for surviving sisters and brothers. When young people, with the help of an effective leader, begin to verbalize, there is a magic in the air. That magic is the newfound capacity to share deep feelings. Just as important, there is the magic of hearing your own sensations, sensations you thought you would have to carry to your own grave, given credence by another. When a young person hears a contemporary say his sister was a pain, it frees the listener to share that same sentiment. The listener, too, can begin to feel perhaps he is not such a bad person after all! To make such an arena available to young people can be the beginning of regrouping what is left of a family devastated by the death of a child.

Since support groups are not always available, an alert friend or relative can help by intervening if he sees sisters or brothers being ignored. Sometimes parents need to be reminded they have other kids. At other times, you might need to be more direct and say: "Your son seems to be really troubled. Have you sat down to talk with him? I think you should." If this is said kindly, it is unlikely there will be a negative response. Even if the mourner seems temporarily annoyed, stick to your statement. Eventually you will be met with real gratitude for your obvious concern.

Dynamics are different when an adult sister or brother dies. There is often a great longing for the good old days of shared birthdays and holidays.

In one family an adult brother had a heart attack, collapsed and died within less than two hours. When his distraught widow called Florida to notify her husband's older brother, he burst out weeping. He ranted, "He was the executor of my estate, for God's sake. How the hell does a younger brother up and die on you like that! Why did I move to Florida when I retired? I should have stayed up north so we could have seen each other more."

The living brother needed some time to deal with his survivor's guilt—the guilt that asks incessantly, why him and not me? What things should I have done differently? Very often survivors become more and more convinced that they are not "good enough" to have been the survivor when the dead person was eminently more qualified to do so.

He also needed time to come to terms with the idea that he

had his own life to live and through the years had made his own decisions. Some worked well while others did not. Florida seemed fine until the death. But is it fair to challenge every decision because it only seemed appropriate at the time? Can someone's dying so unnerve us as to make us examine our every decision? Are we being fair to ourselves when we fall into this trap of feeling guilty for going about our lives given the information we had at the time we acted?

One young woman whose adult sister died cannot come to terms with the enormity of that death: "We fought like hell when we were kids. But as we got older some of the animosity seemed to fade and we actually seemed to be building a friendship. She died before we ever had a chance to resolve some of those old issues. There were so many things I needed to say I'm sorry about. It would have helped me to know she understood. But we thought we had lots of time. You don't think a sister will die after delivering a baby, but that's how she died."

The woman said if there was one thing she would like to shout "from the rooftops" that thing would be to say you are sorry now, today. "Don't put things off," she said, "because none of us knows when our last tomorrow will be."

Certainly the advice is wise. Many philosophers have advised us to live each day as if it were our last. But the people truly able to attest to this, unfortunately, are the ones who have experienced the reverse, most survivors. They are the ones who know what someone's last days really mean. They also know what it means when there is no recourse, no second chance, no longer any hand to be grasped in apology.

But in trying to think clearly about guilt it is important to allow reality to enter the scene. The fact is that most of us *do* put things off and special people die without our giving them the comfort of knowing how much we really care. *Most of us do this.* Just to know this is universal should be of value. No, you are not some unique, one-of-a-kind, selfish monster. You are a real human being with fine points as well as foibles. Certainly there are things you left undone; all people leave some things undone. Learn to be kind to yourself and force yourself to remember some of the things not left undone. Surely in the course of your special person's life you performed some kind acts. Work at recalling them. Hold onto them and they will hold you afloat when you feel you are drowning in sorrow and guilt.

Very often in the course of your life you might have found yourself taking for granted certain courtesies and kindnesses extended by friends. You might even have thought, "What are friends for if they can't understand that I'm having a bad day and that's why I'm rude?"

Many times friends feel great guilt when someone special has died. "I seemed to be so busy. So wrapped up in my own life I didn't even notice that I wasn't seeing her as much as I should. She used to try and tell me but I didn't pay any attention. Now she's dead and there are no second chances."

This feeling is not uncommon. At one time women especially established great networks of close intimates. These were women with whom they shared their innermost thoughts. Sometimes friends would know about events even before husbands did. One of the major advantages of these networks is that women found people who knew how to *listen*. Often, when mourning, that is the sum total of what is required of a friend. It is not always necessary to problem-solve, nor is it possible. But these networks served as a safe place to ventilate pain and guilt and hurt. Because so many have joined the work force, women often claim they no longer have deep, intimate friendships because time no longer allows for them. If this is the case women may have paid dearly for entering the marketplace, for they now find themselves in the same position of emotional distance most men have known. It is then the sense of "I should have done more" sets in.

Men, it seems, rarely find male friends with whom they discuss problems intimately. Just as women are now discovering, the job seems somehow to get in the way. So many demands are made on their time. Big boys aren't supposed to cry, and they rarely bare their souls! Yet that does not mean the need is not there. Men, too, feel guilt over not "having done enough." Men feel guilt over hurtful words they've said or actions they've taken.

Yet it is the rare man indeed who has the luxury of being able to share these sentiments with another man. He is more likely to share them with a woman.

One theory for this is that women tend to listen while men tend to act. Sometimes no action is required. If a grieving male is feeling guilty, a good ear may be the kindest thing a friend has to offer.

As people become more and more immersed in their workaday worlds, as they move from city to city more readily, the days of intimate conversation appear to be on the wane. This does not mean the need for friendship has lessened; it merely shows the transitions we have undergone, and our sacrifice of friendships before jobs.

If your friend died and you are left feeling you should have been more involved, it is valid to question whether you are being fair to yourself. If the old system is no longer a part of your life and you have taken a job and entered a demanding new arena, recognize your reality. You should not punish yourself because your friendship changed. Nothing stands still. You may find comfort in remembering that.

There are others who fall victim to our fast-paced world and despite the best of intentions they sometimes fail to do what they would like. You may recently have experienced the death of a grandparent. Sure, you were going to call her, you were going to take him for a walk. But somehow your days are so full that you never found the time. Now that person is dead and you are left with a huge load of guilt.

One man who has a busy professional career and is an involved husband and father berated himself when his grandmother died. "She was in that nursing home and it wasn't far from my office. I should have stopped to see her at least once in a while, but I didn't. She was so great when I was a kid."

Relationships to grandparents begin very early in your life. Most of the people who mourn but express little guilt about their relationship are people who have grown up with an ongoing communication with their grandparents. It is the rare adult who suddenly discovers Grandma. Most people say Grandma was always there when I got in trouble at home with Mom and

Dad. She'd square things away for me, words to that effect. These are the people who mourn with a genuine sense of having lost a person of significant value.

There are other people who have not been that fortunate. Many people, because they lived in different cities, or saw poor relationships between their parents and grandparents, do not grow up with an automatic love for the grandparent.

"I'm supposed to love her. She's my grandmother," is a common thought. Yet when that grandparent dies there is frequently much discomfort. You might have desperately wanted your eyes to fill with tears but they didn't. You might have wanted to feel a deep emotion like your cousins, her other grandchildren, seem to, but you didn't. It is possible that their relationship with her was much different than yours. She may have invested more of herself in them than in you. Not all people share the same feelings because they didn't have the same relationship. If your feelings were minimal you need not add to them by discovering guilt. You need only understand that the difference in how you feel may be due entirely to the difference in how you related. It is said that people die as they live. It is also true that they are mourned in accordance with how they interacted.

Then there is the other side. Grandparents feel the loss of their grandchild and often a sense of guilt because they are unable to help the child's parents, their own children.

"I feel so guilty aside from my hurt," one grandmother said. "Here I managed to raise healthy kids and enjoy all the pleasure they gave me but my own son is sitting there in so much pain. Why couldn't I have died instead? It would have hurt him but my grandson had a full life he should have lived. Mine is over. I am old. Why him and not me?"

You may have felt this emotion yourself and there is no response that makes things better. Your pain is deep and real. Your sense of guilt, because you, an older person, survived, is an honest emotion. Many people have great difficulty arguing that point. But when all is said and done, for many it is helpful to feel there is a plan; a reason that such an irrational act took place. You may never in your lifetime know the answer to why but if you can accept just the small thing—maybe there was a reason—then at least you have allowed yourself something to hold on to. It can only be hoped that it will help in some small measure.

Many older people have expressed this idea of why him and not me when a grandchild or any child dies. Perhaps to know that this idea is a thread running through many of you in your hour of pain might be of some value. You are not alone, not alone in your bewilderment, not alone in your confusion. If you go through any complex where seniors live you will hear utterances of puzzlement about who lives and who dies. Perhaps, although you are older, your time has not yet been used up. Know your pain is understood. That is probably the best anyone may offer during this dreadful time when you feel guilty for having survived.

If you do not believe there is a plan it becomes urgent to know you have a right to your place on this earth regardless of age. Again, survivor's guilt becomes very strong in such situations. As in many other issues raised by death it is important to stop asking why. You will find no answers and the questioning may become destructive.

While all people know they are separate individuals and not part of a herd, it may be frightening to feel unique at the time a special person dies. Questions like "Why was I singled out to hurt so?" only add a greater level of pain. To know you have not been individually singled out may in the long run be helpful. Don't perceive yourself as a bad person deserving the pain your special person's death has caused you.

To help yourself survive your sense of guilt and become a bit more rational, take a sheet of paper and ask yourself the following:

• Did I actually by intent cause his death?
• Was he perfect?
• Was I always the bad person in our relationship?
• If I had had prior knowledge of his death, would I have moved?

• If I had had prior knowledge of his death, would I have argued with him about money, the kids, travel?

• If I had had prior knowledge about her death, would I have attended my daughter's recital that time instead of playing bridge?

When you read over the answers, ask yourself if you are being reasonable when you chastise yourself.

In living through mourning, when the tide of guilt threatens to engulf you, remind yourself that you are punishing yourself. Always remind yourself the question should not be "Why didn't I act differently?" but *"Did I have prior knowledge?"*

Since few of us are psychic we must learn to be content with our actions as decided upon at the time given the information we had. This is perhaps the best key to diffusing much of the guilt experienced by those who mourn.

Pathways Through Depression

Tears from the depths of some divine despair rise
in the heart and gather to the eyes.
— ALFRED, LORD TENNYSON

There is a story about a teenaged boy who went to his father and asked for an increase in his allowance.

The father, an unhappy man, sat back in his armchair and gazed intently at his son. "If you get an increase, so what?"

"I'll save my money and then I'll have enough to buy a car."

"And if you buy a car, so what?"

"I'd learn about how a car works and become a mechanic."

"So, you're a mechanic. So what?"

"Well, when business improved I could open up my own garage."

"So you open your own garage, so what?"

"Well, with the profits I'd eventually have enough to open an automobile dealership. Then I'd be rich."

"All right. You're rich. So what?"

"Then I could afford to marry a beautiful girl from a real classy family."

"And if you get married, so what?"

"Gee, Dad, then I'd be happy!"

"Hmmm. You're happy. So what!"

This sense of futility is what many people feel when they

suffer the pain of being a survivor. You may well have experienced just this "so what" syndrome. You may have felt there is nothing of meaning or value that you can ever bring yourself to do again. Oh, sure, you have things to do, errands to run, a job to go to, a family to raise, but "So what?"

It is very difficult to attempt anything positive, whether major or minor, when deep in your heart, engraved in granite as on your special person's tombstone, are the words "so what?"

Perhaps the most insidious emotion you will experience after your special person has died will be that of depression. You will frequently feel that nothing will ever be right again. You may think to yourself, "What's the point? Whatever I do will fail. If he could die on me, nothing will ever be right again in my life."

These thoughts and emotions are natural. They are real and they are honest. You have indeed experienced an inexcusable tragedy. Your special person is dead and that is true cause for pain and hurt.

Depression after the death of a loved one means confronting the fact that we will have to restructure our lives without the presence of that special person, according to funeral director Patrick Lynch. This knowledge often leads to a loss of meaning in our lives. When our own lives lose meaning we become frightened and anchorless. We feel somehow we have been cast adrift.

This aspect of grieving has many components. They may include tension, insomnia, and feelings of worthlessness. You may have experienced the sensation that nothing can *ever* enter your life and be joyous and meaningful again. All is lost; every hope and prayer is valueless. Nothing matters now nor will it ever again.

It is one of life's sad ironies that when you are in the depths of your depression and most in need of caring support from people around you, you are most apt to drive them away. This is part of the cycle of depression.

You or someone you know may be carrying around a great weight of gloom and despair. This weight may be like a slab of cement that is almost impossible to chip away in order to get at the real you.

Ultimately, despite the best intentions of kind and caring

friends and family, unless you allow a chink in that wall, people will give up: they will say they feel so helpless, so powerless. That wall of cement often has such a bleak front that you run the risk of ultimately convincing people you cannot be helped! Most of the time that is simply not true.

Someone once said, "Life is a jigsaw puzzle with most of the pieces missing." Never is that more true than when you live in a state of depression after your special person has died.

One mother who worked in an office part-time always had a frantic rush to be on time picking up her daughter at school. When the girl died as a result of an injury the mother suddenly realized she no longer had to rush to meet the time schedule. Her daughter was dead.

"I didn't have to be there at a special time anymore. It hit me that that phase of my life was over and, God, how that hurt. It was like a special purpose had been taken from me, picking her up after school."

Certainly in light of the magnitude of her loss this was merely a component that reinforced the pain, but she said that every day at the special time that once caused her so much frenzy she would find herself nearly unable to get into her car to go home, the pain was so great and the depression so deep.

"I used to tell my husband we needed to move west into a different time zone when two-thirty wasn't the same two-thirty any longer. I wonder if that might have helped. I needed to feel there was some meaning to my life and for the longest time I felt that there was none. In fact, I don't remember exactly when things started mattering again."

One widow used to keep an immaculate house. She was one of those people who pulled an ashtray away when you had just flicked your cigarette into it once. She scrubbed and cleaned and everything in her lovely home shone. Several months after her husband died she was on her hands and knees scrubbing the floor. She suddenly stopped and took a look at herself and all the energy she was using.

"I just stopped to think. Richard is dead. Here I am still scrubbing and cleaning and knocking myself out. What for? What difference does it make whether this damn place is clean or not? He won't be coming home to see it or appreciate it anymore." She burst into tears.

One widower felt the same sense of pointlessness. "When she was alive, I knew certain things. I knew I could call at a certain time of day and she would answer. We never talked about anything important; sometimes I would just ask what's for dinner. That's all. But knowing she was there made all the difference. Now I go home and no one really cares about whether I'm there or not. Oh, sure, I've got great kids and family but it's not the same. It's nothing like knowing someone is actually waiting for me."

These people are expressing the doubts that arise in all grieving people: now that my special person is dead, what is *my* life all about? There is no meaning to my existence. Nobody cares.

Upon hearing such attitudes expressed you might have a strong inclination to say, "Well, the reason you are doing your housecleaning or still working at your job as you did before is that you are doing it for yourself. *You* matter." That sounds fine on paper but if you are recently widowed you somehow do not believe that you matter. You are not important. Only your husband *and his death*—only your wife *and her death*—really matter. When depression sets in, all the negative concepts come to the fore. They are the dominant themes and they permeate your life.

To tell someone that they also count because they are still alive can have a less than positive result. One woman tried to ease her sister's pain with just such words only to be greeted with near fury. Her bereaved sister did not wish to hear words of comfort; she was not ready. You, too, may have encountered such a situation. It is sometimes best to say little and to offer a hug and a friendly hand instead. Warmth may penetrate when words go unheard.

If you, a friend or relative, feel you wish to do more than touch or hug, the kindest way to express in words your sense of sympathy may be to say simply, "This must be such a hard time for you."

If you really wish to lend a sympathetic ear you might inquire about the following:

• Is it more difficult at night or through the day? Why?
• Are there certain things that trigger depression, such as seeing a car like his? Perhaps passing a restaurant he liked?
• Does seeing couples together holding hands trigger depression?

Such questions will likely be met with gratitude because you will show you possess insight as well as demonstrating you are a willing listener.

Sometimes sharing a story that is similar to the mourner's may be helpful. In this a support group can be very helpful. As you are going through depression, there will unquestionably be times when you ask "So what?" For most people, this sensation does ultimately abate. Not everyone can be rushed through this phase of grief nor should they be rushed through it. But if the old maxim that misery loves company is true, a support group may be the most accepting place to deal with your hurt.

Think how difficult it is to contemplate moving or changing jobs, even as a matter of choice. You can always choose not to move or change jobs. You have not lost the element of choice. How different when a special person has died! Then there has been no choice. You did not elect to be a widow or widower or a bereaved parent and yet you are.

One woman has gone through the experience of having two husbands die. Sadly, as people tend to live longer, this is not unique.

"You would think I would know all about this after all these years. When my first husband died I thought my world would end. I rebuilt my life by remarrying and it was a good, solid rebuilding and a good solid second marriage. We were so happy. The kids were grown and we were like honeymooners. We traveled and spent all our time together. Now he is gone and I am really alone. I feel such a heavy weight inside my heart. I'm a lot older now. I don't have the energy to start again, or even to continue my life. Maybe I just don't want to."

Restructuring to many people means starting over. While this woman was willing to make the attempt once, the enormous energy it took to do so has to be acknowledged. Restructuring does require energy. Unfortunately, the need to expend that energy occurs when there is almost none to give. There are those who have said that although mentally they know they should be doing certain things to move their lives along, physically they cannot do anything.

"I keep thinking I should get up, make plans, meet my friends for lunch. But when I make those plans I begin to feel so frightened inside. Will I really be able to meet them? I can't be sure. I don't trust myself during this time, not a bit."

She said she frequently sits curled on her sofa covered with a down comforter and does nothing. She keeps her television set turned on but seems to take in very little of what is said.

If you know someone who is responding in this manner the most important thing you can offer is your understanding; your willingness to make plans with the knowledge that the mourner may not be able to follow through relieves a bereaved person of a great pressure. When a special person dies a sense of failure often sets in for the survivor. Don't heighten that sense in someone who is mourning by berating him for not being able to keep an engagement. This is not what good friends and family do if they wish to be helpful to a grieving person.

Dr. Philip Muskin of Columbia once said, "Bereavement is made of millions of moments." These moments form a patchwork. We cannot be certain just what size or shape the next patch will be. Therefore, bereavement is a time when special attention may be helpful but broken appointments should not cause a further sense of failure and depression.

A good deal of the mourner's time may be spent on the job, as it was before his special person's death. For these people restructuring takes on different forms: the off-hours require reworking.

One man has forced himself to schedule evening activities for every night of the week. "I couldn't stay home anymore. I felt like I was going crazy, the walls were so quiet in my apartment. My children used to say I should come and visit them more. But how much can you visit your kids and not become an imposition? Well, I joined a group of people whose husbands or wives were dead and one of the suggestions that we came up with to help ourselves is knowing there is someplace we have to be every night of the week. I found it very hard to do at first but after a while it became a routine, my routine. Now, at least, I don't sit there with my quiet walls."

He said that this restructuring might sound easy but it was not easy for him. It was hard work. He had to force himself to keep his evening commitments against his inclinations. Although he is not yet ready to begin dating, he has at least acknowledged that he must find a different pattern—one that fits his new life.

While not all people need this much activity—some prefer their quiet time and their time to grieve—many find it helpful, especially early on.

Children very often have the hardest time of all during this restructuring period, especially if they are still living in their parent's home. All too often demands and expectations that far exceed their years are placed upon them.

"I was thirteen when my mom died and everything was different in our home. Nothing was the way it used to be," said one young woman now away at college. "Suddenly I was expected to take over the cooking and the cleaning and everything. I still had to go to school and do homework. I was so depressed because Mom was dead. No one talked to me about that. All I heard was how many more things I now needed to do. It was so unfair. No one took into account my hurt. They used to tell me I was lazy for not helping Dad more. Why didn't they know I was depressed and had no energy to do anything? I was too young to realize what had happened to me emotionally. I didn't recognize depression. I only knew I was sad and hurting. I didn't realize that it is very depressing to know you have to go on with your life and change it to fill in the gaps caused by a mother's dying."

She said all this had fallen into place for her in more recent years. She spent much time angry with her father for not understanding her sadness, and how deep it went.

Sometimes when an adult sister or brother dies there seems to be little if any need to restructure. You may have felt that your life would continue as it had before the death. After all, your spouse is still alive, you have your children, your parents. Yet there are changes and they need addressing because they are painful. Holidays take on a different connotation. You may feel deeply depressed because your sister is not there to share the occasion. Now, your families seem to get together less frequently.

One woman said her brother-in-law, with the best intentions, has tried to keep in touch with her, but since her sister died he has holiday dinners at his family's home. "We've asked him to come here many times, but he says it's so sad and depressing because that's how we always did it that he wants to make changes. They may be right for him, but now we're being cheated of sharing with his children and *they* are all that's left of my sister. They are the bloodline."

Is there a right or wrong to this? It probably depends on whether you listen to the brother-in-law or the sister. Certainly not having her sister present is depressing and painful but perhaps the widower must affect some changes in order to go on. As in so many areas of dealing with death, there is no right answer. What seems helpful to one survivor may be painful to another.

Perhaps she might wish to invite him for a different day or for dessert instead of dinner. Small changes are sometimes more helpful than an all-or-nothing approach. Keeping a line of communication open between family members is important. That way invitations do not come out of the blue, they evolve more naturally when you speak to someone three times a week, or even once a week, than when you make your first call to the home after a month or so.

There are people who have established friendships that have survived as long as forty or fifty years. How frequently has a golf foursome broken up totally when one member dies? The game as it had always been played no longer feels as comfortable. The slot of the dead person may be filled by someone new yet his spectre walks beside the new foursome on the green. One man said he felt such pain that he stopped playing with the regular group. "I needed to find a whole new set of men for golf. Before I did I felt like Mike's ghost was there with me."

He said the other two had opted to continue with the regular game. They still tee off at the same time and have simply added two new players.

Because there are no hard and fast rules, there is no right or wrong to this. It is strictly an individual situation. Just know that the decision must fit correctly for you and you will not be led astray.

It is often very difficult for grandparents to consider restructuring their lives when they are depressed. They generally had looked forward to an old age filled with visits from their grandchildren. When they suddenly find themselves with their dreams in shambles, they find it difficult to adjust. "I even kept a bedroom especially for Kevin," said one grandmother. "He knew it was his room. He had extra clothes in the drawers. When he died I never wanted to look at the room again. I have left everything the way it was. He was my only grandchild."

Whether she will ultimately force herself to take the room apart, at least to remove the clothing and perhaps change to a new style bedspread, is hard to predict. Although it would be wise for her to dismantle Kevin's room for her own sake, she may not wish to do so. If her son, the boy's father, who is fighting through his own grief, visits her and sees the room intact he may become angry because nothing has changed in her home. The reality is there *has* been a change. Kevin is dead. If Kevin's parents are struggling desperately to restructure their own lives, the grandmother may be making this more difficult. She may find her son's visits will become less frequent and more volatile. On the other hand, as a separate entity she does have the right to mourn in her own way. That is the grandparent dilemma when a grandchild dies.

In these times when divorce is an all-too-frequent happening, grandparents often play large roles in the lives of young people. Therefore the death of a grandparent is something that must never be overlooked from the child's standpoint. The degree of pain and depression a young person feels may be enormous. It should not be swept lightly aside and left unaddressed.

One young lady was distraught when her father's mother died. "She was the stabilizing force in my whole world. My parents are divorced; they are always fighting. When things got awful I went to Grandmom. Sometimes I even stayed there. I knew I could always count on her to be there for me when I needed her. Now she's dead and my stabilizer is gone. Sometimes I think I'm more depressed about it than my dad. He didn't turn to her; I did. Now I have to find someone else. But who?"

That is simply not a question an outsider can answer. You may have been in that situation at some time in your life. Was it helpful to find another person? Were you able to find someone special? You are indeed fortunate if that was the case.

Although no one can be a replacement person it is possible to fill part of that void by selecting another confidante with care.

- Make certain the person cares about *you* as a friend or a relative.
- If you have no such person, try to establish a rapport with a clergyman.
- Recognize you need someone and begin trying to fill that need.

Another inevitable part of the cycle of depression is tension. You are ready to snap at the slightest thing that goes awry. Unfortunately, in this less than perfect world, much *does* go awry. Bank tellers make mistakes as do supermarket cashiers. Suddenly it may be difficult to hold yourself in check when you see trivial mistakes that you would usually ignore. You are so raw inside that nearly everything becomes an issue.

One woman whose oldest daughter died in an automobile accident said she was going to try to find a job: "I'm just no good at being home anymore. All I do is scream at my kids for the slightest things. I have no patience with them or with anyone. They're starting to act up more and more and I'm constantly screaming and punishing them. Not only is my daughter dead but I feel that I've lost the most important part of me—my ability to be a good mother. That hurts so. I don't feel I'll ever get out of all this grieving and pain. Ever."

Another woman, a recent widow, said her tension level is so

high she can barely sit through a visit to a beauty shop: "That used to be my favorite thing to do. I would go there, get my hair washed and set, get my nails done. That was how I relaxed. Then Donald died and now I can't sit still long enough to do anything. Even getting a manicure drives me crazy!" She put a smile on her face, a rather sad smile, and said she is not only a widow but she's turning into an ugly one at that!

One widower said men feel the tension as much as women. That rawness is universal, according to him. "Everything *is* an issue. I've talked with other men in my situation and they agree. My sister-in-law called me after my wife died just to say hello and see how I was doing. Well, I was making myself lunch and when she asked me I told her I had opened a can of tuna and put some on a slice of bread. She began to chuckle. What about the mayonnaise, she wanted to know. Did I forget that? At another time I would have laughed right along with her, we always liked each other, but instead I yelled at her. I told her she had no right to laugh at me at a time like this. I nearly hung up on her, I was so annoyed. Yet she really didn't do anything wrong. It's me. I have no patience." This lack of patience often further triggers depression.

The man is probably correct. It *is* him. Things that at one time could be seen as a joke take on different connotations when a special person has died. Ironically, they rarely involve the major events. It is the smaller things, the day-to-day things we take for granted, that become consuming and troublesome after the death of a special person.

Another man who has been a career salesman is finding the tension aspect of depression a real obstruction in his work. "I have found through the years that sales requires the patience of a saint. I've learned to talk slowly and explain my product carefully, and when people ask stupid questions I make them sound not stupid when I respond. Ever since my wife died I just don't have the patience any longer to deal with stupidity. I feel so tense that I want to spring at someone, to lash out. But that's not doing my career any good. Since she died I've lost sales. I should have had them. I just couldn't handle the foolishness."

You may be just such a man in just that position. Perhaps seeing your dilemma on paper will help ease it somewhat. Know the tension does ease after a time but to some degree you must roll with the waves.

• If you find yourself feeling overwhelmed try some of the physical exercises that have now become so popular, things like rapid walking, jogging or bicycling.
• Sometimes painting a room, washing a floor or polishing a car will help ease the tension.
• Above all, help yourself and pamper yourself. You have a right to your pain. Try to be more selective about your customers, if that's possible. See if, in general, you can choose the people with whom you deal. By making choices whenever possible, you can help yourself ease an area of irritation.

If this is impossible, try not to chastise yourself even further for something that is temporarily out of your control.

Another common component of depression is insomnia. If you're not sleeping, you should be aware you have an army of fellow travelers who pace the floors or lie in bed crying. There is an alternative maxim that cautions us that early to bed and early to rise is a bad rule for anyone who wishes to become acquainted with our most prominent and influential people. Early to bed is not something most grieving people are able to do. Perhaps it will be helpful just to know that as you lie there trying to sleep or to make sense out of the great tragedy that has entered your life, morning will come and the dawn will break.

Insomnia creates a "cycle of depression." When you cannot sleep you become exhausted. When you're exhausted, you're more vulnerable to the emotions of grief. When you're more vulnerable to those emotions, you cannot help yourself to fight them off. When you cannot help yourself, you're more depressed.

Many resort to tranquilizers or sleeping pills in an effort to sleep. There is a case to be made for the use of such drugs. The need for sleep does become urgent. When you have not slept enough your defenses are down and depression can overtake an even larger part of you. Then the depression becomes so overwhelming you can't sleep. Some doctors believe sleeping aids are helpful in breaking that cycle.

However, the vast majority of specialists ranging from clergymen to people in the mental health field do not look with favor on this approach. They believe a lifelong dependency can be created, that tranquilizers merely delay the mourning process. They express repeatedly that depression is a normal part of that process and should not be treated chemically. One clergyman said he asks his people to promise not to take a tranquilizer before the funeral. "I believe the entire funeral process including the eulogy should be heard by grieving—not sedated—people. Certain steps occur only at certain times and although there is intense pain involved, especially when a child dies, removing yourself from that pain by artificial means does not help you heal in the long haul."

Unless you suffer from it, insomnia seems like a fairly uncomplicated problem. But if you're alone during the small hours of the morning you know all too well how painful they can be.

One woman called a casual acquaintance at two in the morning crying bitterly: "This was the anniversary of the night my child was conceived. He was stillborn and I never married his father. I feel like I'm crawling out of my skin lying here thinking and thinking and thinking."

The acquaintance said she felt impotent to offer any help and felt that the best she could do was listen well as her acquaintance poured out her pain and hurt.

It would have been far better to have urged the woman out of bed and on into some physical activity like scrubbing floors or walls rather than merely lying there. There is something insidious about feeling tied to a bed when you are depressed and unable to sleep. The best suggestion is to get up. Should you ever be in a position to offer this advice, or should you ever be in the situation yourself where you cannot handle another minute of the bleakness of the small hours, bear in mind there is an alternative. That alternative is to get up and *MOVE*.

One woman who has been widowed for nearly a year found

the same thing: "My doctor said no tranquilizers for me. He explained that eventually they would not work and I would live my life needing stronger and stronger doses. I would be like those junkies you see on television. Instead he said I should join a health club. Can you imagine? I'm sixty years old and now I'm exercising for the first time in my life. I must admit one thing, though. When I go in the evening and work out, I come home and some nights I actually do drop off to sleep. I still can't sleep in my bed but I lie down on the couch and sleep most of the night. I think this is a good thing for me."

Many psychologists would agree and suggest just this type of self-help; it was a good thing for her and probably for a great many people who are grieving.

One widower discovered physical fitness on his own: "It seemed to me that 'working out' was all anyone ever talked about. I get home from work at three-thirty and have so many hours alone that I decided to give it a try. Now I wouldn't miss a day because when I get home I fall into bed and I can sleep. If it didn't sound silly I would almost call it a miracle. I never thought anything would help."

Surprisingly, young people too have a problem with sleep when a parent has died. Although they do not always recognize the term "depression" or "insomnia," both elements are very much present in their lives. When a brother dies and a youngster has shared a room with him, the emptiness of that bedroom can be appalling. One such brother who had never had a sleeping problem found himself with a dreadful one after his brother's death. His teacher finally noticed the dark rings under his eyes and called his home. So distraught were they with their own grief, neither parent was aware that the boy was not sleeping. When it was called to their attention they discussed it with him and ultimately removed the dead brother's bed and totally rearranged the room the two boys had shared. The problem went away.

One grandfather said that as he grew older he seemed to require less sleep; after checking with his doctor and friends, he found this to be quite normal. However, it crossed a line when his grandson died. "Then I'd be lucky if I slept two hours a night. The whole thing was just too much for me, too much to handle. I would close my eyes and see him laughing and playing and I would feel like someone hit me and I would wake up." Although it is slightly better after two years, he still sleeps very little.

Yet another part of the "cycle of depression" is a sense of worthlessness that is common when a special person dies. You feel you were not even worth enough to have your special person live. In this cycle you may feel that somehow you were weighed by a greater power and found wanting, that is why you are suffering the pain you are now feeling. You may feel had you been a better person—done more, been kinder—then you would have been one of the worthy ones, and the person you loved would not have died. This cycle can be seen, for example, when a child dies of leukemia. Parents tearfully turn and say, "But I have heard of so many remissions. This one and that one have gone on to live for many years. Why wasn't I good enough for my child to stay alive?"

When you start feeling this sort of worthlessness you believe your special person's death was a result of your own shortcomings. When you accept this as fact, you blame yourself for the death. When you feel responsible for the death and unable to prevent it, you feel worthless.

This is a common emotion when there has been an untimely death. Although few deaths are "timely" sometimes they are truly out of kilter with normal life. When that happens great depression often sets in.

How unworthy do young parents of a stillborn baby feel when they believe they are being told that they didn't deserve to have a living child? This sense of failure, this sense that they have no value is rarely discussed by them with professionals. It is often a secret the husband and wife share.

"I see people walking along holding their babies," said one tearful mother who was under twenty years of age. "They don't seem any better than me, any nicer. I saw those same kind of people when I was in the hospital. But there must be something about me; I've never had any luck in anything in my life. This is just another example."

When young parents are faced with a tragedy of such magnitude they frequently do focus on what they have done wrong in their lives. When someone is just emerging from the turbulence of a special person's death, it is indeed easy to accept blame for what in most probability was not their fault.

To feel worthless is to feel that life *should* kick you around. You deserve it. You had it coming! How tragic to accept this premise when it is generally far, far from the truth.

There is a widower who's convinced he's making great headway in feeling less worthless. "I'm getting out a bit. But I'm not dating. I know I'm much better but, after all, my wife's only been dead fourteen months. I feel so off balance. In all our talks we were always sure *she* would be a widow one day. That's what the insurance companies tell us. All our life insurance listed her as the beneficiary. We never thought for a moment about taking out a policy on her life. Now when I go to group meetings many times I'm the only man. Why me? Why am I different? She should have been the one to live."

You may have heard such sentiments from a friend or felt them yourself as a bereaved person. It is indeed hard to explain why you outlived your wife. Society focuses so much on widows because of their great numbers that as a widower you may feel overlooked. It is difficult not to feel uncomfortable and indeed unworthy when in addition you feel you are unique. Whether as a widow or widower, to challenge your worthiness to live is a tragedy. The more you allow yourself to feel unworthy, the more depression deepens. How can you enjoy yourself when your spouse is dead and you do not feel you are worthy of being alive? Can you go to a movie, dinner or to the theater with any comfort when you do not believe you deserve to be walking this earth? The fact is you *are* alive. You exist. Be thankful for this and hope you can begin to rebuild your life feeling like a worthwhile person. You know you are worthwhile; deep within yourself you do know it.

Also, this widower, although he's made some progress, is a long way from reaching an acceptance of his reality. Like most of you who are still mourning the death of your special person, he is counting months. As time goes forward if you begin actually working at rebuilding your life you will find yourself suddenly not so caught up in counting: the days and months will take care of themselves. As this occurs you will find some of your depression lifts along with it.

One widow says she hates cancer and says it in such a tone that cancer could be a living thing. She has gone past the time of feeling worthless and blaming herself: "I used to walk around thinking I should have made my husband go to the doctor for that cough. But he was always the strong one, the head of our family. When he said, 'Let's go,' we went. So I didn't force him. Then he died. I felt so unworthy: unworthy of living the beautiful life I lived; unworthy of being his wife, unworthy of just about anything and everything. It hurt so when I felt like that. But then I joined a group of women whose husbands had all died of cancer and they began talking about the disease and how they felt about it. One day I realized I had nothing to reproach myself for. After all, I *had* been a good wife, the kind of wife he wanted. I was a worthwhile human being, a worthwhile wife. When I began hating the disease I felt better. Now I work at raising funds for combating cancer. It won't bring him back but it gives me a purpose and one I am extremely proud of."

Hearing it told this way in so few words, you don't feel the agonies and uncertainties she experienced along the way, the endless time it took to reach a new perspective. This woman made her progress sound simple and it was anything but. How much further she will go away from hating to becoming philosophical about being widowed is anyone's guess. At least she can once again live with herself.

One widower said he sat down with his two sons and tried to respond to their questions. It hurt him when he overheard them talking about how all their friends had mothers who were alive. Why did this happen to them? Well, maybe they just weren't worth much as people.

"I tried to reason with them. I explained that she did not choose to die, it happened as a result of an illness. I said that sometimes there is a greater reason, a destiny. They sat there swinging their legs and looking straight at me but I knew they were not taking in a word I said. I finally realized I was giving more information than they had asked me to give them. So I did something different. I got out of my chair and put an arm around each of them and just hugged them. I told them I was thankful they at least were still with me.

"That was when I got a response. They both started to cry and each of them said they loved me."

According to many in the counseling field, children often have a low self-concept. They may nonetheless believe they can control events by magical thinking. They may believe they can "wish someone dead" and see that become a reality. Young people need always be reminded that there is anger in all loving relationships. If Mom grounded you for a week it would be unusual for you not to be angry. But if she dies you begin to conjure up every negative thought you ever had about her and you convince yourself you were not a good enough person to grow up with a mother.

One young woman is convinced she knows why her sister died of a brain tumor: "It was my fault; I was such a rotten sister. She was always the beautiful one, the one who got all the attention. I used to hate her sometimes because she had it all. I remember how furious I was with her when she borrowed my best blouse without asking and then spilled makeup on it that wouldn't come off. I told on her, all right. She got in trouble. Now she's dead. I was such a rat, I didn't deserve to have such a perfect sister."

How sad this sounds; she's almost saying the wrong sister died. Getting her to acknowledge she was worthwhile and had good qualities became the work of a therapist who ultimately succeeded, but not without a really tough battle.

The therapist would listen to her downgrade herself. Then the therapist would insist she take another look at herself and complete sentences like the following: "I did something nice for my sister when we were kids. I _____." Such exercises bring about a sense of balance.

To do this at home, follow the therapist's format and on a sheet of paper finish these phrases or some like them that apply to you:

- Sometimes my sister was mean to me, too. I remember when she ———.
- I forgave her when she ———.
- She tattled to our parents when we were kids. She did it because ———.
- I helped her when she was ill because ———.

It's hard to feel worthy when you feel left behind and all the attention is focused on the perfection of the person who died. Sample questions such as these can be written about any relationship. Their object is to bring into focus a more honest picture of how things were. By so doing the mourner will not continue to perceive himself as all bad while the person who died was all good.

Then to help yourself begin to believe in your own worth, set up some "I like myself" exercises on paper. Ask yourself, remind yourself:

- I helped ———.
- I showed concern ———.
- ——— told me I was kind.
- I can be attractive when I ———.
- People are nice to me because I ———.
- I am friendly because I ———.
- My (special person) loved me because I ———.

Add some statements of your own. Check this paper once a month and make changes as your view of yourself improves.

If you're a friend or relative of a child who has suffered a loss, you might help by gently reminding his parent or parents to see where the child hurts. See if the child feels worthless, and if at all possible challenge the child about these emotions. By lifting the yoke of worthlessness from a young person you are lifting the yoke of depression at the same time. You will see an improvement in behavior and school grades and, perhaps, ultimately, a return to the zest of living that is every young person's right.

Probably the greatest kindness you can offer someone who is

mourning, someone who speaks of "the wrong person dying," of their own unworthiness, is to affirm their importance in your life. Whether the survivor is a friend, a grandparent, or a grandchild, just to reinforce the idea that they have worth and their lives still touch other people can be a small step forward for the grieving person.

In a discussion of depression, Dr. Philip Muskin of Columbia University explained that phasic depression, depression that comes in waves, is the most commonly experienced. He said this is far different from pathological mourning where the person becomes clinically depressed. That person is depressed all the time, nothing makes him better.

"In fact," he said, "grief is halted by this sort of clinical depression." People who are depressed feel sadness, guilt and worthlessness. They cry and they often suffer from insomnia. It is important not to let depression remove you from intimate relationships.

This is yet another area in which the support group can prove to be invaluable. It is in just such a setting of collective healing that you can monitor yourself and compare *your* situation and ability to cope with that of others in the group.

Roy V. Nichols a funeral director and consultant on death education in Chagrin Falls, Ohio, compiled a list of words that define depression. Use this list and circle the words that fit your state of mind, then date your list. Take a different color pencil several weeks later and again circle the words that apply. Repeat this process on a sheet of paper of your own if necessary as the weeks go by:

surges of emotion	loss of appetite
bitterness	anxiety
fear	anguish
futility	sadness
resentment	disrupted attention span
disappointment	dejection
helplessness	disbelief
nervousness	weight loss or weight gain
yearning	resignation

numbness	panic
sleeplessness	physical reactions
despair	forgetfulness
talkativeness	hypochondria
loneliness	hopelessness
hostility	agitation
guilt	sorrow
emptiness	regret

When you checked back, did you find you'd circled different words? Fewer? This exercise should help you see what is not obvious from day to day: you are feeling a bit better. If you are not, you should consider consulting a mental health professional to combat what may be clinical depression.

There is an apocryphal tale about Albert Einstein's attempt to explain his theory of relativity to a young man. Because he was a gentle man he could not turn the youngster away. He took a few moments to think and then he came up with an explanation that could readily be understood. "When you sit on a hot stove three seconds seems like three minutes. But when you are kissing a pretty girl, three minutes seem like three seconds."

Depression alters our sense of time: time weighs very heavily. You may awaken one morning and decide this is the day you address your pain; you will go out for the day. Bright and early you get dressed up and head for a local department store. You walk through every section and look at all the merchandise. Feeling somewhat pleased with your accomplishment you steal a glance at your watch. It is only 10:30 in the morning. You feel as though you have spent an entire day and you may feel a failure; you may begin to feel anxious at the thought of how many hours remain to be filled. You become depressed anew.

Stop. Praise yourself for what you have accomplished—you got dressed and out and to the store. Try to build yourself up in small steps such as the one you've taken. Time passes slowly when you're depressed, so try to keep active physically and keep in touch with others. If you feel you cannot go out, telephone.

But do remember dealing with depression is not always a steady line forward. There will be times you will feel you are back to square one and your circled words will show you to be correct. Do not panic, because several weeks down the line you will probably once again find you have taken forward strides. This is a basic truth in living through mourning.

Pathways Through Powerlessness

I could not stop something I knew was wrong and terrible. I had an awful sense of powerlessness.
—ANDREI SAKHAROV

Powerlessness is the sense that you lack the ability to make a difference. It is probably the most corrosive of feelings because it encompasses guilt and anger and depression and every other negative emotion in the entire spectrum of human feelings.

Powerlessness can take many forms. Sometimes people become aggressive and do things just to prove they still have some control. Other people perceive powerlessness as painful gusts of wind that hurt but cannot be caught. You may feel like slaying dragons because that might prove to you that you do have some power after all. The only problem is there aren't any.

The object of learning to cope with powerlessness is not to die either emotionally or physically but to live with some measure of dignity and quality despite the emptiness you feel inside yourself.

One of the more difficult adjustments to make when feeling powerless is to recognize your perceptions. Do you feel somehow *you* should have been able to do more, therefore the entire tragedy was caused by your inability to be more than human? To do more than could rightfully be expected of you?

One very common question survivors ask themselves is "Where

did I lose control?" This question is often accompanied by tears and great pain. This is a rhetorical gut-wrenching question for which there is no reply. There are few situations in which you can hope to accomplish something. You are therefore left with frustration and the feeling that you are truly a failure.

The belief you have internalized, that certainty that you are a failure, eats away at your being just as rust eats away at metal. You may feel certain that there was still another doctor, somewhere down the road, you should have tried. People sitting back and listening would jump in shock if you were to say this aloud. Those around you know you did all and more than could be expected. Yet unless you accept this yourself you will continue feeling like a failure. If that goes on long enough and you begin to believe your inadequacy to be a fact, then there is always the danger that you will indeed fail, fail at going forward and living your life. Despite your special person's death you should not allow yourself to be robbed of the power to live yourself.

One woman said she watched her dog give birth to puppies: "She had them, she nursed them and watched over them. She was able to keep them alive. Then I think of myself. I got pregnant. I went full term and my baby was born dead. I couldn't even do what my dog did. If you want a definition of failure, you're looking at her!"

Another man gave up his law practice to fight the painful battle of his son's cancer. His wife was in a state of collapse because of the diagnosis. So he took the boy from doctor to doctor, from city to city. He stayed up nights with his son when the boy became ill from chemotherapy. The man virtually ignored his wife, his other children, his friends: he made the boy his life's crusade.

Despite the best medical care possible, the boy died within a year of diagnosis. When his son closed his eyes for the last time, the man turned to his family, who had all gathered at the boy's bedside, and said dry-eyed, "I failed. He's gone."

Did he fail? The boy's final words to his father were, "Thanks, Dad." Can there ever be failure if the father would allow that memory to be dominant? Can he be a failure when nothing that could be done to help the boy was omitted? Nothing of fathering that he could offer was left out? Can someone who gives everything he has ever consider himself a failure? Does the outcome determine failure? Does the effort put into the venture count for nothing?

The boy was given a terminal diagnosis from the start. That things came to pass just as the doctors forewarned should eliminate this father's thinking that he failed. Yet he just could not accept it. He could not be kind to himself.

If you are feeling powerless you rarely take time to think realistically about the event. You only know your own pain and the sense of loss you are experiencing.

One woman, gesturing in utter helplessness and confusion, says, "I had to stand by and watch my husband die. There was nothing I could do to make it any better for him. After all, if my role in life is to be a wife and mother, I should be able to do those things well. But I failed and now he is dead. There was nothing I could do."

In her grief, she misses the point of what power really is. Although she could not prevent her husband's death she certainly made his life and his last days comfortable. She sat at his side, wiped his forehead with a warm towel, held his hand. She did not lose her power to comfort, but unless she is forcibly reminded of this her sense of failure is complete.

Often widows express a great need not to be bereft of power. They find this most difficult. One woman, a shy, retiring person of perhaps sixty, felt bereft of power after her husband went into the hospital for prostate surgery and died. She did not see the family doctor and could get no satisfactory answer from anyone as to why he died. "I didn't know what to do. All I wanted were some answers. The death certificate said he died of a heart attack. He never had a day's heart trouble in his life. Why then was he so suddenly in trouble?"

She said she repeatedly called the doctor's office and was never put through nor did he return her calls. Finally at the urging of good friends she contacted a lawyer whose specialty is medical malpractice. She said it took only one letter from this man and the doctor mailed her a full report about how her husband died.

"When I got that doctor's letter I felt like a human being again. I was not a nobody whose husband could just die without any explanation from anyone. I had some power at least. I showed that doctor that I am a person too."

Many people feel powerless in this situation. That action, that going to see the lawyer, allowed this woman to prove to herself that she was indeed a person of power, of worth. She merited a careful hearing by the lawyer and an explanatory letter from the doctor. She can now go forward with her life knowing she is not pitched and tossed by every current that comes along.

One widower's sense of powerlessness and failure includes immense frustration: "I own a business and can keep people on their toes by a look or a sharp word, but I failed when it came to my own wife. I should have forced her to see one more doctor, to be more careful. She hated to exercise but the doctor had told her that unless she did, her emphysema would ultimately kill her. I didn't fight her hard enough. But she's dead."

Friends say these were the words he spoke as he stood over his wife's coffin. He was expressing to some degree the futility that many have felt when faced with this finality. Somewhere along the way you might have expressed just what the widower did. He seems to have assumed the role of being all-powerful when in fact his wife also had some responsibility. If she suffered with this crippling disease did she not also owe *him* the best care she could take of her body? Is it fair for him to bear the entire burden of what he sees as his failure? Although she's dead, was she not to some degree less than fair by not maintaining her health to the best level possible? Did she not also fail? Certainly she paid the ultimate price, there is no disputing that, but she did not pay alone. She took family and friends into the morass of pain and suffering she might have averted.

Certainly not all emphysema can be controlled any more than many other diseases. But when you have a commitment to others in this life it is important to understand that caring for yourself is a large part of that commitment. If your loved one did not honor that commitment, it's not your fault. It is beyond what is reasonable and beyond human effort to change some things. You are only human.

Since many children see the world egocentrically, as somehow orbiting around them, it can sometimes be most difficult to rid themselves of the certainty that they failed because they should have been able to prevent their mother's or father's death.

"I can still remember what it felt like watching my mother lose weight every day. I would run to the store to bring her any snack she might have liked but it didn't mean a thing to her. She wanted to send me to camp that last summer and she had her way. I guess she didn't want me to watch her deteriorate any further. But I think it was unfair. Even though I saw her getting sicker and sicker when I was with her, I felt at least as if I was doing something and that way maybe she wouldn't die. Well, I went to camp and it was terrible. My mind stayed back at home most of the time. She died shortly after I got home. Maybe a month or so. Even though this happened many years ago the whole scene is still vivid. I remember feeling so strongly that I needed to be there, that I could make a difference. When she died I felt I had failed. It took me many years to stop feeling like that. Now, well, I just miss her."

Young people feel a sense of events' being beyond their control when a grandparent dies, but certainly that death came in an orderly sequence. From the time we are old enough to understand anything about life and death we are faced with the fact that people are born, they age and when they become infirm enough in their old age they die. To understand that this is the normal sequence of life can help remove lingering feelings of powerlessness for grandchildren. Certainly they may feel hurt and lonely but if they can understand that life has a natural sequence they may well feel peace.

In general when a special person dies, you, like most people, may have felt you only wanted a little more time, and who can blame you? But you were not granted that time. You had no control over when your special person died or, indeed, how that person died. Coming to terms with this is indeed a yeoman's task and more difficult when the death is out of nature's sequence.

One grandmother, her eyes welling with tears, described her painful experience: "I feel like a failure, like I can't help at all.

I couldn't help my grandson to stay alive; I can't help my daughter deal with her pain; I can't help my husband to deal with his. I'm afraid this will kill him. I don't even have the power to help myself, let alone anyone else. There is so much pain and nothing I can do."

Often powerlessness works hand in hand with guilt but is actually a separate experience. The two come together with the sense that the survivor should have been able to prevent the death but didn't. It is important to help yourself go on with your life by changing that sort of thinking. Aren't you taking credit for greater power than you possess? When you hear or feel yourself thinking you should have been able to prevent the death but didn't, be kind and try to force yourself to use the word "couldn't." By so doing you will feel less a failure, less insignificant as a human being.

Feeling small in a big world is the feeling of powerlessness. Suddenly finding yourself tiny in a land of giants is a recurrent theme in children's fairy tales and indeed in adult books and movies. Anyone from Gulliver to Thumbelina may fit the bill. There was one movie in which Lily Tomlin suddenly became tiny and was in danger of being washed down the kitchen drain. The movie showed her swirling around and around in the sink trying desperately to find something upon which to grab hold.

When someone special dies this is frequently how survivors feel. They try to find something upon which to grab hold but are generally doomed to fail when they see themselves as the tiny creature in the kitchen sink.

Powerlessness often manifests itself in a mourner who begins to feel small or vulnerable or impotent. The mourner may feel he is shrinking or the room in which he is standing is getting bigger. Visualize an infant attempting to reach for something just out of his grasp and you are picturing powerlessness. When this occurs attempt to write a short list in which you affirm your control:

- I have control over _____.
- I also have control over _____.
- I can exercise control over _____.

Just making yourself stop and think long enough to know you are not completely without power can help establish some balance.

One bereaved mother put it this way: "I recall sitting on the floor at my daughter's nursery school and feeling strange. My perspective was that of a tiny person. When my daughter died I remember so well feeling it was like being back at her nursery school sitting on that floor and looking up at the world. I felt so small. So inadequate. You asked me to tell you what powerlessness means to me. Well, it's seeing the underside of the table rather than its top!"

How apt a description. If only you who are grieving could believe this is a universal emotion. Your sense of feeling small is a normal function of the grief process, one that you have probably felt but not labeled. To know it is a part of powerlessness may be helpful.

One man whose wife died young had the same sensation: "I did everything I could but it just wasn't enough. I don't like to feel that what I could do was not enough. I feel less manly, somehow. In fact, I don't like to talk about her being dead. I know it makes my friends uncomfortable but that's the way it really is. Why should I discuss something that hurts me and at the same time makes me feel small and less like a man? What's the gain?"

You may well be feeling what this man feels but remember there is merit in sharing your emotions. Whether they are discussed or not they do exist. No matter how deeply you attempt to submerge the pain it is still there. A wound that appears to be healing well may be infected beneath the normal-looking surface. That wound must be lanced and drained before true healing takes place.

When grieving it is reasonable to employ an analogous technique. If you feel powerless, at least have the power to open your mouth and discuss the pain. Use this power and ultimately it should offer you the release of the poison that is gnawing away inside of you.

"You know, my sister lay there dying. She would look at me from her bed and her eyes would plead with me to help her. I was her older brother. But what could I do? Sometimes I felt so small I would just leave the room and later when I would go back she would look so bewildered. She probably was wondering why I left. She couldn't ask because there was a tube down her throat. I felt so inept. So incapable of being useful. I'll probably go to my grave remembering her eyes," said this brother who is now thirty years old. His sister has been dead for fifteen years, yet as soon as he thinks about those days he remembers how small he felt. Unfortunately he did not share this with anyone who might have been able to help him. He was alone with his pain.

Now he wonders if perhaps that early experience of feeling so small has acted as an impetus that affected his entire life. Known as an aggressive guy who "takes nothing from anybody," he says he falls short of being a bully but never again wants to feel powerless in any situation.

While no one wishes to feel insignificant it is unrealistic to say it won't happen because things simply do not work that way. There will always be situations that you cannot control, situations in which you feel powerless. The wisest thing you can do to help yourself is to weigh each issue, see where you can be effective and by all means make certain you act in an effective manner. Yes, your special person is dead but there are still things over which you do have control. You can still control your behavior, whom you see, what you eat, what programs you watch, what you wear. You can control much but perhaps you need this reminder to help you know there are areas where you can take charge. You have charge of *you!* To remember this can offer you great hope and bring measures of satisfaction into your life.

There are many emotions, all negative, that surround you when you feel a loss of control. You feel anger, rage, frustration, fear, hysteria; you kick and scream and weep, often silently. As always know you are not alone nor are your emotions unique to you. Anyone who has experienced the death of a special person knows well how all these emotions intertwine and how little control you feel you have over them.

If you have achieved in this world, if you have built a success of your life, you probably had greater difficulty dealing with powerlessness in the death of your special person. After all, you have proven to yourself and to the world that you are in control. When your special person died you suddenly found yourself in a place that was alien—a place in which you had no control. Here, tragically, was a circumstance over which you could effect no change. Despite your own fine career or professional reputation, your special person still died.

Despite all your efforts—efforts in other areas of your life that rewarded you with financial stability and with prestige—here you have to face something over which you have no control. No say. Events take their course without your being able to affect them.

While you know there are limits to your control in the boardroom, now you must remember your human limitations. No one can control life and death. You did all in your considerable power, all that was reasonably possible.

You must evaluate your self-perceptions. Take a sheet of paper and answer the following:

• Are you a cork on an ocean that merely rises and falls with every wave?
• Do you always perceive yourself as being a victim of whatever sad event occurs in your life?
• Think of when you exhibited some inner strength.
• Recall when you felt you had some say in how things went in your own life.
• Do you perceive yourself as a power person—one who has control over events?
• Are you a self-made success?
• When did you not have control over your fate?
• Did you falter on the ladder at any point?
• How did you feel?
• What did you do when you felt that way?
• Did it help?
• List five things over which you have some control.

These things may be large or small. Just remember they matter. Whenever you can name something that is positive you are reinforcing you are *not* that cork lost on the ocean!

It is hard to believe events are out of your control. Sometimes, however, there is a very sad flip side to the issue of powerlessness. There are many people who have not achieved, not made their mark or left an imprint who also experience the death of a special person.

The sad flip side is that those who have not achieved also feel powerless, but theirs is a powerlessness that is a continuation of all they have lived. They may view the death as yet another one of life's blows. They do not hurt less but they may feel this is just more evidence of their lack of value as human beings.

One woman, poor and abandoned by her husband, had a child who died in a fire. She was wracked with pain and all the emotions anyone feels when their special person has died. During all her mourning and weeping she never said she should have been able to do something about the death. Her acceptance did not mean she had come to terms: she simply perceives herself as one of life's victims, something to be buffeted by every wayward breeze. Her child's death was just one more dreadful occurrence in her life.

There are certainly people who feel they have "no luck." But this woman goes beyond that sort of feeling. There is the sense that she is so powerless that she simply did not deserve anything normal or natural such as her child reaching adulthood. All life had ever shown her was she had no control of events. Her life was run by social workers, welfare programs, greedy landlords and day-work jobs. Since it is never useful or appropriate to make value judgments about who suffers more, none will be made here, but certainly there is much to pity when someone expects things not to go well and takes tragedy as her due.

As a friend it may be more helpful not to commiserate with someone in this situation. Far better to tell her you do not feel that what happened is okay. It is not written in the book of life that she be downtrodden by life *and* death. It is not okay for her that life has dealt her such an unfair blow.

If she becomes angry rather than complacent she may at least feel that some life is being breathed back into her. You may do her a favor by showing her that all the unfairness in her life is not to be expected. If you can help her come up fighting after this dreadful tragedy you may find she will indeed feel less powerless and less content to live her life as she has lived it up until now.

In living through mourning there are still other aspects of powerlessness that need understanding when a special person has died. There are countless cases where a person is killed by a drunk driver and the driver is merely given a slap on the wrist. The pain and anguish of people whose loved ones die this way, their powerlessness, is difficult to behold. Sometimes at the worst of times people come face to face with the reality that not everything is fair. Many people have come to realize there is not always justice despite having been raised to believe there is.

One woman, Ms. Candy Lightner, became enraged when her child was killed by a drunk driver. She organized a group, Mothers Against Drunk Drivers (MADD), which is now national. MADD has helped people to feel less powerless when dealing with such situations. The group also works to see that some fairness is displayed in meting out justice.

A couple whose son was killed by a drunk driver just after he graduated college listened to their pastor's eulogy quite carefully. In it he urged them to forgive and turn the other cheek. If they did not do so, they were not being good Christians. So they suffered silently and brooded separately and neither shared with the other the thoughts of vengeance and rage they were experiencing. In their determination to do as the pastor had urged, they even debated whether they would attend the driver's trial. In the end, they opted to go even though it was being held some miles from their home. When they arrived in the courtroom they were dumbfounded to find nearly a dozen men and women wearing huge blue-and-yellow buttons which read MADD.

"We suddenly saw we were not alone. There were other people who cared about our son and what had happened. We were not alone in how we felt, either," said the father. "We went to lunch after the hearing and talked. These people all told us about how angry they were when their children had been killed. My wife and I turned to each other and suddenly felt like a couple again. Here we were, each trying to do what the pastor had said and now, finally, we were with people who *knew,* really knew what we were feeling.

"Sure they are angry. They were robbed of the life of their child just as we were robbed. I don't feel so beaten by the world now that I can shout how angry I am. And even more, to know there are other people out there just as angry."

The woman said she fully planned to sit down with her pastor and have a long discussion about anger and vengeance and eulogies. "It's fine and good for him to say 'vengeance is Mine saith the Lord,' but Johnny wasn't his son!"

She said that his counsel at the time of the funeral was divisive; it made them each feel less than good, as though, if they had been better people, this would not have happened. It also made them feel they could not share their innermost ugly thoughts with one another.

"But being with this group has shown us both that although our son is dead we are not sheets on a clothesline flopping in the wind. We are real; we are people. We have been injured as the others in the group have been injured. Knowing we too can go and sit in a courtroom and possibly make a judge think a little harder before sentencing a drunk driver gives us a sense of some power. We weren't able to save our boy but we can at least work at seeing justice done when other parents are in our position," she said.

One widower feels powerless because he will not take the law into his own hands *as he most assuredly should not.* "I ought to get in there and kill the bastard," he said. His wife had been killed in a robbery at their home. "Now the guy is in prison but my wife is still dead!"

Certainly, anyone who has suffered the death of a loved person as a result of homicide has felt just what this man feels. Although he cannot do anything about the circumstances that occurred, he certainly can prove his life has some meaning, that he does have some power. Perhaps he can help organize a neighborhood program where people watch for strangers more closely. Sometimes, however, people wish to remove themselves completely from the cause of death. He can find any number of organizations that are always looking for volunteers to do worthwhile projects. At a time when you are feeling utterly powerless in the major scheme of life, nearly any action you take will bring you a bit forward. Since you cannot expect to be healed quickly, know that any step, regardless how small, is an expression of power. You are telling yourself, the most important person, that you can still move your feet. That is indeed urgent when a death has robbed you of your sense of having control over your life and the life and death of someone you love.

Perhaps the group of people who feel most powerless are those who have had to come to terms with suicide. It is the rare individual indeed who does not feel some degree of helplessness when a person dies as a result of suicide. Implicit in that type of death is the thought that somehow you should have been able to prevent it. You should have known. You begin to challenge your own sense of understanding of others, your own sense of compassion.

These people live, nearly always, with a deep inner regret that they failed, with the conviction that their love was not strong enough to keep their special person alive. They begin to believe they are powerless. There is no question they were unable to control the events that made them bereaved people, but they are not powerless to continue their own lives.

You may know someone or be someone who has spent years with a suicidal person. You may have hauled that person from social worker to psychologist to psychiatrist to mental health clinic. Years of your life may have been devoted to trying to save that person just as many people have spent years trying to save someone dying of cancer or heart disease. In the end, if you can only be kind enough to yourself, you will give yourself permission to see that you did all you could. You worked against a terminal disease. . . . People who die of suicide are considered by some experts to be just that, terminally ill. . . . You were unable to accomplish what you set out to do. The other person, the one who died, managed to accomplish what he set out to do. He is dead and that is what he wanted.

As time goes along it is hoped you will realize you do not

have the power of life or death over another human being. You do have the power, however, to restructure your own life. You can take the steps slowly that will help you attain that power. Especially as a helping person dealing with the survivor of a suicide it is urgent to remind the survivor that he only has power over himself.

Although your special person is dead you have not lost the power over yourself. For a while you may have hidden it away under layers of mourning and grief but that power is still there. It needs to be dug up once again, and the digging may be very hard. But know that it can be done. Trust yourself.

One woman whose father killed himself when she was in her mid-thirties said she felt she had no substance. How could her father have done such a thing knowing she was pregnant? Her mother was dead and now this woman, expecting her first child, was orphaned. "I tried so hard. I knew he was unhappy. I knew he had a lot of problems, my mother was dead. But so do lots of people. Then he killed himself. He used to say he *would* one day and I begged him to go for help. But people who are older—he was sixty-five—don't seem to be willing to run for help as much as most of us who are younger. He refused. So I would call him twice a day. I begged him to move in with us even though my husband did not want it and my father refused. He liked his life. That's what he told me. Liked his life! Then he took an overdose of pills just to prove how truthful he was. I should have known. I should have been there. I might have been able to save him."

How often these last words have been repeated by grieving people when there has been a suicide! How difficult to recognize that there are events over which we have no control, no power. Whether someone decides to end his life is usually one of those situations. There is a difference between those who threaten and make *"safe"* attempts and those who are truly serious. Surely no threat should be ignored. But you must understand there are limits to what you can do; to what you could have done. Self-blame is unjust. While you did not have the power to keep the person alive, you do have the power to live your life to its fullest. The death, certainly, will intrude at times. That is its way. But the opposite of powerlessness is power. You can prove to yourself that you, the living, still matter.

Most people who feel powerless believe that not only were they unable to prevent death, they are unable to make a difference in life. But sometimes there are things that can be done. If your loved one was murdered and the judge handed down a light sentence for the accused, you may call this to the attention of the media. Recently in Detroit a young Chinese man had been beaten to death by two Caucasians. The men were given sentences of probation and fined some $3,000 each. The mother of the boy was so outraged that she made her son's case a cause that became known to the Chinese community throughout the country. The two men ended up being retried on another charge—that of violating the dead man's civil rights because it is alleged racial slurs were involved. No matter what the woman's degree of pain, she was at least shown she still had power. An ordinary mother, she who would not allow her son's murder to go unvindicated.

In the case of homicide there is generally little you can do in dealing with the perpetrator. If you cannot muster the energy to demand a new trial or hearing you certainly can help yourself by proving you have the power to form a group or attend one for those who have suffered a homicide. Your special issues will be discussed in those meetings. That is proof of power. You can talk and ask for suggestions and sometimes even offer your own. You are not impotent when you can act. To act is to have power.

As life has grown more complex for many people, issues are often not as clear as they once were. An example of this is that most dreaded of issues confronting those who feel powerless. In light of present medical progress, you need to address at least to some degree the question of having too much power. In other words, the question of "pulling the plug." This is never a simple issue. You certainly did not grow up and live your life believing you would ever be put in a godlike position, and many view pulling the plug as just that. You, an ordinary lay person, or you a medical professional, are suddenly confronted with what King Solomon wrestled with in Ecclesiastes. He said in that text there is a time to be born and a time to die. Nowadays that time is not always decided by health, plagues or famine. Life and death are often decided by how long a medical procedure may be prolonged, how long someone can be kept alive by machine.

Ironically, not all progress means going forward. People were much more comfortable when they were not faced with issues like whether or not to put a child, wife, husband, brother or grandparent on a life-support system. Now families agonize dreadfully over what is the right thing to do.

It is very easy to sit back and intellectualize about how you would handle a certain situation. You know all the right things and have all the right answers. But being on the firing line and having to make a decision about how much longer your son or daughter will live is far more difficult. Most of the time the doctors will come forth and offer their opinions about whether to use life-support systems or not. But ultimately the decision seems to rest more and more with the family of the person who is ill.

One mother said making the decision not to allow extraordinary means was the hardest decision she ever made. "My son had cancer. Each time they would come to me and say they had a new treatment, an experimental treatment and would I give my consent. My son and I would talk it over with my husband and each time we agreed to go on, to try something more. Finally, my boy was in a coma. The doctor came out and said the end was near, did we want to try any of the life-support systems. My husband and I looked at each other and we both began to cry. Our boy had suffered enough, we decided. It was time to bring all this to an end. I was shaking when I told the doctor not to try any further. My son died three days later and he looked so peaceful. Thank God we had the strength to do what was right. He had suffered enough."

These people appear to feel at peace with themselves and the world about this most traumatic decision. Not all people are so fortunate. One widow said she fought her entire family because they felt it was inhuman to keep her husband alive artificially. "I always believed where there was life there was hope. If anyone held out even a bone to me, I felt I had to take it. I couldn't just say pull the plug. We were married nearly forty years and I felt I owed it to him.

"But he lived for two weeks in an intensive care unit and he suffered and so did I. I don't know if what I did was right. But I did the only thing I knew how to do and that was to preserve life at all costs."

One woman was told by her doctor that if only he could keep her seventy-five-year-old mother alive just a while longer he could control the emphysema that was killing her. The mother finally reached the stage where she was dying. The doctor called the daughter out into the hallway and said all he needed was to buy some time; he *knew* without question she would improve if he only could have the time he needed with her. The daughter went against everything she believed to be correct and morally appropriate and bowed to the argument of the doctor. "What else could I do? The man was telling me, not hinting, that he could make her better, that she would be well enough to leave the hospital. Who in their right mind would not have bowed to that pressure? Well, I did. My mother lived for two weeks in intensive care. She had a respirator and an arteriogram and every other hellish procedure imaginable. She did not pull through; she died. She died in fear and discomfort. I am furious that I allowed the doctor's judgment to outweigh what I knew to be right. My mother died afraid and that was unforgivable."

Whether there is a right or wrong answer to this latest of major issues is certainly not clear. Like much of life, it is heavily tinged with gray. But there is one thing you can do for yourself and even more for those you love who might be placed in this most untenable of positions. In your own handwriting spell out just what you want done. Do you wish to be kept alive artificially? For how long? The use of a standard printed form is not as helpful to a family member as seeing your wishes spelled out in your own handwriting. Then you are guiding them and they know what you wish.

Because most people die of a lingering illness or an incapacitating one, the question of life-support systems becomes more and more important. You can be performing the greatest act of love if you will make it your business to put in writing just what your feelings are. If you are a survivor you know even more how difficult these decisions can be. Spare those you love and help them to know they are carrying out your wishes whatever those wishes may be.

It is as dreadful to have too much power as it is to have too little. Bear that in mind as you determine just how you will deal with your own illness and help those you to be free of the decision-making process. They will have to endure all the pains of being a survivor. Help them at least to avoid having to decide your fate, whether you will live or die. Let that be your decision. That way you will set those who love you free. It may well be your final legacy—an act of daring kindness. You, and only you, have the power to do that for the people you love and who love you.

Faith . . . One Pathway

Religion is not asking. It is a longing of the soul.
—GANDHI

There is an old tale about a philosopher and a theologian. The two men were engaged in a debate and the theologian tried to undermine the philosopher by likening him to a blind man in a dark room looking for a black cat which wasn't there.

"Well, that could be so," said the philosopher. "But a theologian would have found it!"

Both men were being derisive, both sarcastic. But when you have survived the death of a special person you are often caught between just such extremes. Like the philosopher, you grope in a seemingly endless darkness hoping to find something of substance upon which to grab hold.

Because you are facing what is probably life's ultimate tragedy, your search often becomes frantic. You begin a mental rather than a physical search: you seek what you could have done differently, how you could have better helped, how you could have been a better person. And ultimately that search leads you to explore your relationship with God.

Like the theologian, who undoubtedly would have found the cat that wasn't there, you are grasping to make something tangible out of what is in your soul. You are trying to make something concrete out of a concept. To your dismay you can rarely do this. It is difficult to hold onto an abstract idea—the existence of a supreme being, of a greater plan to lend meaning to your tragedy.

The truth is that faith cannot be seen or touched. It is something you must know even though no proof to warrant faith is offered to you.

When a special person dies there is a great struggle, frequently, about the question of faith. There are those who are drawn closer to their God because they feel a desperate need to know there was some reason, however obscure, that this terrible tragedy took place. To feel there was a greater purpose, a greater plan, can offer immeasurable support when everything around you seems destroyed.

There are endless stories about people who have grown closer to God after the death of a special person. One father, whose two children died soon after birth, said all the pain he and his wife had suffered proved to them there was indeed a God. "The time will come when we do have a child and we will have so much more love to give because God has made us understand about loss. When you come to know pain you are more willing to give pleasure. We both believe this."

Another bereaved parent, the mother of a child who died as a result of heart disease, adds to this idea: "God was merciful. Had he lived my son would have been incapacitated eventually. He would have been one of those who sit looking out the window while other children play. There was no surgery that could help him back then and he died. God spared him the pain of being a looker-on at life. Although we miss him and it certainly hurts us that he is not here, we are also thankful that he was spared a life of pain."

How fortunate such people are! People who believe in a good and merciful God can at least derive some measure of peace in the midst of tragedy. They are like Emily Dickinson who was able to extract certainty from a belief. In her poem "I Never Saw a Moor" she wrote:

I never saw a moor,
I never saw the sea;
Yet know I how the heather looks,
And what a wave must be.

I never spoke with God,
Nor visited in Heaven;
Yet certain am I of the spot
As if the chart were given.

There can be such comfort in knowing without question that your special person died for a good reason, and, even more important, is now in a better place. But there are many who believe no such thing. Some have never believed in a world after death. They feel that they must be the best people they can in this world because they only pass through life once.

Many such people, called humanists, have lived with the philosophy that they must do all they can in the here and now. Certainly they mourn when a special person dies. Certainly they hurt as anyone hurts at a life ended too soon or too painfully. But they rarely face the difficulties experienced by many people who have believed there was a benevolent God all their lives only to suddenly feel betrayed by that God.

One father felt that truly all was lost and there could be no hope if his daughter was dead. "What meaning can anything have? I was always a God-fearing man, a person who felt there was a greater plan in this life. Now, Lynne is dead. What plan can have been made that allowed a fourteen-year-old girl to die? She never really lived and now she is dead. How can there be a God?"

Of course, there are no answers, easy or otherwise. Because for every mother or father who feels as that father felt there will be another who works at becoming comfortable with the idea her baby is now with God. "Certainly I cry," said one mother, after the death of her son. "It hurts me when I see the other kids out there playing. But I know my son is with God and nothing will ever again hurt him."

It is not our function here to raise religious disputes. We need only know the most basic truth: no one has the right to make judgments about how anyone else perceives faith. Certainly it is more comforting to believe that your special person is in God's hands. But it is not appropriate to make a value judgment and attempt to force your beliefs upon anyone else, especially when they feel vulnerable and defensive and hurt. When a grieving person is faced with endless pain he cannot avoid, it seems needlessly cruel to increase his conflict by making him defend his belief or lack thereof.

The widow who believes God is watching over her dead husband can perhaps sleep more peacefully than the widower who is certain that once his wife died there is nothingness and she was totally short-changed. But to force your way of thinking upon someone else is simply not fair; nor is it appropriate. It is, in fact, cruel. When people are hurting and feeling vulnerable they are already beset with countless things that challenge their thinking and their faith. There is much they wish to share. But they do, in fact, live a rather secretive life when it comes to their negative thoughts. Just as people are fearful of sharing how angry they are with the dead person for abandoning them, many people who believe there is a God are enraged that He allowed this tragedy to occur.

One woman who had always believed in God suddenly lost her faith when her daughter was murdered. She found herself in a panic. A lifetime of certainty had been buried along with her daughter. Where should she turn now? What should she feel? A part of her soul had been removed not only by her daughter's death but by her newfound certainty that there was no God. What was now right for her? She no longer knew. This woman lived in a rural community where people spoke frequently of God. When they did, she would turn away fearful lest they see the disbelief she felt showed in her eyes. She feared her lack of belief in God would make her an outcast in her community.

"My people were really kind. They would come and sit with me and bring food, but then one of the women suggested that we all take hands and pray together.

"I couldn't handle that at all. I had been hearing a bunch of meaningless platitudes, meaningless words. They didn't tell me how I was going to survive the day. People only said 'Trust in God' just like on the dollar bill! They tried to assure me if I did that all would be well. I just exploded at a group of women who had come to visit me when they asked that we join hands. They were all from the church. I told them it was easy for them to offer me all the moral support in the world, it wasn't their daughter who was buried the other day, it was mine. I told them I didn't even want to think there was a God because if there was, He was cruel and vengeful and evil!

"I was probably being unjust. They were doing what they felt was the good Christian thing but I just could not hear that prattle any longer. They were babbling as far as I was concerned, just babbling. They left my house shortly after because no one seemed to be able to answer my rage, and that included me. I think back to that time and my only regret was that I lacked control and good manners. But as far as my feelings about a god, well, they just have not changed."

To make matters even more complicated the women told the minister that she was "behaving strangely." She said when he came to see her she was no more polite to him than to them. Since that time she claims to find only icy responses when any part of her community deals with her. "Sometimes I feel I brought it on myself and other times I think life brought this about," she says.

Countless people find themselves in the same situation as this mother. One widow who was an integral part of her church simply could not handle the magnitude of being alone when her husband died. Her church friends would come and visit often. But one day, when she felt everything of value had been lost to her, she blurted out to these women that she was no longer certain she believed in God. She went into a small oration about why there could be no God and if by any small chance there was, well He was a God who inflicted pain.

These people who came to offer comfort certainly were unprepared for the tirade. Their affiliation with one another was a church affiliation. How could she have expected them to respond? They did the obvious thing and left as soon as possible.

Now the widow sits and bemoans her fate. Not only did her husband die, but her friends abandoned her. She does not see that she helped create the predicament. Certainly she could not have prevented the death, but despite her pain and anger she would have been wiser to select other people with whom to share her questioning of God. Although the women perhaps represented religion to her because she knew them from church, there are things that need to be remembered even in such extreme times. Not all things are for all people's ears.

If this woman with all her hurt and pain could go to her minister and tell him what she is feeling, knowing that he would listen and care about her when she is through describing her hurt and disillusionment, then she could be comforted. Sometimes to do such a thing takes courage. If she does not feel capable of seeing her minister alone, maybe a friend or family member could accompany her. If her support person sees the conversation is going well, he could excuse himself and allow the minister and his parishioner private time. If he sees this woman is having difficulty articulating her hurt and despair, he could perhaps help her express what she is feeling. If this woman has joined a support group, her facilitator might make the visit to the clergyman with her.

Most of all, it is important for her to meet with her minister both for her sake and his. If she does not share her anger she could well turn away from God. If she is a lifelong believer this could mean yet another major loss in her life. If the minister does not respond appropriately with kindness and an open mind he will have lost her as a parishioner.

It might be helpful for her to write out some of what she is feeling before she sees her minister. As a friend you might suggest this approach. If she can put her feelings on paper she will give him a chance to digest what she is experiencing and perhaps be able to face her without judging her. By being a good listener he will certainly have gained a friend and most likely have avoided the loss of someone who was always a believer.

One of a clergyman's most fundamental duties, yet one for which he is least equipped, is that of counseling people when there has been a death. Most clerics leave their seminaries ill-prepared for the arduous tasks of dealing with families who are distraught and raging with grief. Certainly a clergyman's task would be made easier if that rage were directed at anything but God.

While many members of the clergy believe it is their function to defend God, one Catholic priest said it best. "God does not need me to defend Him. It would be arrogance on my part to think I could fulfill that task."

This priest works with dying children and has seen much pain in his ministry. He said he merely listens when someone vilifies God. He does not refute, nor does he try to explain.

"When people are in such a state of rage and pain they are really not hearing. And if they do hear, they must come to their own realizations about God and His infinite goodness. I cannot do that for them."

It is terribly sad to feel the need to challenge your views about God when a crisis of such magnitude occurs. One man had been raised to believe God was all-seeing and loving. Then his young wife died and left him with a small child. He found himself in the terrible bind that afflicts most male bereavement: he was unable to cry in front of others and rarely able to cry when alone. He, like many men, found it very hard to express his emotions to anyone. Finally, feeling as if he might explode, he went to the minister who had been a lifelong friend of his family. This minister had performed his marriage ceremony as well as his wife's funeral.

The minister invited the widower to his home rather than to the church where interruptions and distractions were the norm. He sat quietly and asked the widower nonabrasive questions. Slowly the man began to feel a bit at ease and shared all that had been pent up within him. He even reached the point where he told the minister he questioned his belief in God. The minister, rather than immediately jumping to God's defense, took in all that was said, and merely told the man how sorry he was that things had taken such a dreadful turn in his life.

"It wasn't easy for me to go see him but then I found it even harder to leave," said the widower. "I finally felt, here was someone who would listen. I expected him to slap my wrist when I told him I didn't even know about God any longer, but instead he took it all in stride. He said I was not the first person to question nor would I be the last. What a relief that was!"

The young widower said gradually he began attending church again and eventually, instead of merely continuing a habit, he found he was deriving some benefit from being there. The minister could have done many things when the young man came to see him. He could have preached at him. He could have been scandalized by this man's lack of faith. But instead, he did what the man needed. He merely listened and did not pass judgment. Perhaps that is why the man could return to his church and even feel he was being helped.

How much more positive this experience than that of the woman who went to her minister after her son died and found the man unable to fully comprehend what she was experiencing. He seemed so removed from her reality that she did not feel the freedom to tell him she actually hated God: "We sort of skirted around the issue. I said I was disappointed that all my praying wasn't heard. He kept trying to reassure me that God still loved me. That wasn't what I needed to hear. He was less than helpful, really. At that moment there was nothing I could possibly have been told that would have had any meaning. I just needed him to listen."

Sometimes ambivalent behavior may be seen in those who mourn. You may be angry at God but you are not ready to turn your back on Him. This confusion about feelings can heighten an already intense state of anxiety for someone who is grieving. If faith has been a part of your life until the death you will feel even less anchored, more adrift, if you turn away now.

This type of emotion can well be likened to what occurs when a child and parent quarrel. There may be anger, resentment, hostility. Yet at some level these quarreling people love one another and feel a bond toward one another which must be preserved despite the temporary battle. This is why it is so important that the minister not make bad worse by condemning someone who is feeling betrayed by God. If left without pressure to sort this through most angry bereaved people will return to

Him just as most children and parents do reunite even when there has been very bad feeling in the family.

Ministers have a very difficult time in dealing with a family when a child dies. All sorts of things can be said about the deaths of parents and siblings and grandparents. But when a child dies and a parent is confronted with his own loss of immortality the task of a minister is hard indeed. Some clerics, faced with their own sense of uselessness in this most dreadful crisis, turn to platitudes. They quote scripture, which may be helpful to some. Yet there are far too many others who are left cold and feeling deserted by these expressions.

One woman went to her temple and heard the Old Testament story of Abraham willing to sacrifice his only son Isaac because it was God's wish. This woman's son had died six months earlier. When she heard this story, and it was not a new one to her, she heard it from the standpoint of having involuntarily buried a child she loved. She heard it differently in the retelling and questioned how anything could make sense when a patriarch could even consider letting his child die! She said it took her many years before she could walk into her temple again. She labeled the entire experience a "turn-off."

Perhaps the most difficult situation of all is the one described in the chapter on anger—the story of the mother who, after her son died, kept asking the minister why, why did this happen? The minister took her by the hand and in a solemn voice responded, "This was God's way of telling you you need to be a better person!" The woman never set foot in a church again.

You might have been victimized in some such way by a clergyman but it is important to remember that not all clergy are the same. There are caring and loving members of that difficult profession who do understand pain and do genuinely wish to help. While you are in such need it could only benefit you to try to church-shop and minister-shop until you find someone compatible with whom you may speak freely.

Many members of the clergy from all parts of the country maintain that not enough grief-counseling classes were offered in their theological seminaries. They were taught scripture and told to use biblical examples but very little more. Therefore, they are sent into the worst possible situation not fully prepared. After all, most people, whether bereaved or not, view the clergy as being God's representative on earth. When that minister does not live up to a standard you have preconceived, in your grief you feel not only the minister has failed you but God has also failed you.

One Ohio minister acknowledged it is always difficult to know just what his parishioner needs. Some people in mourning, he said, do prefer biblical parallels, while most people want something more tangible.

"I have found the most helpful thing I have to offer is a hug. It seems to say all that needs saying. The touching, the sense of human warmth seems to do it for many of my people. Often, months later, bereaved people will come up to me and thank me for my understanding and help. Yet I rarely say much. Perhaps I convey all my sympathy for their pain because I believe in touching," he said.

The minister may well have hit upon an important key to the problem. Words seem not to hold much meaning to many bereaved parents when a child dies. They seem to slip through a sieve that has become the parents' life. But actions such as touching and the indication of love that comes with sharing time, sometimes in silence, sometimes with listening, can be very helpful.

While living through mourning, you probably have experienced one of the greatest losses aside from death when you felt those pangs of "Is there really a God?" Those thoughts, for people raised to believe in a supreme being, are much more than unsettling, they are frightening. All you have ever believed in your life is suddenly tumbling down around you. You believed that your God would watch over you and all the people most precious to you and *that* did not happen.

You may feel God has turned his face away from you, or you may feel there is no God. In any event the end result is the same. At the time you are most desperately in need of stability you find yourself grasping at air. You are faced with yet another void in your life—not a tiny pinprick but a huge chasm that is empty and dark and frightening.

A young widow whose husband died in an automobile accident is in her early thirties; she was left with two young children aged ten and eight. The woman, although financially able to manage, felt alone and isolated from most people: "I found that my friends were either married, single or divorced. I could not really connect with the married ones. It was just too painful for me. My single friends were into the bar scene and that is just not my life-style. My divorced friends spend hours complaining about their former husbands. I can't bear hearing what they have to say. I would have given anything for Ken to be alive and all they do is bitch about the men they were once married to!"

Not being able to find her place ultimately led her to attend a Sunday morning church service, something she had not done since her childhood. As she looked around, she saw some people who came as couples, some who came alone; all had what she described as a wholesome manner.

"While I could not be sure how they spent their leisure hours I at least found myself in a healthy environment and it was the first time in a long time that that had happened."

She said after the service she waited until the other people had left and asked the minister for a few minutes of his time. She explained her plight and that somehow she had not found a place in which she fit. The minister told her there was always room in his congregation and that everyone "fit." He took her name and telephone number—which she debated about leaving but finally agreed to leave. Within a week she was contacted by the church women's club president. She was asked about her interests and her children and the types of things she liked doing. Although she was reluctant, she agreed to attend a meeting. The president promised to meet her at the door and that promise was kept. In short order, the young widow found herself helping with the annual picnic, an event in which her children could take part.

"Some of the women were married and some were not. But because we were working for the betterment of the church there was an entirely different atmosphere than I had experienced previously. It felt good. I felt like a person who belonged and a person who did not have a label. I was not a 'widow' in that environment so much as another person lending a hand."

The question of labeling is one that all bereaved people need to explore. Do you wish to be specifically identified with your loss? Would you prefer to melt into the crowd unnoticed? These are individual issues and must be decided by those who are bereaved.

Without question there are numerous cases where the church or temple acts as a perfect melting pot, a place where you know your help is needed and you will not be labeled if you choose not to be. Also, as a bonus, it can be a place where your presence is appreciated. You might find this sort of environment brings out something of your spiritual side. Even if you are going through a period of questioning about your faith, you still do have a spiritual side.

Perhaps spirit can be defined as your essence, the thing about you that makes you the unique human being you are. One of the great losses you sustain when your special person dies is so often the sense that you have lost your spiritual side; that side that is your inner reserve. Certainly if you love someone a part of you is buried with that person; anyone who has loved deeply would attest to the truth of that. However, when you feel you are diminished because you are no longer someone's mother, wife, husband, child, sibling, then your spiritual side becomes even more important because that is the side of you that is *you* unlabeled.

More scholars and theologians than ever before are beginning to look deeply into the question of death and religion because they can see the great impact one has upon the other. Many who were deeply committed to their faith simply dropped away after their special person died. They are bitter and angry. You may well know such a person. You may indeed be one.

On the other hand, you may never have given God or faith much thought until your wife or some other special person died. Then the picture changed dramatically. Suddenly you were flailing around for something, anything, upon which you could grab hold. When the something that ultimately became God initially entered your being, you might at first have been incredulous, for certainly this was a new concept. But as time has gone on and you have found something upon which to lean and something that offers some meaning to the death and to your life, you may have started to accept the idea that there is indeed a greater being.

You may have been helped by this belief. But bear in mind not all people respond the way you did. To attempt to force others to see what you are seeing is to set up a situation that can create great discomfort. Certainly you might suggest that someone attend services with you and even call on the day you plan to attend but beyond that you can be most helpful by sitting back and allowing each person to find his own place in the scheme of religion. This is far too personal an issue; you can never force your opinion upon another.

Sometimes bereaved parents will differ in their approach to religious belief. If this is the case, each person must function as an individual. Grieving is not always done in a team. Religion is often an issue of people doing what is best for them *singly*.

It is important to remember that you most likely have been raised to feel it is wrong to question God or His wisdom. You are, according to some religions, committing a sin by so doing. Yet the truth is you may experience much rage at God when a special person dies.

Although you may feel it is a sacrilege it is sometimes almost easier to rant at God than at another person who will respond with equal anger. Sometimes when something cannot be seen it is easier to vent frustration on it. You probably find it easier to say no to a salesperson on the telephone than to one you see in person, for example.

If you believe there is a God you must remember that He is a forgiving God. If you had bursts of anger during your mourning it is reasonable to expect to be forgiven for your rage and for your doubts. Do not give yourself yet another whip with which to beat yourself by allowing yourself to feel guilt because you viewed God in a disparaging way. Remember your disparagement was built of your despair. Be kind and forgive yourself.

Reverend William Wendt, an Anglican priest who heads a

bereavement counseling establishment at the St. Francis Center in Washington, D.C., said two-thirds of the population is buried out of funeral homes and not out of churches. "We must restore and renew the church's ministry so that people will return. Rituals such as wakes should take place in the setting of the church."

Reverend Wendt said that religion's apparent incapacity to deal with death stems from his belief that many ministers went into the clergy with a fear of their own death. "Because of this, the church has been the greatest abdicator in helping people deal with death. If we wish people to return to religion we must create a real ministry."

Having a family member or members do the eulogy would be Reverend Wendt's preference. Also, he would like to see incorporated in the wake its original intent: "The wake was established as a forum in which to tell stories about the dead person. They may have been sad or funny but most of all they had to be real."

And Reverend Wendt would like to see families more involved in the ritual of preparing the body of the special person who died. He said one popular senator's family came and washed his body and prepared it for the burial thereby making it a far more personal and intimate experience.

Another idea he would like to see incorporated in the way we deal with death is the Jewish custom of shiva, in which all members of the community go to the mourner's home and pay their condolences there; it is not enough to make an appearance at the funeral.

The idea of shiva serves a deeper purpose than merely saying you are sorry. By going to the surviving person's home you are immediately removing the pain of setting the mourner apart from general society, an act of great kindness in itself. While some Jewish people complain the atmosphere at some homes during shiva becomes almost partylike, the opposite situation of sitting home alone and wondering how you can prepare a meal appears to be a greater burden on the survivors.

Despite all the pain and anger people generally feel when a special person has died, there are lessons that may be learned.

Nothing is irreparable except death. We all have the opportunity to see things differently and change our views as long as we are alive. To have felt and expressed rage against God is not an unalterable act. As Reverend Wendt says, "God is a God of love."

If we love we learn to forgive. Certainly to chastise yourself for doubting and questioning is an act of futility. Take that energy and help yourself grow to understand your new situation as a survivor and nurture yourself with love.

As you complete this chapter about religion and faith there are some suggestions you might write down and try to answer:

- Did I have faith before my special person died?
- Have I lost that faith?
- Am I certain it is not still there at some level?
- Do I need a break from thinking about God?
- Would I be wise to stay away from my church for a while?
- Would I be wise to push myself to attend services?
- Was my minister helpful? How?
- Did he add to my pain? How?
- Should I seek another minister?
- Do other family members feel as I do? Do we all need to learn tolerance toward one another's attitudes?
- If you are a bereaved parent it is possible your spouse does not share your religious point of view. Allow each other to practice or not as suits the individual. This may mean attending church alone.
- Most important, after you have written down your thoughts put them aside for a month or so. If after that time you still feel angry or lost, in the kindest, most tactful way send your thoughts to your clergyman by mail. Then wait a while and see if you can set up an appointment with him to go over some of your feelings.
- Encourage him to establish a support group within your church.
- If you do not believe in God begin doing some reading of poetry and philosophy and see what others who do not believe in God have discovered to help them on their path. A lack of belief in God need not destroy you. It merely establishes you have a right to your own point of view.

• If you do not believe in God begin a clipping file where you save works that will help you in your grief.

• Perhaps begin looking at artwork to see how artists have depicted death when they do not use angels in their paintings. You may gain strength from this and ultimately find your own peace.

If you are fortunate enough to believe there is a Supreme Being, Someone or Something that does have a master plan for you and all the rest of humanity, you perhaps somewhere along the line will find some comfort in knowing there was a reason God took your special person. You may never know what that reason was during your lifetime but the certainty that such a reason exists can be a soothing balm on your heart.

When you have gone through all the various facets of coping with the death of your special person it is hoped you ultimately will find some acceptance in your new and ongoing life.

Acceptance . . .
a Pathway

To teach men how to live without certainty and yet
without being paralyzed by hesitation is the lesson
of learning acceptance.　　　—ANONYMOUS

Acceptance is the net result of a healthy grief process. It is the
ability to recall one's special person without pain. Acceptance
does not proceed from a denial of the death but rather through
confronting the event. The only way around grief is through it.

Although it may be far too early for you to think of your
special person without great hurt, be assured that you will reach
such a time and you will be of good mental health again. You
may be tempted to ask just how long it takes for good mental
health and acceptance to set in. The answer to that is there is
no exact time schedule for grieving. You have your own individual clock just as everyone else does.

There have been many issues you have explored as you traveled the pathways toward healing. You have dealt with denial,
your first response to the news your special person had died.
You have explored and shared the stories of others who have
had similar experiences. You have felt, as they felt, the incredible
sense that you would not allow yourself to believe such a tragic
event had occurred. Indeed, that is a major hurdle to overcome.
One of the first steps in dealing with your denial was having to
address the funeral with all its decision-making and ritual. Those

days of visitation or shiva were hard and bleak times. You often wondered what you were doing there, why all the people were coming to see you. You questioned whether any of this was real. And, indeed, that questioning was important. It made you face up to the pain and mystery of death.

Those early days were filled with bewilderment and constant questioning. How did this happen? Why? Why to him? Why to me? What comfort to know you are not alone! All these thoughts and many others that have crept insidiously into your mind are not unique to you. While not everyone feels the same about each of the painful issues involved in the normal grief process, certain things can be of comfort. Knowing you are not alone heads the list!

When your special person first died, you probably found yourself in great conflict between your tending to deny that the tragedy occurred and the necessity of dealing with the funeral. There you were, at the time you most wanted to be removed from it all, being thrust deeper into dealing with the death. You probably had to decide what your special person would wear at his burial. You had to think about clergymen and eulogies. You found yourself with endless tasks and viewed them either as meaningless or as overwhelmingly important.

Before the burial you possibly wondered to yourself; why all the fuss? All this pomp and circumstance. You may have walked around in a daze looking from face to face; knowing these were familiar people yet not quite recognizing what they were all gathered around you to do. This is certainly not unusual. You may have wondered why the importance about what your special person wore. You may have questioned why the need for a eulogy. After all, you knew quite well what you had lost. All that was occurring around you was meaningless. Or so it seemed.

Then there are other people who become intensely involved in planning their special person's funeral. You may be like them. You may have wanted to select every item of apparel. You may have elected to have him buried with his watch, or placed a picture or lock of hair in the coffin. You may have spent hours with the clergyman discussing how he would present your special person to the people who came to the funeral. You may have found some solace in hand-picking the hymns played in the church. You may have derived much comfort in knowing that others before you have done just such things. Again, you found yourself realizing you are not alone. You are part of an endless chain of people who have come before and suffered in their agony over what decision would be correct for them. You are, in effect, woven into the fabric that makes up all of life and death.

It has been said that to speak when you are angry will allow you to make the best speech you will ever regret. Anger works that way. You may have endured endless hours and weeks, perhaps years, of rage because your special person died. There are many people who have great difficulty knowing they felt such anger. They are the ones who are shocked to learn that there is anger in all loving relationships. You may be such a person. You may have felt hurt by your husband or wife or child for dying and leaving you in such pain. You may have felt fury at God, the being you had always trusted to see you through the storms of life, for allowing this tragedy to occur.

Now, sometime down the road to healing and acceptance, you may look back on those bitter, hurting days and think how irrationally you viewed everything. Yet you know now that you were one of many people who share these same "irrational" thoughts, who have felt this same sense of injustice you experienced. Certainly you may regret raging at your special person because he died, but this anger is an emotion most mourners experience. Anger is a normal reaction to grief. When you have been conditioned, however, since early childhood, not to display anger because it is not ladylike or gentlemanly, you feel, aside from all that grief, a discomfort over your own behavior. But to feel so much pain and hurt and then to question your own values and sanity is heaping too heavy a load upon yourself. Knowing that so many have shared your experience can be a safety valve of great value when you are working toward accepting the death of your special person.

There are others you may have felt anger toward. Perhaps your clergyman, the funeral director, or the doctor who attended your special person. As time goes forward it is to be hoped that some of that anger has dissipated. You cannot hold on to anger indefinitely and really take steps that move you along. As you work your way toward acceptance remember that while your anger may have been something to hold on to at a given point, there comes a time when it is okay and helpful to let it go. That is the time to move on and begin rebuilding your life.

Some people have said they could not reach the stage of acceptance that their special person died without taking some action: confronting the doctor or starting a lawsuit against an automobile company if a car was involved in the death. They needed public recognition of their pain. They needed news-paper headlines and juries to agree that a great injustice had been done. Sadly, all too often when the fuss had died down, these people who were so angry still had to deal with that anger. No financial settlement in the world can make up for having a child die as the result of a faulty automobile design, for example. What has to happen ultimately is that the anger must be let go in order to allow your heart to heal.

Another problem you have explored along the pathway to-ward acceptance is your attitude toward guilt. You may have been somewhat surprised to see that many share your feelings and hurts. You may have had to weather the all too painful guilt brought about by your having survived your special person's death. This is not unusual. You may again experience that nag-ging sensation of "Why him and not me?" You may feel guilty because you felt you did not do enough while your special person was alive. Why weren't you more loving, more caring? Certainly all of us should work diligently every day at being the kindest people we can be, but there are times in all relationships where kindness flies out the window. You may have experienced many moments of irritation and short temper with your special per-son, yet you thought nothing of it when that person was alive. The feeling you had, that tomorrow is another day and you will make it all up then, is universal. How sad that that other day never came: you are left wishing to say you are sorry and you have no one to say it to!

Perhaps the most pervasive emotion you have experienced

throughout this long ordeal is the depression that seems to have completely overtaken your life. No matter what you do or where you go the feeling of depression sits with you like a weighted cloak. Certainly you may laugh, go to the movies or enjoy the company of amusing and interesting people but most of the time you feel as if you have two faces: one that you show to the world, and the other that you know *you* will have to face alone when all is quiet and the amusing people end their visit.

In current mental health thinking there is much discussion about emotional peaks and valleys as the norm in human mood changes. Picture a peak as an emotional high point, and picture a valley as an emotional low. Then picture a graph or chart of these Vs and inverted Vs. You will realize that every valley has its promise of a peak and every peak a forewarning of the valley to come. This kind of emotional cycle is far different from the depression that overtakes you when you are mourning. When you are in a depression, you picture no high point to be reached ultimately. You see merely a swamp that has no bottom and no top.

To come to terms with the certainty that you will wake up in the morning feeling just as badly as you did when you finally fell asleep the night before can be of some help. You are learning to accept that for the time being, at least, there will be a period of hurting that simply will not go away. Certainly there will be those special moments when the hurt leaves you for a while but it probably will be helpful if you do not expect it to go away quickly.

Another area that has probably been difficult and painful for you is the knowledge that there are events over which you have no control. Your sense of powerlessness with its accompanying frustration and feeling of worthlessness is hard to combat, especially while you are wearing the cloak of depression. Yet, like many other components of grief and mourning, powerlessness can be broken down into manageable pieces. You are faced with a great challenge. Do you allow yourself to let this lack of power overtake your life completely? Do you reach the point where you accept without question that you are merely an object swirled by the wind? Are you the leaf on a tree or its trunk? Certainly in the early days it is virtually impossible not to feel like you are swaying to and fro but as time goes on you may reach the point where you no longer can accept the sense that you are merely an object to be moved by the wind. You are a person. A somebody. As that somebody, you may have decided to take small things in hand and deal with them. Assert yourself. Even if the issue is small, you will derive immense satisfaction from having done just that. You may even come home and look in the mirror and congratulate yourself because you have proven even in a minute way that you are somebody who has the ability to make a difference. When you felt you made no difference whatsoever in this life you were deeply hurt. You were vulnerable to every bit of pain imaginable. But once you take control over even the smallest thing your overriding certainty that you are powerless may begin to erode. When you realize that erosion is starting to take place, you will have helped yourself up yet another rung of the ladder of mourning.

While dealing with the death of a special person is in no way a positive experience, there are certain discoveries that you may find *do* emerge once you have reached the stage of acceptance, and they may be helpful forever. One such discovery is the knowledge that you have challenged your faith and come to some sense of clarity about it. You may have decided you no longer believe there is a God. If that is the case, is it possible that you questioned all along, well before the death? If that is your decision, know you have a right to it. Having decided there is no God may not make you the most popular person on the block. It may, in fact, be wiser to just keep that view to yourself at least for a while. That wise old saw about never discussing politics or religion may be something to consider. But if you have reached the decision that you cannot accept the concept of God you may have worked through just what it is you *do* believe. There can be much merit in the process of working through a belief.

On the other hand, you may be someone who has always believed there was no God. Therefore you were never wracked with the uncertainty and pain and disappointment of those who have felt betrayed by God when a loved one has died. You had accepted, long before the event, that there is a natural order of things and no supreme being governs it. For you, there were no decisions to make. No challenging of your values. But still you had to deal with your loss.

But you may be one of the many many people who through most of your life have felt like a good person, a person who has tried to do the right thing, a God-fearing person who attended religious services fairly regularly. Why then did this catastrophic happening occur? Why did God see fit to punish you and allow your child to die? Your husband? Your sister? When you are a believer you rarely seem to challenge God but rather you question your own unworthiness. What did *you* do wrong that God should have punished you so drastically? How could this have happened? As you work toward an acceptance of your special person's death, it is often impossible not to question your relationship to God. Most people do. Yet you are perhaps the most fortunate because you know in your heart of hearts there is a God. You may not understand His ways or why things happen as they do, but you never question His existence. Religion has been described by its detractors as the opiate of the masses. Some disparagingly call it a crutch. But what is wrong with a crutch if your leg is broken? You need it. It helps you move about. How much more necessary is a crutch when your heart is broken? The difference is that a broken heart is invisible. All sympathies lie with those who wear casts on legs and arms, those who need wheelchairs. How helpful it would be if people who hurt in their souls and hearts could wear an outward cast to let others know their pain.

One woman went to a therapist thirteen years after her husband and only two children died in an automobile crash. When she first saw the therapist she was apologetic and said anyone who was still deeply in mourning after such a length of time must be crazy indeed! The therapist hastened to disabuse her of this notion, because time is only one of the factors in the grieving process. You will stay in mourning until you are willing to take up the pieces of living and place them in your own two hands again. Thirteen years without going forward may be that woman's personal time clock. Certainly it is a protracted period of time. Possibly had she been approached by any one of a number of support groups that could have helped her in her fight, she might not have needed such a long period of time. Most people *do* begin dealing with their grief and mourning in a much shorter period. And that does not mean you have turned your back on your special person. It merely means you have not turned your back on yourself and your own needs. That is a most important concept to remember. As you work toward accepting the reality that your world is different now and will never be the same, you must remember that *you* matter. You have rights and needs. You are still alive.

In ancient Egypt when a pharoah died his slaves were buried with him and obviously soon died for lack of oxygen. But you do not live in ancient Egypt. You live in the twentieth century; man has landed on the moon. It is urgent that you realize you still do have the right to live a full and decent life. When you begin to understand that, you will be walking toward acceptance. The walk may be long or it may be short. It makes no difference. What does matter is you have taken the steps and begun your journey forward.

Many people who are willing to take a few steps forward run into obstacles. That goes without saying. It is the rare football player who runs the length of the field without anyone trying to bring him down. When dealing with mourning it is not necessarily people who are trying to bring you down; events, too, will cause setbacks. Choose your beginnings carefully.

One couple whose daughter died after a long illness was invited to her friend's sweet sixteen party. Their daughter, who would have been sixteen, had been dead nearly a year. The parents debated about whether to attend and ultimately decided that they should. By attending the party they would make their statement that they were indeed functioning. Well, the outcome was nearly predictable. They got to the restaurant and saw all the prettily dressed young women who were their dead daughter's contemporaries and both of them bolted for the door.

"It was silly. Just too early for us. We had no business being there," said the father. The mother merely nodded her agreement.

As a bereaved parent you may have found yourself in similar circumstances whether it was a high school graduation, a Bar Mitzvah, or a sweet sixteen birthday party. You may have decided to go before you had reached that point of acceptance. If you did indeed try, you probably did not meet with success. Few do who attempt such major steps before they are ready.

That couple might have been wiser to begin by just dropping a gift off at the girl's home and spending a few minutes with her rather than attempting the giant step of attending a full-fledged party to celebrate one of the peaks in a girl's life.

As you work toward acceptance, you must learn to protect yourself.

One woman made the same mistake in different circumstances. She had a favorite restaurant, an elegant one that both she and her husband always enjoyed. She was feeling depressed and needing to prove she could "do it" so she got all dressed up and went to that restaurant.

She said she got a very bad table because she was alone and she left without finishing her meal because wherever she looked all she saw was couples. Her husband had been dead for nine months and for her the wounds were too fresh.

"I might have been smarter to go to a cafeteria. People often go to those places alone," she said. "I was foolish to attempt going to that restaurant because I knew it was a couples type of place."

Another woman who is now a widow said she wishes people did what she and her husband did when she was alive. When they went to a casual restaurant they would frequently spot a man or woman sitting alone and approach him or her and ask if they wished to have some company. More often than not they were gratefully invited to join the person at his table. Certainly they asked for separate checks but they felt they were making a humane gesture. "How I wish people would do that for me now," the woman said.

Sometimes making your first excursion out into the big world is better done spontaneously. You may have sat home night after night pondering whether to attend this or that, or go here or there, and finally you simply decided not to go. But you may find that at the right moment you can just pick yourself up and go somewhere on the spur of the moment. That may be the only way to begin. Once you have met with an initial success or two, you will find it much easier to try a third time. You will be surprised at the pride you feel in yourself because you have learned you can manage, albeit something small, by yourself.

One man whose wife had died only weeks before decided one evening to eat his dinner at a restaurant rather than at home. Because she had been ill for so long, he had learned to cook and clean and could manage quite well for himself. Retired, he had no job that required public outings even for lunch. When he walked into his first restaurant after his wife died, the hostess greeted him with a friendly smile and said, "Just one?" He said he felt his eyes fill with tears and with that word "just" he turned and walked out of the restaurant. To use such phrases is an act of insensitivity. Rather than using the word "just," why not merely ask "One?" Just as any hostess would do with a party that was larger in size. To use that word diminishes the person who comes in alone.

You may have experienced a similar lack of tactful handling. Rather than turn on your heels and leave, perhaps you can assertively stand your ground and tell the hostess, "No, not *just* one. One." You will probably feel a bit better for having spoken up and she may have learned something valuable in her dealings with people who are alone.

Spontaneity is fine for a while but on your long pathway forward you must come to grips with the knowledge that some plans need to be made in advance. You do not have to make complicated plans nor do they have to involve large groups of people, but some plans are important just to prove to yourself that you can do it. Part of attaining acceptance is knowing you are capable of making such plans, thinking in advance, and following through. Sometimes acceptance merely means acknowledging that there is a tomorrow and that you will be a part of it.

One of the greatest obstacles to acceptance is the sense you may be experiencing that if you do indeed begin to live your life again you will be leaving your special person alone, unmourned. Of all the problems bereaved parents face, this ranks high on the list. There is a sense in many of these parents that the only bonding they have left with their dead child is the bond of pain.

It becomes quite easy to see why people do not assiduously work at going forward when they feel by so doing they will leave their special person behind. Perhaps it is important that you be reminded that as long as you live your special person is remembered. It has nothing to do with any activity in which you may engage or any degree of pleasure you may find for yourself. Your special person will live on in your heart and be remembered with fondness as the years go on.

Widows often find themselves enmeshed in this bonding with the dead. How often have you thought, "I shouldn't buy that dress; John didn't like to see me in blue." Although this may sound harsh, it is helpful if you can internalize the fact that you are now John's widow and *not his wife*. To work toward acceptance of your new life you must realize this. You may find it frightening at first to confront this new reality, you may feel anchorless and afloat. But ultimately you will have to accept its truth. You are now in the time of your life where you are no longer responsible to a spouse for any choice or action you may take. This can be very difficult to accept after a long-term marriage. After all, you have become accustomed to sharing your thinking and decision-making with another human being. Now you must learn for yourself to make those same decisions.

A widower of two years remained in the home he had shared with his wife for forty-five years. He followed a daily pattern that was always the same. He stacked the dishes in the dishwasher just the way his wife had stacked them. He hung his clothes exactly as she had hung them for him before. When his living room needed redecorating he simply had the painter use the same colors that had been on the walls before. When asked why he kept everything as it had been he said, "Well, my wife always liked things done that way." You may be thinking long those lines. Does repainting your walls in the same color seem a fitting or necessary memorial? You might try asserting your new role in life by intentionally changing something you had always done in a certain manner when your wife was alive. That too is a part of acceptance.

Sometimes young people must display great courage in the face of a parent's death. That too is accepting the reality of your present situation. While you will always be your mother's or father's child, there are alterations you must make in your life as it progresses. Your dead parent would probably not wish to feel you were following a course that was no longer in your own best interests simply because you discussed it with that parent. What seemed an appropriate choice then might not be now.

One young man had to come to grips with just such a difficulty. "I had always told my father that I wanted to be a doctor just like him and his father before him. It was something we used to talk about a lot. I used to play with his stethoscope when I was just a little kid. Well, my father died and two years later I went off to college fully planning to go into medicine. Along the way, though, I discovered engineering and I loved it. I didn't know what to do. I asked my mother what she thought and she just kept saying I should remember what my father would have wanted.

"That sat in my head for the longest time. Then one day I took a long walk around the campus and did some serious thinking. If she kept saying I should remember what my father wanted, why was it not possible that he would want me to do what was right for me? The more I thought about it, the more sense it made. I finally changed to an engineering program and am so happy I did. It took my mom some time to come around but she eventually did."

Maybe being the son of a dead father means incorporating "to thine own self be true." After all, to remain in a locked position because you cannot discuss an issue with a dead father does seem less than fair. Being true to yourself is perhaps the finest proof of the upbringing you received from that dead parent. There is a saying that a good parent gives his child roots and wings. If you are caught in the quandary of making independent choices now that a loved one is dead it may prove helpful to you to remember this.

The difficulties of coming to acceptance can be especially hard for friends who are used to sharing a great deal of one another's company.

One woman whose close friend and contemporary died at the age of fifty always found the game Scrabble to be an outlet when she was anxious or troubled. Whenever things became rough she and her friend would play together or try to form a foursome. When her friend died she found this was the one time she could not hide in a mind-stimulating game. Since she had always used it as an escape along with her friend, to go ahead without her would only have added pain. She said it became imperative to find new hobbies that did not have the same associations with her dead friend. "I took up knitting, of all things. Before that I always felt I had all thumbs. But I find knitting satisfying and there is a sense that I am creating something and somehow that does seem to help the pain I feel because my friend is dead."

She is not alone in having found this outlet or one that is similar. Many bereaved people stumble onto just such methods to help them in their grief. One woman said there is something almost like a reaffirmation of life when she does calligraphy. The fancy scroll writing has a level of creativity about it and somehow it makes this woman feel that not everything is dead all around her; she still has the ability to create something from scratch, to bring something forth. There is much comfort in this for many people who are hurting. Some even take to paint-by-number kits and derive great satisfaction from working at putting paint on canvas.

There are no hard rules about what sorts of things do the most good. But know that, even for someone who is all thumbs, finding a creative endeavor might be useful in your quest to deal with the acceptance of your special person's death.

Another facet of coming to terms with acceptance is the importance of taking a long hard look around you and seeing how your family is dealing with all this pain and shifting that the death has caused.

When you reach the point of being able to examine these changes that have taken place, you may be surprised at how great the changes are.

There are parents who have not really explored surviving children's reactions to all the pain and suffering produced when a sibling dies. They often are so immersed in their own pain there is simply no room to help those around them to come forward. When you begin to accept the truth that your child is dead you may also be willing to accept the reality that your surviving people need to regroup along with you and build a new unit. Know that no matter how you try, this unit will never be as complete as it once was, but it can still be a good and functioning family group.

In fact, sometimes this regrouping may shift too far, too intensely. You may find that the bonding is so great there is little room for new people to enter your life; new spouses of your children and their families, for example. This is not uncommon.

One mother said the feeling her immediate bereaved family has is one of a tight fist where there is little room for anyone to enter. "My daughter just became engaged and we are working very hard as a family to learn to accept 'outsiders' and it is not easy. But we do understand, intellectually at least, that it is necessary to make this sort of adjustment and deal with what *is*."

Bereaved parents are not alone with this problem. One woman, widowed five years, was most anxious to remarry. She had found a man with whom she thought she could spend her remaining years in peace and harmony. But the tightness of her unit with her children was such that it was an upward battle to even attempt to have this man accepted. "They thought it was fine for me to be seeing someone. But at the core of us all was my dead husband and no one would allow us even to share the special feeling we had for one another as a new couple. I felt like a noose was being tightened around me and drawn closer each time I brought up the subject of my remarriage," she said.

"One day," she continued, "this dear man and I decided we were adults and as such had the right to make a decision, popular or not, that we knew was right for us." That is what they did. Rather than the wedding she had hoped for in which her family would participate, they were married by a judge and then announced an accomplished fact to her family. The new husband added, "We put the ball in their court and it worked. They were not prepared to lose their mother and feel orphaned."

He said that when they told her children they excused themselves from the room and talked things through in one of the bedrooms. "When they came out they were smiling. Her son extended his hand and welcomed me into the family."

Perhaps this action did more than satisfy their own needs. Because of their decision not to seek approval, they showed her children that there comes a time when it is important to accept what is a fact. They helped her children really come to terms with their father's death and their mother's right to continue with a productive life for whatever years she had remaining. Sometimes acceptance does need a nudge or shove. When you have thought and reasoned carefully, there is no need to fear that asserting your position in the world is wrong. To accept your new status and realize that certain changes will occur with that status are steps toward strengthening your position in your new world and new life.

Remember that some people pursue happiness but others create it.

Very often the distinction between the two becomes evident on holidays and special occasions after the death of someone you love. Frequently, especially in the early days, you have a sense that perhaps you would be better off if holidays would simply go away and not rear their "ugly" heads. Yes, indeed, they do appear ugly when you are bereaved. They become yet another announcement of your loss, another time and place to feel the pain of emptiness already so familiar to you.

To help yourself deal with reality remember that early on most bereaved people do not wish for any happiness or anything positive. In fact they will work assiduously to avoid taking in any such experiences. After all to be happy means letting go of your pain just a little, and you may not be prepared to do that yet. Certainly when you are trying to avoid acknowledging a special person's birthday or another important event in his or her life you are not apt to be one of those seeking happiness; you would much prefer to run away from it. That may well remain the case for a long or short period of time. As in all other facets of dealing with grief, when you are ready to enjoy a holiday depends on your individual time clock. But after a certain period you gradually might find you are willing to partake in celebrations of the birthdays of your living children and other family members.

There is no question that the holidays hurt when you are grieving. That is part of the spectrum of mourning. Every special occasion carries with it the spectre of how your special person felt about that occasion; it carries with it the newfound emptiness of not sharing it with him. But then the day does come when it is important to begin the reentry process. Part of that process is renewing your participation in family holidays and the special occasions of friends.

In early days you may certainly not feel as if you wish to pursue with vigor the birthday of a living child. The death date of another child may be the bigger milestone in your life. But as you have come forward you probably have come to recognize that along with the pain must come some pleasure in the things you have left in this life. That is not to say one child replaces another; still not to acknowledge with gratitude that you were spared at least the remaining children is not to go forward. You must also remember that the living child needs to have *his* life confirmed.

One woman whose ten-year-old child died of cystic fibrosis found it difficult to acknowledge that her two remaining children had any worth. She had no desire to have a birthday cake to celebrate their birthdays or even buy clothing for them. She was still so immersed in her pain that she did not see the absolute rejection she was creating all around her. This was someone who certainly would not pursue any form of happiness. But her daughter, a girl with quite a temper, let that temper show one day before her birthday. She stamped her foot and shouted at her mother. She reminded her mother that she, the daughter, was still alive. She had rights. She had the right to a birthday party. Because her sister died did not mean she could no longer grow up!

"When she started shouting at me, it was as if she woke me from a long, deep, nightmarish sleep. I suddenly looked around me and saw that I had created a black hole into which no one but me was allowed to crawl. I didn't know how far I had sunk until she berated me so violently. I did end up making her an ice cream party with a few children. My heart wasn't really in it. But I think I took my first step toward accepting that my life would go on when I made the effort."

One widow, after some time elapsed, was able to go a bit further. She opted to pursue happiness and chased it with vigor. Certainly there were days, her anniversary for one, that were setbacks but there were many others where she made a point of having family and friends over, on Thanksgiving for example. She used her best dishes and worked very hard at creating an enjoyable environment. There were some difficult moments. Her husband always tended the bar and now she was left alone. Rather than make a fuss she asked a close friend to fulfill this function for her and he did so with grace. What could have been a "downer" in the middle of her pursuit was turned into a plus. The friend was very honored that he had been chosen to function in such an important role in the woman's home.

Then, of course, there are those who create happiness. They are the people who work diligently to establish an atmosphere that is pleasurable. A widower who spent four years sunk in a pit finally worked himself through to the point where he knew, really knew, things in his life would not change unless he changed them. He set about doing so by going to a local orphanage and inviting all the ten-year-old boys to a football game. For as long as they live those children will probably remember that day.

"I decided to do it that way because I didn't want to pick who would go and who wouldn't. That way, anyone of a different age could not feel hurt and even more abandoned."

The widower found that he spent more and more productive time among those who were without parents. He said he understood all too well the pain of being alone and if he could alleviate it for them they benefited. But, equally important, those youngsters filled a void in his life.

"Yes, I do have grandchildren," he said. "And I do see them a lot. But they have mothers and fathers and their need is not as great as my kids at the home. I'm fun to my grandchildren but more of a lifeline of support to the orphans."

He may indeed have found the greatest pathway to acceptance and that pathway means judging where you are most needed and giving of yourself. Those who do so always know they get back more than they give; this widower found deep contentment in carving out his own special place.

Not everyone has the financial resources, the time or even the inclination to become involved with an orphanage as that widower chose to do, but you do have at your disposal any number of outlets where your help will be greatly appreciated, especially at holiday time. If a special person has died it can be helpful to attempt to find new ways of observing the holidays you used to spend together. Perhaps inviting a fellow recently bereaved person to partake of your holiday meal might be valuable. The introduction of a new face in the old crowd makes a statement aside from being an act of kindness in itself. It says loud and clear, "This is my new reality and I have come to accept it."

When you can do something so important you know you are on your way toward feeling some measure of comfort in your life.

Finally, to know acceptance and its importance you may best help yourself by making changes in "how you always did things." If you opened Christmas presents in the evening when your son was alive, change the time. The presents will still be special. It is not always a virtue to think, "We always did it this way."

If your husband died and you always spent your birthday in your home surrounded by those you love, change the setting. Perhaps hold the gathering at an adult child's home or a restaurant. You will still feel his absence, certainly, but it need not permeate all you are doing and any pleasure you might find.

If your wife is dead and she always made a fuss over your birthday with a gathering of the clan, you might wish to change the system dramatically. Ask yourself if you were comfortable with all that fuss. If you were not, perhaps you could keep it small, invite a few people to a restaurant for cake and ice cream. If you enjoyed those large parties, order in different food and perhaps choose a different time of day for the festivities. These changes, no matter how small, are extremely important in coming to accept that things are no longer the same nor will they be again.

Sometimes adult children in their striving toward acceptance find great difficulty with their parents' anniversary. They do not know quite how to behave around the surviving parent. Should they ignore the date completely? Should they talk about it? Perhaps merely inviting the survivor to dinner in your home that evening can help ease the hurt for all of you. Acknowledging that this is a painful day is certainly appropriate. After all, you, the offspring, shared in their anniversary for many years.

Sisters and brothers find these times very hard also. It is not easy to enjoy Christmas when you find it no more than a mixed emotion not only in yourself but in those around you. How should you behave? Should you be happy because you received a gift that gives you pleasure? For some, the season itself brings a sense of mirth and joy although far too few people understand that this is a time when there is also much sadness. Again, regardless of the age of your dead sibling, make changes in how things were always done. You are helping yourself when you do so by reminding yourself that you still have the power to affect change. When you recognize this you are beginning to understand acceptance.

There are many occasions you shared with friends that were special and complete in their way. Now you have turned around and your friend is gone. Two women born two days apart always celebrated their birthdays on the day in between. This had become a custom of more than two decades. When one friend died, the other woman simply did not see how she could enjoy her birthday ever again. Indeed, for the first two years she asked that no one honor her on that day. Her husband stepped in the third year, however, and insisted he did not wish to let the day go by unnoted. He suggested that instead of going to dinner as they always had he would take her to the theater and a late supper. At first she was reluctant but after a time she agreed and saw the wisdom of what he suggested. She maintains it was not the happiest of times but she faced reality on that birthday and began to accept the fact that her friend was dead but her birthdays would still be going on. It took some creativity on the part of her husband but it did, ultimately, become a happy birthday for her once again.

In the final analysis, reaching the avenue of acceptance is a road fraught with twisting and turning bypaths. It is not easy. You may place a smile on your face but your heart will still hurt because your special person is gone. Ultimately you will reach some inner peace, but that is *not* how it begins: it begins with the attempt.

William Makepeace Thackeray in "The End of the Play" wrote:

> The play is done; the curtain drops,
>   Slow falling to the prompter's bell:
> A moment yet the actor stops,
>   And looks around, to say farewell.
> It is an irksome work and task;
>   And when he's laughed and said his say,
> He shows, as he removes the mask,
>   A face that's anything but gay.

In the beginning, under your mask, you too will have a face that is anything but gay. But remember, without that smiling mask, without that performance as a first step, it becomes ever harder to take another and then another. Without those first, perhaps even false steps, you cannot reach the point where the smile comes naturally under the mask.

When you have reached the point of knowing that smile is there you have indeed found acceptance in the face of all your pain and hurt.

As you sum up your pathway through pain give some time to thinking about your responses to all the components that make up mourning.

• Have I thought through what I feel because my special person is dead?

• Do my moods continue to fluctuate?

- Am I less fearful about this?
- Have I put the funeral in its place—behind me?
- Have I dissected my anger? Where is it directed?
- Am I being fair? To myself? To my family? To the loved one who has died?
- Have I thought through any guilt I may be feeling? Is it based on fact or the wish to punish myself because I have been left alive?
- Can I give myself permission to acknowledge that I am in fact powerless to control life and death?
- Have I come to terms with my feelings about my faith?
- Have I talked with my minister if I feel it is needed?
- Can I acknowledge I have a right to live and make that life full and fruitful?

Write our your responses and check back on them from time to time and measure your forward progress toward acceptance.

A Support Group Manual

This support group portion of *Living Through Mourning* is dedicated to Rabbi M. Robert Syme, who, along with Rabbi Harold Loss and Cantor Harold Orbach of Temple Israel, West Bloomfield, Michigan, helped assure the success of the pilot group.

My appreciation also to Eileen Abel, Karen Amber, MSW, Barbara Begun, Dr. Gerald Gold, Lily Goodman, Dr. Jacqueline Grekin, Lillian Schwartz, David Tisdale, Dr. Richard Traitel, and Dr. Gerald Weinberg, all of whom shared and contributed to this work.

I would like to thank the former executive director of the Ohio Funeral Directors, Zelma Bishop, who traveled throughout the state of Ohio with me in order to establish support groups sponsored by members of that state's funeral directors.

Introduction

We have identified the people who are mourners: parents, widows, widowers, surviving offspring, surviving siblings, friends and grandparents. While each group has its own unique set of difficulties, the majority of the problems are the same. How a mourner deals with denial, guilt, depression, anger and the entire spectrum of his or her pain can be effectively improved if the person wishes to become involved in helping himself.

Support groups, where people can share emotions and pain in a nonthreatening environment, seem to have the most to offer a person who is suffering from the death of a special loved one. While a group should not take the place of private therapy for specific problems, it can serve the function of displaying for the mourner just what is in the average range of emotions for a given period of time. If a group member sees he is very far off the mark it is recommended that he seek private counseling. Many therapists do recommend this be done while continuing with the support group as well.

The following manual is designed for lay people who wish to form groups. It outlines how to get one started as well as how to conduct the meetings. While such groups must be tailored to meet specific needs, this general format, if followed, can prove supportive.

Organizing the Group

Support groups for people who are grieving may be formed along many different lines. Sometimes churches and temples decide they can best serve congregants by sponsoring groups for mourners. In many cases the needs of a congregation cannot be met by the one or two clerics who serve it; there are simply too many members and too few clergy.

Groups may be formed independently by one or two people or families who have a need. All such people need do is call a few other people sharing a death and they have a nucleus.

Funeral directors could serve as sponsors of such groups. If they choose to do so, they can share the names of those who are mourning. They could act as a powerful force in this ever-growing movement.

Community complexes, apartments, subdivisions, villages and cities could offer those who live within their confines the concept of group meetings for people suffering after the death of a loved one.

In short, any time there are two or more people who share the painful experience of trying to cope with the death of a special person, there is a place for a group.

Groups will not and should not be homogeneous. They will be comprised of people who have suffered a diversity of deaths. In general, there is no need to break meetings down to the special needs of any one set of members because every session will pertain to all. Every session will address a different aspect of grieving. Every aspect should be known to every person who is in mourning. When people are grieving, pain is universal.

It is helpful if groups are organized under any number of different umbrellas, whether church, temple or civic organizations, because through such institutions greater numbers of people can have access to them.

To achieve the most effective results it is wise to meet every two weeks. While some groups meet monthly many members find this too infrequent. Other groups meet weekly and that may be too intense. By meeting every other week the entire program will be completed in four months. For some this is enough time. Others may wish to reenter the group for another sequence or even two.

Groups should also meet in the same place each time. This lends continuity to the group.

Groups may be of any size. There are those who prefer a larger group because it offers more perspectives. Others prefer a smaller number—four to six people—because they like being able to speak more often. If a group is so large that members leave frustrated because they have not had enough time to verbalize their feelings it might be wise to break into smaller groups.

It is always important to review what was discussed at the previous meeting including the introductions. Sometimes people need to feel that they have fallen into the groove before they are ready to speak. This review is helpful even if there are no new members. Different people take in different information at separate times.

Group members may be found by using lists provided by funeral directors, clergymen, mental health professionals and by family members. A potential member should be called personally by the facilitator or a member of the group and should be asked to attend an opening meeting. It is helpful to offer to meet a potential member at the door of the meeting or even to drive him to the meeting. As an additional backup, sending a letter to prospective members from a doctor, funeral director, clergyman, school teacher or indeed anyone in a position to recognize a need would be most helpful.

There are two basic tenets members of groups *must* understand. If they cannot handle these rules, another form of help would be more productive.

The first rule of functioning within a support group is maintaining *confidentiality*. What is said within the group stays in the group! While incidents and insights are shared, names must not be. If you do not believe you can handle this rule you should look elsewhere for support. It is acceptable to use names within the group but that is where they must remain.

The second rule is that participants must be *nonjudgmental*. People must *not* be berated for feelings because feelings are things all people have as a born, innate right. If members begin to believe they are being judged, they will lose faith in the leader and in the group.

Facilitators can be of any age group, and of either sex. They must be people who have a demonstrable degree of kindness, the ability to start a discussion, the ability to listen well and to *learn* from those in the group. When a leader stops feeling he can learn, he is also demonstrating that he is no longer experiencing. When that occurs, his effectiveness is diminished.

Facilitators need not be professional mental health people; lay people often function superbly. They *do* need one basic experience that will be common to the entire group. They, too, *must* have suffered the death of a special person.

Frequently that death will have occurred some years back. There is value in this, as time lends perspective. Occasionally, people feel they are ready to lead a group within two to three years following the death. Such people are also valuable because their insights are fresh.

The reason for using only bereaved people as group leaders is evident. It eliminates the question "What do you know about this?" that mental health people are often asked and creates an instant bond between the leader and the members of the group.

Before someone is asked to facilitate a group, he or she should go through some screening process. Within the religious community, the clergy, together with some lay people, may select *members* who will be trained. Volunteers should not be called for. People who have experienced a death are sensitive. It is unhelpful to heap on the added burden of rejecting a volunteer because he does not have the kind of personality needed to run a group.

Within every community, there are people who are automatically turned to by others in times of crisis. Very often these people are facilitator-caliber. They have an aura of caring and a perceptivity that is obvious to many around them.

In order to be effective, facilitators must be taken through a fairly rigorous training program. It will include going through the meeting portion of this work and in a group setting actually dealing with the issues. Because of the exposure to other people who have *their* views on grief and guilt and anger, facilitators will learn first-hand what to expect when they head a group. With an elected or appointed leader, facilitators will be trained by using the same material they will be asked to cover for their members. By the time they have completed the eight meetings, their comfort level in leading should be well established.

Group leaders are not therapists. They are there to facilitate members and to help them verbalize what they are feeling. They are there to encapsulate emotions. They will ask questions that will help members draw their own conclusions but they are not there to do therapy. This must be remembered at all times.

When a discussion threatens to make a leader sound like a therapist—and this can occur when he is asked a direct question by a member—he is free to call upon his own experiences and ask other group members to share theirs. That is as far as he may go unless he is a member of the mental health profession.

Sometimes a facilitator will be faced with a situation where he sees quite clearly, as will other group members, that individual counseling is necessary. The person in need should be supplied with a list of names of therapists who have made a specialty of working in the field of death and dying. The leader may offer his suggestion privately, with compassion and with the knowledge that the group will remain a part of the member's healing process.

Counseling will be in addition to the group.

Facilitators will be responsible for inviting speakers. These speakers should be screened carefully. Many people have a view on death and coping with it that is unrealistic. One clergyman known for his erudition tells grieving parents "anything after three months is bad theater." Support group members must not be exposed to such destructive ideas. When someone is grieving years can be like hours, and that must be remembered.

Facilitators should give speakers specific topics, preferably relating to the discussion planned for that evening. They should be asked how they view the grieving process as a screening measure. If facilitators detect judgmental thinking or narrowness of viewpoint, the speaker should *not* address the group. The facilitator can simply thank such a speaker and say, "We will be in touch."

Facilitators should establish a maximum time limit of thirty minutes for the speaker, after which questions will be invited. The speaker should leave after the question period in order to allow the group to maintain confidentiality during the discussion that follows.

In most instances, a facilitator does not specify exact words or phrases to be used in meetings. The group will take on characteristics of the facilitator's personality and the personalities of the various members as well. Therefore, questions must be asked that will fit that particular group of people.

Facilitators will be supplied with a general format: how to introduce the topic, inviting group participation, and how to tie things together at the end of a meeting. Since it is assumed facilitators will be sensitive and bright, the tools in this manual will give them a sense of security while offering enough latitude to allow them to deal with issues that may arise.

Understanding the Issues

In order to understand the needs of those who will be group members, it is important to understand the issues with which they will be wrestling. Sometimes they will express their needs and concerns, but they are not always capable of doing so. By bringing some of these issues to the fore, you may shock a person in mourning into sharing his feelings because the issue has struck so close to home.

Compounding the awesomeness of being a survivor are many problems, some self-manufactured, others not. Frequently, those who have survived feel a great sense of guilt for having done so. They seek ways to punish themselves. They struggle to find things they did "wrong" in relation to the dead person rather than fighting to remember the good they shared and did for one another. Frequently survivors will search their minds to come up with some minute thing that could have been done better, something they should not have done at all.

Mourners need reminding that they are human—human in their good qualities and human in their frailties. That means having good days and bad days, having loving days and hostile days, having days of pride and days of shame.

One of the greatest impediments to coping with grief is the dreadful problem of feeling "If only I had." Mourners are beset with the "if onlys." Those "if onlys" slow the healing process at best; sometimes they totally destroy it. It is important to tell these people that by wallowing in the "if onlys" they are doing themselves and their loved ones a great injustice.

When people allow themselves to remain immersed in pain, actually push themselves further into it, it depletes their already low energy level and leaves them nothing to help fight their way back. They cannot undo things that were done, nor can they change what was not done. People can only live today and perhaps go forward. They can realize their errors and make certain they are not repeated with those who survive. But to bemoan what cannot be changed, to regret what is unalterable, is not only futile, it is destructive to whatever time someone has left.

Often, bereaved parents feel guilt over things that might be laughable were the circumstances different. Many whose children died very young and very suddenly blame themselves for being annoyed at the baby. Every parent has at some time been exhausted and fallen into bed only to be awakened shortly thereafter by a baby's crying for a middle-of-the-night feeding. People call their friends and share these little war stories because, while annoying, they are still amusing. Amusing unless the child dies, that is. Then suddenly this lapse they felt in themselves, this idea that for a few moments they were irritated by their child, takes on a much graver perspective than it actually should. Parents beat themselves with their alleged shortcomings when there is no need.

As children grow older, the problems often grow greater. They misbehave, stay out late at night, are willful, do not clean their rooms, do not study hard enough, don't call when they promised.

If things go normally, each issue is treated as it arises. Anger is vented. Parents resort to punishment, grounding, the repertory of behavior that comprises parenting through the growing up years. When a child dies, however, parents suddenly review these issues and find themselves wanting. They were too harsh, they were too mild, they should not have let him take the car, should not have let her go out with that boy. Why did they have such a fearful row over something as trivial as a messy bedroom? They are so bad, so ignorant, they did not deserve to have their children live!

If only bereaved parents could understand that these minor conflicts are normal in a normal home. The only thing that has changed is the situation. The child is dead. That does not mean the behavior of the parents was wrong. Because the child is dead, parents attribute mystical importance to normal happenings in ordinary daily living situations.

What a waste of energy! Most of the time, bereaved parents forget they were only doing their jobs in the best manner they knew how.

But not only bereaved parents suffer the pangs of regret so common following a death. It is the rare widow indeed who does not review her years with her now dead mate without feeling sharp pangs of the "if onlys."

"There were the times I refused sex. How could I have been so cruel?" Many widows have voiced this frequently. Perhaps they should be heard by the bereaved mother who will no longer have sex with her husband. Although her reason might be that she does not wish to feel any pleasure, the issue of sex is a real difficulty and one the group should discuss.

These people don't think of the times they gave themselves freely and lovingly. No, it is only the negative which they recall in their grief.

"All he wanted to do was travel. But I didn't like the way he drove so I wouldn't go. Now he is dead and he never went anywhere."

Never went anywhere? It is doubtful that in the course of a lifetime a couple remained at home, totally stationary. Yet so often widows will forget what they did do and mourn instead the things they didn't do. A widow will think to herself, "If only I had gone fishing with him or camping." The fact that she hated these activities no longer carries any importance. Instead, she thinks only of how she denied her husband.

Even such things as "He liked fish but I hated to cook it" are blown out of context at this time. It is so painful to see a woman suffer the devastating loss of her husband and then to see her make it worse and ultimately intolerable by remembering only the things she did wrong. Yet this appears to be the pattern many widows fall into.

It is in this area that the group can be of great help. Generally when someone gets involved in this convoluted type of thinking a group member will challenge the mourner and stress the idea that no one lives an idyllic life all the time. Coming from a fellow mourner, this challenge is generally acceptable and will inspire some inner reflection.

Widowers, too, pull themselves down with this sort of faulty reasoning.

"I was not a good provider" is a common statement. "She really didn't want much and I couldn't even manage that."

"If only I had worked *less*. The money wasn't all that important. I should have spent more time with her."

Many men in their grief have uttered these regrets in their effort to find some bit of self-blame.

"She always begged me to talk with her and share my thoughts with her but I didn't. I would come home so tired. Now she is dead and I'll never have the chance to tell her I love her." Again, a common regret many widowers feel. Rarely do they allow themselves to remember their nonverbal statements of love. Each week when he brought home that paycheck he was saying "I love you." Each time he helped clear the dinner dishes while the kids ran off to play, he was saying "I love you."

What about the times he bought her a Mother's Day present because he was afraid their grown children would forget? Was he not then saying "I love you?"

Yet, tragically, men forget these things in their grief. They only remember their omissions. Rarely do they recall their kind little acts; even the times he took her for a ride and got the ice cream cone she wanted are forgotten. Yet, above all, she loved doing just that.

When these sad reflections arise during a group meeting, the leader or a fellow member will ask about the positives even in the worst situations. While the positives do not always arise readily at such a time, they should at least share equal billing with all those negative memories.

"I was not good. I did not listen. I drove her to an early grave." These are not uncommon sentiments expressed by children, and even worse, sometimes left unexpressed. All the regrets about not listening and not obeying instantly set in. Children, after all, are only younger old people when it comes to grieving. In more simple form, they feel the same things all of us have felt. Above all, there is the sense of somehow being to blame for the tragedy, to blame for not always being perfect, for not always doing as they were told, for not always being on time.

Teenaged children suffer terribly when they recall the acrimony that often became part of the family disputes. Many young people have stormed out of the room after talking to their mother and thought silently, "I wish she was dead." No one ever takes the time to explain that wishing someone dead does not make a dead person.

Youngsters need to understand that part of growth is the need to establish their independence. In fact, they were behaving normally.

Sometimes this process of gaining independence is accompanied by power struggles. The need to assert is deep within young people. Parents know this, yet must use their own judgment in allowing freedom. Often these issues are resolved with anger, then apology, then a hug and kiss, then they are forgotten—unless the parent dies. Then, tragically, all that is remembered is the quarrel. The bitterness. The momentary flash of hatred.

Never, while grieving, does the child recall the kindness she showed, the little pictures she drew, the little moments of thoughtfulness. She generally will perceive her parent's death from the perspective of "Mother was perfect and I was a rat." This is furthered by the eulogy and well-meaning relatives who visit and speak only of all that goodness now gone. The child takes that in and subtly begins to feel worse not only because of the loss but because of her own behavior toward this "perfect" person.

What an imbalance! What an injustice to do to oneself! Yet these children all too often keep these thoughts to themselves, fail to tell any adult what they are feeling, and bury their pain deep within themselves, sometimes so deeply that years of therapy are needed to unburden themselves.

Married children find themselves almost consumed in their own lives, lives filled with the needs of their homes, their spouses, their jobs and their own children.

When a parent dies, older children, too, have a set of "if onlys." They frequently regret things that cannot be changed: the birthdays gone unacknowledged, the times driving a parent became an annoyance, the guilts for not having called more frequently. "If only I had been a little kinder" is an often-repeated regret.

But after the death it is all wasted energy. It is simply too late to make changes, to undo, unless there is a surviving parent. Then, perhaps, consciously making the efforts that were not made in the past, an older child can hedge against the guilt the "if onlys" bring about.

Surviving siblings suffer many of the same negative emotions experienced by offspring of dead parents. In addition, the pain of feeling "why me?" is sometimes never reconciled. They think privately that the wrong child is dead. He was the good one. She should have lived. Why was I left? Would my parents be mourning like this if it were me?

All of these thoughts are there churning and fomenting and rarely expressed. One woman hearing a facilitator in training discuss how he felt when his brother died during their childhood suddenly sat up. She told the group she had never discussed her son's feelings about the death. She was advised to initiate the topic the next time she saw him. When she did, the first thing the young man said, much to her amazement, was, "I was waiting for you to bring it up."

He then proceeded to tell her openly how he felt. She said when he was through she could see the beginning of a new and special closeness that up until then had never been formed.

In the course of a group setting the leader will discuss offspring and siblings. There are some suggestions that might be helpful:

- Talk to them. The need for individual attention is great.
- Do not allow a breakdown of discipline in the home. Discipline means security.
- Talk separately with each child, regardless of age. Ask enough to elicit any feelings of guilt and anger that may prove corrosive in later years.
- Remind youngsters of their good acts just as you remind older offspring of the same.
- Explain they were not bad because they quarreled with a sibling or parent; it's normal. The regret they feel after a death needs to be put into perspective.
- Explain that wishing a person dead does not make a dead person. Siblings and offspring believe in their own omnipotence whether dealing with death or divorce. They believe they should have been able to make things better when in reality the issues were often out of their hands.
- Religion is a very sensitive subject. Simply saying it was God's will can create an atheist instead of a believer.
- Don't condemn children for laughing during the first days following a death.
- Do not push anyone of any age to go to the cemetery. Some people need more time.
- Do not canonize the dead person. The offspring and siblings will begin to believe you and feel they can never measure up.
- Do not avoid talking about the dead person. He or she did exist. It is wrong to obliterate the dead.
- It's all right to allow your grief to show. After all, you are human. In fact not showing your grief may make it harder for other survivors to show theirs.

The group will usually find these suggestions valuable.

Grandparents suffer dreadfully when a child or grandchild dies. They are placed in a situation of literally walking on eggs. They know all too well that their position is tenuous. For example, if their son dies, they can be removed from their grandchildren by any whim of their surviving in-law. It takes enormous wisdom to avoid the pitfalls of being ostracized. Perhaps the most prudent yet difficult thing a grandparent may do is *not* to visit unless he is certain his emotions are under control. The in-law all too often loses patience and gradually begins to make the grandparent unwelcome.

If there is a remarriage the eggshell walk is even more delicate. While no grandparent feels it is moral for their grandchildren to forget the parent who died, a new spouse has the need to establish his or her own domain. All too frequently he or she feels this can only be done by eliminating the former spouse's parents. While the group can do little to make this blatant unfairness equitable, it can serve as perhaps the most sympathetic of sounding boards. Occasionally, a sensible suggestion might even arise.

Aside from the "if onlys" there are other equally potent emotions that fight healing every step of the way. One of those emotions is the very basic one of anger.

There is no greater fury than the fury generated when a loved person dies as a result of someone else's action, whether it was a medical error or a car crash.

There is no rage to equal the rage against someone responsible for your loved one's death, none anywhere in the world. When it comes to this issue there is no such thing as a regional difference, no such thing as different strokes for different folks. Some people will go to greater lengths than others to vent their rage but all those who have grieved have a deep understanding of anger.

Sometimes in the case of bereaved parents this anger takes very extreme forms. Several years ago a man named Khalifa Hamaas Abdul Khaalis and a band of fellow Hanafi Muslims held more than one hundred people hostage in three Washington, D.C., buildings. They demanded revenge against Black Muslims convicted of a 1973 mass murder in which seven Hanafi children, four of them Khaalis's, were slain.

On the surface their behavior seemed just another act of terrorism: a situation for a SWAT team, a television plot. On the surface.

There are many bereaved parents who, learning of the episode, heard it differently. They heard with the experience of having their own children die. What they heard was the story of a man who came home from grocery shopping and found four of his children butchered. They heard his rage!

Certainly to respond by taking hostages is not acceptable in society. Certainly it avails no one of anything positive—including the bereaved parent. But it is useful to know just how huge a bereaved parent's anger can be—how great! The desire for revenge can become all-consuming. To some parents, unacceptable as it was, there was at least a flickering of understanding of Khaalis's anger.

There is no question that in most instances anger is a negative emotion. It does little in most human encounters. But that it exists is a real and honest thing. People generally do not feel like world-savers and great humanitarians, and they don't feel like turning the other cheek when they have endured the experience of having a child murdered, mistreated medically or killed in an accident.

The most important thing to remember is that no revenge—none that we of this earth know or understand—will bring the dead child back to a bereaved parent. The responsibility these parents have is to themselves and those with whom they spend their days. To the living. To the other children. To their families. Anger, unless channeled, can eventually destroy our capacity to function rationally and that is its main danger.

The Hanafi Muslim is in jail. His act of anger availed him nothing. His four children are still dead. Had every hostage in the place been shot his children would *still* be dead. There is nothing positive to be gained from such destructive anger.

Yet there is a frustration about such circumstances that anyone with a dead special person can understand. That frustration should be brought to the group. Often it can be diffused.

There is a widow who lives a life of poverty and bleakness since her husband was killed by two men who robbed his small grocery store.

She can go for several days—and it has been three years—

accepting the fact that the robbers have been caught and imprisoned but then her anger always returns.

"They are alive. My husband is dead. They will be paroled one day and my husband will still be dead. Sometimes I lie awake at night plotting and thinking about them and what they did to my life. Sometimes I cannot bear the fact that they are alive and I am alone."

In spite of the frustration to the group members who will so wish to help her and who have generally retained a sense of justice, simply hearing her in a nonjudgmental way has been of help. The value of the group to that widow is immense because they are hearing her, really hearing her.

There is something to be learned from this experience. There is a sense of needing to understand that not all things are as we were taught they should be, in our homes and schools. This intense anger is real. The truth is some things are not just. Some issues cannot be rectified. This is a bitter truth indeed. A bitter lesson for all.

There is a need among those who are survivors to feel a sense of justice has been served, but all too often these people walk about with a sense that nothing equal to the magnitude of their loss has been meted out as punishment.

Although it often goes unsaid, many survivors also feel anger at the dead person for having left them alone and bereft.

Remember the young man who was just about to be married. He expressed great rage that his brother, who had died ten years previously, was not there to be his best man.

"Jack should have been here. He should have been at my wedding!"

Illogical? Certainly. Yet few people who suffer the death of a dearly loved person don't at one time or another think just that same illogical thought.

Often anger is directed against the medical profession. One young widower, left with two small children, bears great hostility toward his late wife's doctor.

"I don't know whether she got the right care or not. I've had no contact with the doctor. Nothing. My wife is dead and he pretends she never even existed!"

Sometimes surviving children get caught up in great bursts of such rage—especially when they are left orphaned.

"How could they have driven in one car? Didn't they know they risked making me an orphan? Now I have to live with an aunt. She's not my mother. I hate her husband. Why didn't they drive separately?

"How could they have done this to me?"

Since cancer is a leading cause of death there will be many youngsters who feel particularly enraged at having been abandoned by parents who smoked cigarettes. Commercials on radio and television continually bombard the youngsters stressing that cancer is caused by smoking and smoking kills. Unfortunately, many adults who know intellectually that smoking is wrong are addicted and cannot break the habit.

What happens when a parent dies in such a situation?

"If he loved me he would have stopped" is probably what runs through the heads of many young people. And this is a most difficult problem to deal with when a youngster cannot understand addiction.

Sometimes there is anger at omission. There is a great difficulty when a loved one dies as a result of a car accident, for instance. If you survive and your passenger is killed, are you welcome during the mourning procedure?

Should you come to the home and pay your respects? Should you risk the anger of the family which can only compound your own sense of guilt?

When such a situation has arisen it deserves to be discussed in a group setting. Sympathetic people will hear the anger but may be able to introduce some balance which could prove helpful. For anger, when it becomes a festering wound, can infect an entire human being.

Sometimes bereaved people enter into lawsuits to help dissipate the anger they feel: lawsuits against doctors, hospitals and businesses.

One man won an enormous settlement from Ford Motor Company. He had been driving a Pinto and was hit in the rear. The man was able to pull several of his children to safety as the gas tank exploded but one boy was stuck in the car, his foot lodged behind a seat. The father tried frantically to pull the boy out. He even tried to break the boy's leg to help unwedge him but to no avail. Until that father dies he will probably hear the child's voice crying, "Daddy help me. Daddy help me."

That lawsuit served one basic purpose: that of shouting, "Someone is to blame! I want fault acknowledged! Someone else is going to be hurt as I was hurt!"

But in the final analysis some of the people who have won major lawsuits come to the tragic realization that once again they must draw upon their energies to rebuild their lives. Although there has been a monetary gain, the loss they sustained far outweighs anything else.

Sharing his pain with the group can be more of a catharsis than appearing on a witness stand, for the group will enfold this man but a jury can only offer cold cash or insufficient justice.

The problems someone must endure whose spouse has suddenly died following a recent move are vastly increased because the people whom he trusts and loves and grew up with are often thousands of miles away. There can be little comfort from a neighbor one has known for a few months in such a situation. People need to be cushioned by knowing and loving friends and family at such a time. Even if these people do fly in quickly to help during the crisis, the moment of truth always arrives when the new widow must decide whether to remain in the new place or go back to her old home. Should the widower sell the house or not, disrupt the children in the middle of a school year or not? This must be done without a support system because no one can make all these decisions in the few days when they are around.

Our mobility has created great stress upon families who grieve, simply because we need the people closest to us at this most disastrous of times.

As retirement age still finds many people feeling vital and active, they often move to warmer climates. Often, too, they find themselves in adult communities where they meet new people and form different associations. What happens when such a couple suffers the loss of a child, sister, brother or grandchild and they are in this new environment far away? How can they share with strangers the depth of their pain? Even if they fly to their children's home, their old hometown, the time to return to their own new home comes eventually.

Many seniors' spouses die while living in new surroundings. While they can feel the comfort of having many contemporaries about, they lack a basic support—that of their own family, their own children. And at a time of such crisis, that support looms very large.

We cannot be reminded often enough that Americans live in an instant society. There is instant coffee, Instant Breakfast®, instant oatmeal. Flick on a switch and immediately there is radio or television. Push a few buttons and there is electricity, there is heat, there is air conditioning. All done with the click of a switch.

All of these are comfortable and nice things, fun and pleasurable, but the concept of instant gratification is destructive when dealing with grief. Grieving is a long process. If people begin to feel it is taking "too long" to heal, they begin to panic. Something is wrong, they are certain. After all, if every other sense can be instantly gratified, certainly this horrible pain of grief should work the same way—or at least that's what we think.

Parents are fearful when years elapse and they still hurt. One woman's son was killed in a bomber mission in 1944. She missed him until the day she died in 1978. She was very upset about how long she had mourned simply because everyone told her she was not in synchronization with society. She found this very frightening.

Widows and widowers are often victims of the desire for instant cure. Often they begin to date while their hearts are still heavy. They come home alone after an unsuccessful evening on the town and moan to themselves: "How long? How long?"

Widowers particularly are pushed into dating before they are ready. There are far too many eager friends and single women who begin thinking of "fixing him up" almost immediately after the funeral. He, like most men, needs time to adjust, time to think things through, yet it is unlikely he will be granted the courtesy of this time by well-intentioned people.

Children, missing mothers or fathers, wonder if ever there

will come a time when they will *not* feel that loss. Certainly, the time will come when the loss is less acute, less a conscious part of their everyday lives, but there will always be moments when they will be sorry their parents did not live to see this or that achievement of their own or of their children.

Although there is no instant cure, as days and weeks and months and years elapse, there is indeed an easing of intensity. There is relief. But to worry about how long this easing will take will only create a further anxiety and one people who are grieving don't need.

People who are mourning *have* deep needs. Needs for comfort. Needs for kindness. Needs for warmth. While upon them rests the dreadful burden of having to reach within themselves to supply the grit to come out of their grief, they will reach a little more confidently with the help of a caring, loving support group.

Although there are many supportive and caring people out in the wide world, they need guidelines. They truly wish to help but feel inept and overwhelmed when confronted with enormous grief. Just as there are those who are physically repelled by the sight of a friend whose arm has just been severed, repelled by the sight of the raw wound, some people react with the same fear and horror to an emotional wound.

This fear and horror often makes outcasts of those who mourn. This must be stopped! Now there is a place for people who have suffered the death of a special person and that place is the support group. It is there, in a setting that offers shelter and love to all who enter because all who enter are also grieving, that a survivor can receive his just due—a place where he *fits*, where he belongs, where he can safely work through the problems of being a survivor.

Facilitating the Meeting

MEETING ONE

Topic: An overview of what will be covered in the program. The group will discuss deaths sustained by members and introduce themselves.

Objective: To teach members to speak freely about death; members will learn to discuss *feelings* openly

The purpose of facilitating a support group is always to make those who need help comfortable. As a unit you will, in a special sense, become family. You will serve as a support system in a world whose members are becoming increasingly isolated.

This first meeting is designed to help members become acquainted with one another. It is not necessary that the group plunge itself immediately into deep problem areas.

Since there will be apprehension on the part of many newcomers to the support group concept, it will be helpful if you can outline to them just what will be covered in your sessions.

Briefly tell the group that you will have a specific agenda of material to cover during the weeks you meet. The areas of discussion will include denial, which is the sense of "This can't really be happening." Also, you will cover funerals to some degree as well as anger and how insidious an emotion that is. Religion, both pro and con, will be addressed as it has great impact upon a mourner's perspective of death. The topic of guilt will be the subject of a meeting as will that of depression. You also will discuss powerlessness and how it can overwhelm someone who is hurting. Finally you will address the issue of acceptance. Recognizing that most group members are recently bereaved, this last should be addressed as an eventuality somewhere in the distance. It is not reasonable to expect any group member to come to terms with an important death in just a matter of four months. You will, however, by that time, have shown the path toward acceptance and, equally as important, you will have shown the steps each member has available in order to help attain that goal.

Since each group will have its own personality, how you initially greet members will depend on how you feel comfortable. Shaking hands, holding onto someone's hand for a moment, placing an arm around a shoulder are all acceptable greetings.

After everyone is seated around a large table or in a circular arrangement of furniture, *begin slowly*. Give the group your name and tell the members who the special person was that died in your family. After that, go around the table and ask each person to tell a little about himself. If possible, avoid allowing a spouse to serve as spokesperson for the couple.

Questions should include:

- What is your name?
- Who is it you are mourning?
- What is his or her name?

Note each answer so you may address people by name and use the name of their deceased. It will create intimacy. After you have gone around the table and as many people who care to answer have done so, start again with the first person who spoke.

Questions should include:

- Cause of death
- Age of the person who died

Introduce the topic with a statement like the following: "I hope we as a group will become very close. In order to do that, we should know something about each other's special person as well as something about one another."

Explain to group members that the sense of being able to share what the dead person meant to them, how painful their absence is and how each person as an individual responds to this traumatic happening is in large measure what the group is all about.

A man of sixty whose eighty-year-old mother died can suffer as intensely as a parent whose child has died, especially if the two have been sole survivors for many years who shared a home and depended upon one another for companionship. The group must never take an attitude that "my loss is greater than yours." Each loss is great or the person would not be in the group. This, too, should be carefully explained.

You have already given the group the overview of the entire program. You have also had them introduce themselves to one another. As the topic of the first meeting, try to explore something of each member's attitude toward the death.

Go around the group once again and ask, "What was ———'s most endearing trait?"

When all who care to have responded, go around again. Ask members if hearing what others have said has brought up any additional special things about the dead person they wish to share. When addressing members, always do so by name.

Whenever names are used the sense of intimacy within the group grows. There is a feeling of camaraderie that is almost certain to be felt when someone's special person who is dead is referred to by first name.

Since many of the groups will be sponsored by a church or

synagogue or community center, it is very possible that other group members knew of the deceased. If that is the case, ask the members to share what *they* remember about that person.

Also, it is possible that members in the group know one another. Ask if this is the case. If so, discuss what others see as the group member's strengths. Sometimes when someone is grieving, they forget they even possess the power to think. By having positive traits reinforced, a group member will be reminded that he is still a functioning person.

Another aspect to cover that will be of help to the facilitator in getting to know his group is to ask each member by name what the most difficult part of the entire death process was. The answers here will vary. Some may say, "Watching him die" if they have lived with a terminal illness. Others will mention the funeral. Since the funeral is the topic of the second meeting, tell members you will go into that issue at length the next time.

Some other members might discuss how empty the house is now that everyone has stopped visiting. This is a very real issue. Ask other members if they have experienced this too. This is guaranteed to open a lively area of mutual interest.

If, along the way, you have any additional remembrances of your own experience that would pertain, by all means take your turn as you go around the table. This will help the group to feel more at ease with you and not set you in a position that will remove you from the emotions they are feeling.

As the meetings progress you ultimately hope to help achieve a sense of balance about the person who died. It is urgent for someone grieving to regain a perspective anchored in reality, a necessity as they go on with the rest of their lives.

You hope to lead the group into sharing not only the dead person's good qualities; you want to help people retain an honest memory of the dead person. If you can achieve this, you are doing a great service to these survivors. By trying to encourage an honest memory, you can help avoid the trap of having the dead person placed on such a pedestal of perfection that no living mortal could ever achieve such rarefied status. That is too much of a burden for children, siblings, spouses and other survivors to live up to.

Explain the concept of keeping an honest memory and why it is so important. After all, if someone has erased the humanness from their special person, who is he mourning? Explain that all people are fallible. Not a single person is perfect. Perhaps your dead person had a particularly annoying mannerism that you might wish to share by way of example. Ask what were some of the things that *bothered* you about your wife, your child, your brother?

By putting it just that way, and assuming there were indeed things that were troubling, you are in effect telling the grieving person that it is okay to have negative thoughts. You are telling them a very important truth.

As you work your way through the group, you must remember that a facilitator must be *nonjudgmental*. You will not be dealing in good or bad, in right or wrong. You are dealing in what is. Explain this to the group.

You will never use expressions like "I know how you feel" because every situation is different. Instead, work with the philosophy, "Tell me how you feel. Share your thinking with me. Share your hurt. Together, we as a group can try to work it through." Of course, much of this must be put in your own words, but the essence of this is imperative to bring home to members.

At this point, take a coffee break of fifteen minutes maximum.

After the break, group members are feeling somewhat more comfortable with one another. At this point, the members should be at least somewhat receptive to beginning to understand their feelings. Start by defining bereavement, mourning and grief. Thomas P. Lynch, a funeral director, in his booklet *On Dying, Death, Grief and the Funeral*, published by the National Funeral Directors Association, outlined the different nuances of the death process:

> *bereavement*: Refers to a period of time in one's life following the death of a significant "other." It says nothing of the quality or duration of emotion but only signifies a date within a personal history. Bereavement is the *event* in personal history that triggers the emotion of grief.

mourning: Refers to a *process* of recovery and adjustment to the death of a significant person in one's life. Mourning is the method by which the powerful emotion is slowly and painfully brought under control.

grief: Refers to the *response* to any loss or separation, real or imagined, actual or symbolic, of any emotionally significant person, object or situation which is perceived to be of an irredeemable or permanent nature. Grief is always more than sorrow. It is the raw feelings that are at the center of a whole process that engages the person in adjusting to changed circumstances. These feelings include the deep fears of the mourner, of his prospects of loneliness, and the obstacles he must face as he finds a new way of living.

See if any member has something further to add. Sometimes the definitions in and of themselves become the tools of a dialog. If you heard discussions during the break which you believe the whole group could benefit from, begin to explain what you heard. Then ask the person you overheard to take over for you and explain in his own words what was said. Very often this move will bring about additional dialog.

As a facilitator, you will do very well to speak less yourself and have group members speak more. This will aid them. You personally do not need answers at this time. Remember that. You may draw upon your own experiences, good and bad, and share them. It is not the role of a facilitator to attempt therapy but rather to provide a warm, comfortable setting in which people may share their feelings.

Tears are natural. Try not to fear them. Don't be afraid for the people who weep. Tears are merely emotion turned liquid. You have been listening to people verbalize their pain. Do not offer tissues or handkerchiefs but make them readily available. If someone is crying, they feel they must no longer do so when they have been handed a tissue because they are, in effect, being told, "Time's up."

If someone begins to weep and quite obviously cannot continue speaking, simply say in as gentle a voice as you can, "We will go on to whoever is next. When you feel you want to continue, please join in."

Remember, you will be working with people within the group who are fresh in their grief. They should not be frightened by tears. Try not to allow them to frighten you.

As the final discussion of the evening go around the room and ask each person by name if he has any closing comments he wishes to make, any thoughts he wishes to take home and ponder, any insights he has gained. By doing so, you are asking members to summarize the meeting at which they have been present. If any point of importance has been left out take a few minutes to reiterate. Members must never leave a meeting feelings things are "up in the air" because a sense of closure is urgent to someone who is grieving.

Ask each member to bring a picture of their special person who died to the next meeting. Announce where and when that will be and repeat the topic of the next meeting.

MEETING TWO

Topic: Denial and a discussion of the funeral

Objective: To show that denial is often the first step in the mourning process

The second meeting is often more successful than the first because many who were reticent to speak the first time will feel more comfortable doing so at this session. They may, in fact, feel an overriding need to do so, for they have had the chance to go home and ponder the dynamics of the first session. Very often they will feel geared up to speak in order to catch up with the others.

If, in the course of discussing the topic of the evening, a question is pointedly asked of you, the facilitator, please remember *you are not a therapist*.

If someone were to ask, "Why am I so angry?" do not attempt

to give a psychologically approved answer. Instead, respond by saying, "I remember when I felt such anger and I too was confused or bewildered." Then throw the discussion open to the group. Ask others about their anger.

There is nothing wrong with veering from an exact agenda. You are dealing with people and their needs. That is the most important thing to remember. Because they are real, living people, they cannot always compartmentalize their feelings, but at some time during the evening the scheduled topic must be discussed. It is important to leave time for the planned-for topic because it was announced at the close of the last meeting. Continuity counts. So does predictability.

Since you have been selected to facilitate a group, it is understood you are a reasonable, thinking person. While this manual will contain certain suggested opening and closing dialogues, it will by no means put words into your mouth. You have grieved and survived; you have *experienced*. Draw upon your inner knowledge and resources and the questions and answers will come to you.

Again, begin slowly. Remember it is not urgent that the group plunge itself into deep problem areas immediately; there will be ample time for this as the meetings continue. Go around the room and ask each member:

- What is your name?
- Who is it you are mourning?
- What is his or her name?

Just as at the first meeting, go around the group a second time asking:

- Cause of death
- Age of the person who died

As each person starts to speak at the second round, ask him to pass the picture of his special person who died. Seeing the person can be helpful to fellow group members.

As a reminder, if possible, avoid allowing a spouse to serve as spokesperson for the couple. Also, do not force anyone to speak who is not ready to do so. In time, when a person feels safe within the nucleus of the group, he will take as active a part as he chooses. If someone opts not to speak, simply go on to the person sitting next to him.

If someone does not speak, this does not indicate you are a failure as a facilitator. The choice to speak or not is that of the bereaved person and has nothing to do with your ability!

Understanding the dynamics of the grieving process can be most helpful when one is going through it. Understanding will not necessarily change reactions but will allow people to know why they are feeling as they do. Emotions should be addressed in a logical sequence; the subject of denial is the first issue at hand since it is most often an immediate response.

Denial is our automatic response to the news of a death. One of the first things we say is, "No. I don't believe it." *If denial is allowed to persist, it can hamper normal grief and mourning.*

Share this definition with group members.

Go around the group and ask each person if he recalls this feeling. When did it begin? Was the sensation immediate? Has it left them yet? If so, when? If there is someone in the group who recognizes he is still gripped by denial, work a discussion around by asking other members if they consciously worked their way through denial or if it just abated by itself.

Explain that it can serve as a real reinforcement to bereaved people if they know that they have at least made an inroad toward healing. It is almost like a checklist to a mourner when someone can sigh and think, "Well, at least that's *one* behind me." Even though there will be many steps to climb, there can be comfort in knowing group members have at least mounted the ladder.

Feeling they have faced denial and perhaps even addressed it can be the first step toward mounting that ladder! If a member can recognize himself in a stage that has been defined by "experts" he will feel somewhat more secure amid all the insecurity of the grieving process.

Disposing of the dead person's belongings is often a symbol

of conquering denial. All too often there are people who simply cannot let go even though to do so is an affirmation of going on with one's life, of not being trapped in a time warp. There are those who can't throw away a half-eaten sandwich, a half-finished bottle of soda; can't make a rumpled bed; can't change a radio station because each of those things is a sign of the dead person. By introducing this to the group and sharing these examples, you may run across people who are doing just such things.

Do not make judgments. Merely ask why that person has decided to act in that manner. Invite the group to join in with their comments about "mausoleums." From fellow bereaved people who have retained a few possessions because they are cherished, a person unable to take apart a room can perhaps learn to do so. It might not be surprising to have a fellow group member even offer to help!

Ask if people kept things and why. Sometimes they may not know. If they do not, throw it open to the group.

Questions like "Why do you suppose he kept his wife's comforter?" may be very helpful and enlightening to the group after discussion.

Very often the first smatterings of dealing with denial will begin at or after the funeral. Ironically, all the pain and horror you recall from your own experience is generally the beginning of the healing process. The funeral acts as cautery on a wound. It is then that you must face the painful reality of being a mourner. That reality is there in the very stillness of the person who died.

Since the object of the group is to deal with current issues and current pain, the funeral will become the second half of the evening's topic. Even though the event is over, it is so significant that it must be addressed. However, really belaboring its horror can sometimes be counterproductive.

Questions to group members may include:

- How old were you when you attended your first funeral?
- Whose was it?

Perhaps at this point you may question whether we culturally overprotect people from death—something which all people know they must face eventually. This will allow a somewhat philosophical discussion about funerals in general and might help diffuse the intensity of the individual experiences.

Explain to members how the funeral can act as cautery. Ask:

- Can you still remember the funeral vividly?
- Has it blurred?
- Was it blurred for you when you were going through it?
- Do you remember the eulogy?

While no one must be denied the right to speak of his funeral experiences, remember there is a time factor and others who wish to share as well. A member may be reminded of this kindly and gently—but firmly—by the facilitator saying "We must move on to the next person now."

Another point to discuss is the treatment of the family by the funeral director. Very often, and frequently unjustifiably, people are angry at funeral directors. They become the focal point of all the rage and frustration and pain bereaved people are experiencing. If there has been a glaringly incorrect situation, this should be discussed with the group. Then suggest that a letter be written by the member who is unhappy directed to a specific person in the funeral home. By and large, funeral directors try as hard as they are able to make things as comfortable as possible. Of course, they are working in a situation where there can be little comfort, but some things are outside the norm and should not go unaddressed.

If, on the other hand, there have been good, positive, helping experiences, the group members should also let funeral directors hear about *them*. Writing a letter of appreciation can be very heartening to the director and a positive experience for the bereaved person. This is an appropriate suggestion for a facilitator to make.

Generally, this second meeting will fly by in no time. But if there is room for further discussion you may well draw upon your own experiences as a mourner. Introduce the topic of "things people say" that you personally recall. Some may be profound and might have helped while others are so foolish as to be ludicrous. Things like, "I know how you feel," "Well, you had him forty years," "You can have other children," are as insensitive as they are common.

Following the heaviness of the discussion about funerals and denial, this area can generate some lively and even amusing responses.

In closing this meeting as in all meetings that will follow, time must be allowed for something positive with which the group may leave. Sometimes summarizing with such things as how a member worked through denial in a healthy manner might be reinforced. If no such concepts surface, ask group members what steps they might be considering taking to help themselves after the discussion at this session.

Someone will come forth who will be able to offer his insights simply because group members are never exactly at the same place in mourning.

Grieving is not an exact science, nor does it allow an exact progression. Group members should be made aware of this for their stages will be individually their own. No two people grieve in exactly the same way or in synchronization.

Ask members to write a few sentences at home dealing with their feelings about death and anger.

Announce the time and place of the next meeting and that the topic for that meeting will be anger.

MEETING THREE

Topic: Anger

Objectives: To allow members to vent their anger and to seek positive ways of dealing with it

As you begin this meeting you most likely will find that group members have started forming a sense of group. In case there are newcomers to this particular session, be sure you, at least by overview, make them current. Invite members to help you in this task.

Just as you have done at every preceding meeting, begin by having each group member:

- Give his or her name
- Age of the deceased
- Cause of death

Go around again and ask:

- What is the name of the deceased?
- When did he die?

If you have newcomers, be certain to invite them to take part in this procedure but begin with someone who has been at several meetings.

After you have started by discussing denial and/or the funeral, ask another group member to help you by picking up on the overview of the last meeting. Have yet another member continue to do so.

This is a particularly effective way in which to invite members not prone to speaking to share. They are in a position of possessing information that newcomers lack and generally will be pleased to be called upon. Also, this enables them to further expound upon their own conclusions.

Meetings must always allow this flexibility. Although the previous session did not seem very long at all and generally participants were reluctant to leave, it did in fact offer much to ponder over. By going back you are helping those who are grieving to verbalize their feelings and perhaps reinforce the positive support they were given.

Keeping an eye on the time and recognizing how long new material takes to cover, there will be a point when you hear repetitive statements. When this occurs, step in and call the group back in session by announcing the topic of the meeting will be anger.

Anger is the emotional agitation of no specified intensity aroused by what is considered outrageously unjust, mean or shameful.

In general, when attempting to cope with the death of a special person, anger has at least five targets. People feel anger toward:

- The doctor
- The clergyman
- The funeral director
- The person who died
- God

In the case of murder or accident, anger may be directed at the person held responsible. With good group and therapeutic help it would be hoped in time a mourner could ease this anger as it serves no real purpose, but that is not always possible.

Explain that not everyone experiences all of these emotions, but most people feel at the very least a twinge of anger against at least one of those focal points.

Go around the group and ask each member what he has written or thought through about his specific anger at this time. Again, by assuming he is angry, you are freeing him to share his feelings openly. You may ask members whether they feel the doctor, funeral director or clergyman was helpful. Were there problems?

Some of the responses you might receive will be:

- The doctor should have done more.
- The funeral director is nothing but a money grubber.
- The clergyman did not abide by my requests.

These statements are common. Group members may agree or disagree. Allow them that.

Sometimes people will state they are angry because the doctor never answered a telephone call. Ask the group how they feel this should be handled. You may hear some very creative suggestions the grieving person may opt to act upon. If it is not mentioned by anyone, suggest that a registered letter, return receipt requested, be sent to the doctor. The letter should explain the urgency for communication. Most of the time people need to know a bit more about why their special person died. They need the reassurance that everything was done that could be done. Those are basic and simple courtesies anyone who is grieving has a right to expect. By writing a letter, the mourner helps himself alleviate some frustration which often becomes mingled with anger.

The same course of action should be suggested for the clergy or funeral directors. Very often, we are angry at the doctors, clergy, and funeral directors because these people serve as symbols and reminders of the death.

Aside from these three categories of tangible anger, there are at least two intangibles that go deeper and hurt longer. People often feel unwilling to discuss them aloud and yet, because they are silent, find themselves hampered in working through their grief. Most people at some level of consciousness find themselves keeping the terrible secret of being angry at the person who died. Yet this is perhaps the most common anger of all!

"I loved him so much and he went ahead and died! How could he have done such a thing? How could he have left me alone and in such pain?"

Just such a statement would not be unusual for someone to feel, indeed, to express. As blatant as the words sound, as illogical, they are real and the feeling is a true gut emotion.

By introducing the concept of anger to the group you will be helping members realize they are not alone in this frightening sensation. That, after all, is the purpose of the support group. Members come away with a sense of not being isolated even when they have "nasty" emotions.

Once again, facilitators are not therapists. It is necessary to remember this when entering such a sensitive area. Assert that not everyone feels the same emotions but that this is indeed a common problem experienced by those who grieve. There will be people in the group who are recently bereaved. They may not yet have experienced this raging anger. How fortunate for them that they will be forewarned!

You can always avoid quibbling by speaking in generalities.

When using expressions like "most people" or "sometimes," in fact any equivocating word or phrase, you are not setting up defensive situations. You are allowing people to *listen* and *participate* by internalizing information rather than being concerned with how they will *refute* you.

After you have defined the various targets of anger you might share a personal experience. "I remember when I was angry at ———." From there, perhaps go around the room and ask group members whether they are feeling any anger toward their special person who has died. You will find some members will admit to this freely, others reluctantly and some not at all.

Not every stage of grief hits everyone at the same time; therefore, everyone in the group may benefit from this round of questions. For some it will be an affirmation that they are normal, for others a forewarning of things to come. To be forewarned is to be forearmed!

It is possible you have not experienced this anger in any *recognizable* form. If this is the case, feel free to draw upon my personal experience: When I was home alone after my son died, I would walk from room to room screaming, "How could you have died? How could you have done such a thing? How could you have left me in so much pain?"

At the time I was shouting to the heavens, I felt a part of my brain telling me I was doing something "wrong." I was doing something iconoclastic. I was eroding some holy concept such as only speaking well of the dead.

Along with my grief I felt shame and guilt. I did not understand then that my feelings were normal, that I had a right to my feelings just as all people do. I never discussed them until I wrote *The Bereaved Parent*. I spent five years, 1,825 days, with this secret buried inside of me! I needed to be given "permission" to be angry with my son. When I interviewed people and asked them about anger, then and *only then* did I discover this was common, ordinary, garden-variety grieving!

During this discussion, the issue of being angry with God will most likely surface. Explain that the entire question of death and religion will be the next topic you as a group will address. Try not to get entangled with it during the session on anger as there are different lines you will draw when talking about religion.

In order to allow group members to leave the session with some degree of comfort, no discussion of anger should be allowed to end with ragged edges. Instead, they must be smoothed to give a mourner a sense of balance. Before the meeting ends try to help those who are feeling anger to offer something positive to the group. Although they may be angry at the doctor, the funeral director, the clergyman, they will also most likely have some kind words to say about them. Ask specifically for a good thing these people offered the group member. Balance always matters.

Since there is not always enough time to cover everything, each person should be heard from for at least a small portion of time. If someone has not spoken about any anger, ask if a family member said or did anything untoward. Did they say foolish things, insensitive things? Instead of harboring a deep resentment, a mourner, by having his feelings brought out into the open, may be relieved of the rage he has possibly displaced upon an inept relative. In general, group members have probably been conditioned to believe it is "not nice" to be angry and so they deny and try to bury it. That doesn't work.

Generally a group member is angry because he is in pain, because he feels abandoned, because he feels life is unfair.

Anger, when carried over to those around the mourner, can all too easily cause further problems by eroding his support system. Make group members aware of this.

By acknowledging anger, you have removed a burden which otherwise could keep a mourner crawling on the ground forever. Be certain in your closing comments that people leave the session a little more at ease with their feelings, a little less intense.

Ask members to write out at home briefly whether they feel their religious faith has offered solace. If so, share how. If they have no religious faith ask them to write out what does offer them solace.

Announce that the topic for the following session will be religion and death.

MEETING FOUR

Topic: Religion

Objective: To develop a rational concept of the impact of death upon religion

There are people who will suddenly pull closer to their faith when faced with a special person's death and people, sometimes long-time observant, religious people, who will suddenly turn their backs completely on God because they feel God has turned his back on them. As a facilitator it is not your responsibility to force belief onto those who grieve. What is important is to offer a *nonjudgmental* ear to someone in distress. The tone you set will be the tone adopted by others within the group. You must always remember this while conducting sessions.

It is helpful to mourners to publicly name their special person and how he died because they are rarely given this opportunity in the normal routine of their day. It is their time in a non-judgmental atmosphere to mention the name, give the facts and be heard compassionately.

As in all previous sessions, begin by asking those present to share their "vital statistics." By this time, of course, you and all the group members will know one another by name. Therefore, when you call upon them, do so by name. Ask:

- The name of the special person who died
- How old the special person was

Go around again and ask:

- The cause of death
- When death occurred

Unlike speakers on other topics it is extremely desirable that a clergyman be present at this session. It would be very helpful if that person was somewhat unflappable, as there likely will be members who will challenge whether there is indeed a God. Attempt to discuss this with the clergyman before he agrees to come to the session. Since clerics, whether rabbis, priests or ministers, whether Methodist, Lutheran or Baptist, are considered by many as God's earthly representatives, it is helpful for a mourner to be able to confront this representative about his doubts and pain. A secure clergyman, comfortable in his faith, can be helpful by listening well, not becoming defensive and answering questions to the best of his ability. To say, "I don't know" is not a sin.

After you have gone around the group and introduced yourselves and the clergyman who is present, introduce the topic of God. You may do so by explaining there are no right or wrong emotions. How people choose to act on these emotions makes the difference.

Explain that following the death of an immediate family member, there are people who instinctively cling to their faith. Basically, those who cling are the lucky ones. You can explain there are some excellent options open to them. They can accept the idea that God had a greater plan. You will meet, perhaps, with some derisive comments if you say this, although other group members might agree. Should you meet with derision, you have your opportunity to explain at the *outset* that we are not gathered to make value judgments. People have a right to this concept and no one has the right to mock or belittle their belief.

It is important that you recognize you may well be dealing with a dichotomy here. Although your group might be religious-based, people attending may still profess a hatred of God or a disbelief in Him. Accept this information as you have accepted all the other forms of anger—by giving the speaker the dignity of authenticating his feelings and by not judging them.

Whenever possible in your facilitating, use third-party stories. They can be real-life experiences, anecdotes you might have run across, or something biblical to illustrate a point you wish to make.

An example of this is a Talmudic tale of a rabbi who came home from a trip and asked his wife to see their twin sons. He did not know both children had died during his absence. Rather than immediately lead him to the boys' bodies, she first asked: "If someone loans you precious jewels and asks that you enjoy them while they are in your keeping, do you have the right to complain if the same someone asks for their return?"

The rabbi thought for a moment and replied, "Certainly not. They must be returned without complaint!"

Hearing this she took his hand and led him to the room where the twins lay. "God wanted his jewels back," she said.

Some years ago, the poet James Russell Lowell wrote a poem entitled "After the Burial" following the death of his daughter Rose. There are several stanzas that apply very well to those who no longer believe—or who think they no longer believe.

> Console if you will, I can bear it.
> 'Tis a well meant alms of breath,
> But not all the preaching since Adam
> Can make death other than death.

> Communion in spirit, forgive me,
> But I, who am mortal and weak
> Would give all my incomes from dreamland
> For a touch of her hand on my cheek.

At this point, if you are fortunate to have a clergyman present, tell the group you have attempted to give an overview of both sides of the question. The clergyman will now address the topic of the impact of death upon religious belief and the impact of religious belief upon death. Tell members what they have written or thought through about what did or did not offer solace will be the core of the discussion following the clergyman's half-hour speech.

After the speech, invite questions for the speaker.

When the speaker has finished go around the group and ask how different members now feel about religion. Some may be comforted, others angered. Which philosophy comes closest to their way of thinking—that of the rabbi's wife or that of the poet?

Ask if people in general view themselves as accepting. Do they believe, despite their pain, "What will be, will be"? Remember, some people have been raised to feel it is forbidden to question God or His wisdom. These people may be in the minority at such a meeting. Since one of the tenets of the group is to be nonjudgmental, remember to protect their rights to the way they feel. Ask a true believer to explain his feelings to the group. People may profit from his thinking. Ask the group to keep their minds open on this issue.

- Do people view themselves as comforted by their religion?
- Do they feel angry?
- Why?

The more people are asked to verbalize what they are feeling, the more they have to deal with some sort of logic rather than the nebulous emotions that swirl around and never find a foundation.

Go around the group and ask each member by name how he perceives God at this specific time. People in grief find constantly changing attitudes as their pain ebbs and flows.

During the discussion on religion, you will often hear much anger toward God. Understand this is something that should within bounds be allowed to be aired. If someone is raging at greater length than is fair to the rest of the group, in a kindly manner ask him to remember that time must be allotted to all group members and others might wish to speak also. By doing so—with kindness—you are not negating his anger but instead making him also pause and listen to other thoughts, fresh input, hopefully positive.

Remember, as always in dealing with grieving people, you are attempting to deal rationally in an irrational situation.

You will also have to deal with those in the group who, rather than being angry with God, insist there is no God. They may, in fact, have felt deeply religious before the death but have allowed bitterness and anger to overtake any positive feelings about God.

As ever, you are not there to make judgments. You are not there to convert anyone. You are there as a sounding board. If you can assuage, within the confines of the group, some of the negative emotion toward God, the grieving person will be better able to make a decision about his personal attitudes that is right for him.

You cannot make that decision for him.

Just understand there is questioning, doubting, uncertainty and none of these are unusual nor are they extreme—nor are they necessarily permanent. Often they are a stage.

Know these negative feelings must also be given credence. People who do not have a faith bear an even greater burden than others. Sometimes, those who believe can rationalize. They can feel their special person is in a better place with a loving God.

That is not true when one does not believe. There is no room for any consoling spiritual influences. These people are hurting and hurting desperately. If you see that someone in the group is having great discomfort during the discussion about God, again share Lowell's poem. Ask the clergyman to offer his views. Give legitimacy to the member's feelings. Let him air why he no longer believes. Ironically, if that person does not get the "expected" argument about why he should have faith he very slowly may begin to reconsider his rejection of God and possibly come back into the fold.

During the course of discussing negative views, you may see others interrupting and becoming angry. Hold them in check. A support group is not a popularity contest nor is it there only to bare "nice" thoughts. It is no one's job to defend God. His shoulders are strong, as one priest so aptly put it.

When someone is angry with God, or someone who no longer believes is through expressing himself, ask:

- Did you ever believe in God?
- Were you bar mitzvahed? Did you take communion?
- Did you have a civil or religious wedding ceremony?
- Have you ever had a close relationship with a clergyman?

These questions are designed to help an angry, bitter person remember some positive religious experiences. Sometimes if the right questions are asked, a balance in the anger might be struck.

This will be a very difficult session. It is usually easier to have a clergyman in to perhaps explain a bit about how your faith (or faiths) explains death and to answer questions people may have. Remember, there may be recently bereaved people in attendance who are angry with the clergy. Control the meeting to the extent that your guest not be made to feel an onslaught of hostility.

Ask group members to share what they have experienced during this session. Go from member to member and invite specific comments. Inquire whether points that were troubling them have been cleared up. Acknowledge that not everyone believes the same way. Nor is a particular view of religion—especially one that is new after a death—necessarily permanent. People change. They mellow. If the meeting has offered more information, perhaps some of the anger will abate in direct proportion. Tell members, above all, to work at keeping an open mind.

Suggest to group members, regardless of their religious preference, an ancient Jewish tradition that can effectively be translated for all people who are mourning.

In Judaism, there is an eleven-month period during which mourners attend services daily and sometimes twice daily. This custom can be translated for anyone. Believers and nonbelievers alike may avail themselves of the following daily exercise:

Have group members at a given period of time each day select a special chair, take a prayer book or a poetry book or some object belonging to the special person who is dead. Tell members to allow themselves half an hour to think about the dead person, his life, and how the member thinks *he* may continue with his own life.

Tell group members to get up and out of their chair after the half hour is over. Tell them to do something physical. This is known as establishing a "grieving time." By telling someone he will have a fixed time daily, you will help him free some time to begin functioning again without feeling guilty because he is "abandoning" the grief of dealing with that special person's death. He will know at the end of the day or in the beginning, there is a special time reserved for his mourning.

Also, for those who do believe, if a church or temple does hold a daily prayer service, suggest members avail themselves of it. This, too, can be very helpful.

If at all possible, invite your clergyman to stay for the entire session as different questions will arise during different parts of the meeting.

Announce the time and place of the next meeting during which the topic will be guilt.

MEETING FIVE

Topic: Guilt

Objectives: To understand the dynamics of guilt and its destructiveness; to learn to look at guilt rationally

By this point group members should be acquainted enough with one another that you, as the facilitator, will ask the questions that open a meeting by calling upon members using their names. Since you all know the basic ages, causes and time sequences of your special person, it is time to move forward.

Begin by asking group members:

• Did you attempt the "grieving time" concept discussed at the last meeting?
• Did it work?
• Have you done it regularly?

Go around the group again and ask each member by name:

• Have you done any reading about death?
• Was it helpful?
• What books did you find to be of value?

Allow the group less than half an hour for this discussion as the topic of the evening generally consumes the meeting time completely.

Take notes about which books were of value and which were not. The helpful books should go on your list of possible referrals.

Explain to members that just as during the last two sessions dealing with anger and religion you are again in a very sensitive area. This session will deal with guilt. *Guilt is a legitimate state which a mourner endures almost universally. In reality, it is the act or state of having done a wrong or committed an offense; culpability, legal or ethical.* However, rarely is a mourner's guilt based on fact.

During this discussion you may find people of any age in the group who, during the course of their experiences with the person who died, felt anger at him at least some of the time. Remind members there is *anger in all loving relationships!* Very often, when someone dear dies, we tend to forget this basic tenet of involvement. We have been culturally conditioned "not to speak ill of the dead." Since no one is a saint, these two ideas are in conflict. A husband, a child, a parent may indeed have been extremely tiresome or difficult. While that person was alive, somehow his foibles were accepted and looked at squarely. It is only after his death that people tend to negate his negative but very real traits.

Tell members that most people share thoughts like the following:

- "I should have done more."
- "I should have called another doctor."
- "I sometimes was mean to her."
- "Why didn't I recognize the symptoms?"

Ask whether anyone in the group has ever had such ideas cross their minds.

What other thoughts does the topic of guilt bring to mind?

Are members at ease in their memories about their relationship with the special person who is dead? Invite them to share their feelings.

Is there a particular facet about the relationship they wish could be changed? If so, ask members to attempt to share this with the group. It can be enormously helpful for a member to bring such a negative to the surface rather than to bury it deep within himself. If it is placed on the table, it can be examined, explored. If it is submerged, the member runs the risk of becoming infected with the poison that guilt so frequently gives off.

Other situations that evoke feelings of guilt will be discussed further along in this meeting. As you introduce each issue to the members, ask if anyone has experienced guilt over that issue.

If the group has already discussed in part some of the guilty feelings a member might have, turn to that member and ask him to share his thoughts once again with the group. Then invite other members to respond.

If you had experiences of your own in which guilt played a large part, be certain to include them and let group members know how you felt then and how you feel now. This will be helpful to everyone because you are further along in your healing process than they.

Let members know that all these and many more such insidious ideas breed like bacteria within a grieving person's thinking process. Somehow, most people who grieve force themselves to reach and stretch until they find some big or little things upon which to hang self-blame. Most of the time this blame is undeserved. But as people thrash around looking for the mystical answer to the inevitable why their special person has died, they all too often end up feeling they themselves are at fault. Has any group member felt this?

When you hear self-blaming statements, avoid saying things such as, "Don't feel that way." We *never* have the right to tell people how to feel. Instead, a comment like, "It must be very painful for you to feel so responsible," is much more acceptable. You are commiserating without making a value judgment. That is always the appropriate response but sometimes it is hard to give.

Depending upon the trust bond within the group, you may hear some surprising tales dealing with guilt. It would not be impossible for a grieving spouse or a bereaved parent to burst forth with the information that he cheated on his mate and God punished him by having the mate or child die. There is, of course, a basic illogic there! If God was indeed being punitive, why have the innocent party die? After all, while a survivor mourns because he has lost a special person, it must be remembered *that* special person lost everyone!

People will blurt out just such statements in their need to blame themselves; this situation has arisen at support group meetings in various parts of the country. Rather than displaying reactions such as shock or distaste, this is where your humanness must come into play. A statement like, "It must be very painful for you now," lends sympathy and support to someone already in deep turmoil.

In general, it would be a very shallow and unfeeling group member who would jump in in an accusatory manner and agree with the grief- and guilt-ridden person. If this should occur, you must intervene and restore the sense of equilibrium the guilty-feeling member deserves.

Sometimes people will express guilt over having placed a special person in a nursing home. Statements about how they should have cared for their special person are also common. It is not always realistic to keep an ill person home: sometimes finances prevent this, sometimes work factors play their part and sometimes people simply are not emotionally strong enough to handle a terminally ill person in their home. To do so can mean feeling imprisoned when there is no one else to help.

If the nursing home situation arises, hear the member out and then ask whether the member *truly* had alternatives. Was keeping the special person at home something that could have been worked out in the world of reality and not fantasy?

Remind grieving members who feel trapped in these situations that most people do the best they can when faced with hard and painful probems and choices.

There will be people within the group who have had to deal with suicide. Rarely, at the outset—and this is when you will be seeing them—do people whose loved one died of suicide think: "Where did my loved one fail? Could *he* have done anything to avert this disaster?" Instead, in the beginning, the survivor, who is also a victim, only sees his own failure, his own sense of not having done or given enough. While some people take their lives as an act of aggression, to "get even" for real or imagined slights, there are other people who take their lives because they simply cannot live. Things have become so painful for them that it just hurts too much to go on.

The most important thing the group can offer someone so painfully victimized is an understanding ear and heart. Tell the group this. As a facilitator, unless you have experienced suicide, your major role will be to listen and learn not to look away even though the member feels a deep sense of shame that is again unjustified.

Sometimes the suicide will be described in quiet, gentle terms and other times you will hear rage. Try not to let either end of this spectrum overwhelm you. Simply be as sympathetic as you can.

Remember, special people who have died this way die *of* suicide, they don't commit it!

Once again remember that you are not a therapist; your function is to help establish an ongoing dialogue between people who are grieving. You cannot resolve guilt problems for anyone. You can offer sympathy, perhaps some insight, some similar shared emotions, but you cannot make it "all better." If you see that someone is being consumed by guilt and continues to be for many sessions, begin to suggest he seek professional help.

There are several ways of making this suggestion. Foremost in the discussion is the idea that one-on-one therapy should *not* exclude the group as another source of help. By this time, members have entered a mutually caring relationship. To break this off would add a further sense of loss to an already grieving person.

First of all, it is important to be certain *you* are comfortable with the idea of suggesting therapy. Next, be sure you have a list of members of the mental health community whose specialty is working with death and dying.

During a break—or perhaps even by telephone, as long as you deal with the person in a *private* manner—explain your group is equipped to handle general grieving problems. You are seeing such intense pain in the member who is feeling guilty that you believe it might be helpful if he sought professional help. You are not asking him to leave the group. On the contrary, you hope he will remain. You do, however, care enough about him to hope he will avail himself of some psychological assistance in order to work through the guilt.

If you can do so, place an arm around the person you are saying this to. When you have made that decision, the person is probably already aware of his need for help, because the group often serves as a self-measuring stick for emotions. Most of the time, you will be merely reinforcing what he already knows.

Dr. Jacqueline Grekin, a psychologist, has another suggestion for wording this delicate issue of suggesting professional help.

"If you broke your arm I would sympathize with you, go to the doctor with you, sit while you had it X-rayed and set. Then I could drive you home and be concerned. But the one thing I *cannot* do is set your arm. That requires a professional who is trained to do so.

"As a facilitator, I am trained to help care about you but I cannot set your arm. That is beyond my expertise. I have the names of some therapists who might be helpful to you."

Emphasize again to the member that you hope he will continue with the group and that it is perfectly acceptable to "shop" for a therapist. If one helping person is not to his liking, by all means he should try another.

Because guilt is so large an issue, be certain that enough time is left for closure. Go around the group and ask each member by name how they feel about hearing the person next to them express feelings of guilt.

Did the listener learn anything of value from hearing someone else? If so, what?

Make certain each person has input into this essential summarizing. What did they hear? What did they learn?

Ask members if they have any suggestions to make to one another—or indeed for themselves. Perhaps members might, when that wave of guilt overtakes them, condition themselves to remember a key word that will establish a healthy sense of proportion. Ask members what such a word might be. One suggestion might be the word "rational." There are certainly others; and the group might have already adopted some expressions as its own.

Have members go home and think about a book they might have read, a movie they might have seen, a television program they might have watched in which a character was falsely accused of a crime. Have the members try to remember just how they felt at this injustice and perhaps even invite them to write a few words on the topic. Explain that being accused of something one did not do is not so different from accusing oneself!

You will then be taking a situation in which a member has been myopic and widening his lens.

Announce that the next meeting will deal with depression.

MEETING SIX

Topic: Depression

Objectives: To analyze the components of depression; to learn to deal with them in a healthy manner

Before announcing the topic of this session go around the group and ask members if they were able to recall movies or literature dealing with unjustly accused people. Ask:

- Did you identify with the person accused?
- Were you angry at the injustice?

Go around the group once again and ask:

- What was the date of your special person's death?
- What was the date of that person's birth?

Make notes on the above answers as they will dovetail into the topic of depression. You may vary the opening questions as you see fit. The main object is to get members into the concept of speaking at the meeting. Also, someone may have worked through something from the previous meeting that could be of value to the group. This would be a good time to share such insights.

Introduce the topic by explaining that depression is perhaps the most pervasive emotion anyone experiences after the death of a special person. There is all too often a sense of futility that overtakes the grieving person. "Why go on?" "There is no point to anything anymore." These are not unnatural questions or feelings. In the searching for answers you have personally fought to discover, you know how deeply you can be pained by these negative concepts.

Continue by explaining there is a dreadful sadness that begins to fit over those who grieve almost like a second skin. Nothing seems to hold meaning any longer. *Depression is the knowledge that we will have to restructure our lives without the presence of our special person.*

This knowledge often leads to a loss of meaning in our lives. When our own lives lose meaning, we become frightened and anchorless. We feel somehow that we have been cast adrift.

Depression has many components. It includes tension, insomnia, feelings of worthlessness, bitter self-accusation. There is a sense that nothing *ever* can make life joyful again. All is lost. Every hope and prayer is meaningless. Nothing matters now nor will it ever.

It is ironic that although depressed people need support the most, they make it nearly impossible for anyone to offer them comfort. Their aura is so beset with gloom and hurt that it seems almost impenetrable. Frequently, after a prolonged series of attempts to help, friends, sincerely caring people, will simply give up because they feel they are trying to do something useless. That is one of the dangers of depression: others eventually may remove themselves.

This danger heightens one of the "cycles of depression" those who suffer have to endure. They create an atmosphere that makes it impossible for others to come close, then they feel doubly hurt because they feel isolated in their hour of need. When they feel isolated, the sense of depression they are experiencing is heightened.

Go around the room and ask each person if he is feeling any of the components of depression: tension, insomnia, feelings of worthlessness, bitter self-accusation. Name these components separately. If a group member does not feel any of them, feel free to ask what he is feeling. Check again with the group to see if anybody else is experiencing what the member has described.

It is possible that a group member might say that while it is very helpful to come to meetings, it is very difficult to go home alone. That is quite a legitimate feeling, for going home alone often feeds into depression. Take this statement and turn it into a positive. Tell the member how pleased you are that he at least has *this* respite from feeling isolated with his grief.

There are many things that trigger depression and these should be discussed with the group. You may personally have felt the pain of the change in seasons: it is summer and he is dead; it is winter and he is dead. This is not uncommon. Just to know others have felt that way can be helpful.

Anniversaries and birthdays can be another source of great pain whether it is the birthday of a group member or that of his special person. Bring up the issue of these occasions and acknowledge how painful they can be. Refer to the notes you made during the opening of the meeting and check whether any special event has passed or is impending. Ask members for suggestions about how to deal with these days. Did anything work for you? Did you go to the cemetery? Did you stay away? Was there anything at all that helped *you*?

Any discussion about depression is likely to evoke tears. After all, there is much pain in sharing with a group why one does not feel like getting out of bed in the morning. On the other hand, fellow members may have suggestions to offer that can be of real value. Do not let the tears impede the discussion. If the group member cannot go on at a given time, simply turn to the next person in the group and ask about his feelings, or tell the member you will return to him when he is ready.

Another cycle in ongoing depression, the "vulnerability cycle," is by far the most difficult problem with which a depressed person must contend. When someone is depressed, she cannot sleep. When she cannot sleep, she feels exhausted. When she feels exhausted, she cannot cope with being depressed. That is when she cannot sleep and so it goes. Ask members if they are experiencing this cycle. The majority probably are feeling at least parts of it. By acknowledging the problem is universal, you have already aided members. Suggest that members not nap during the day. Eventually they will sleep and that sleep will help break the "vulnerability cycle."

In this very difficult area, it is most important to remember you are not a therapist. Instead, you are offering an arena for people to ease the burden of feeling isolated and alone. Easing that burden to some degree can help break into either of the cycles.

On pages 175-176, there is a list of words that define depression, put together by Roy V. Nichols, a funeral director. Pass out copies of this list to those present.

These words describe how members feel. Read them aloud to the group, slowly, in order to allow for their impact upon members. Ask members if they are feeling responses to these words. Remember that not everyone feels the same thing at the same time and remind group members of it. Some people will say they are experiencing every one of the emotions and sensations; others will only relate to one or two. Ask them how this emotion is affecting them. Is it impeding their day-to-day life? When you are through, ask if there are other words that might also describe their hurt. Since the list is long and many may wish to address these descriptions, do not feel rushed into cutting members short. You may not complete all the words during this session. If you do not, save them for the next session because they are important.

Try to keep a careful eye on the time, because the cycles discussed and the "depression words" can create a very involved dialogue. Make certain you allow time to ask group members what has been helpful during the evening if only for a short span of time.

In closing this meeting ask members whether attending services at a church or temple has been helpful—especially on an anniversary date. This might be a suggestion to offer.

Go into your own background and try to recall anything that might have been of help to you. Also, remind members about the concept of a grieving time—time allotted daily in which to pray or contemplate, followed by becoming involved in something active even if it is only housecleaning. Sometimes small physical things can be of benefit: walking for a given time, bicycling, preparing dinner, washing the car, cleaning the oven. All these things prove to the person who is grieving he does indeed have some worth. There is *something he can do!* Keep careful track of suggestions and refer to them when necessary.

Ask group members whether they feel comfort if others remember their special anniversaries. Suggest that a visit to the cemetery might be valuable on a special anniversary as might calling friends and family. Remind members not to wait for sympathetic phone calls but rather to reach out and tell people their comfort is needed on this date. Ask how they would feel about having a birthday, death day, or anniversary calendar. Compiling such a list can be helpful to you as the facilitator. It may also be helpful to assign one or more members the task of accumulating the list of these important dates. Perhaps group members who tend to sit more quietly during sessions could become involved in this activity.

Inquire whether group members would appreciate hearing from other members on their important days. They might feel gratified to receive a card from others who attend meetings with them. The card need simply say, "I'm thinking of you and I care."

Since you will have dealt with so much emotion at this meeting be certain you tie up as many loose ends as possible. Try to have each member speak to the question of what might be helpful to himself or another person in the group. Above all, work at having the meeting end on an "up" note. Discuss the positives as much as possible: the positives are the things that can be of help.

Have members go home and study the words dealing with depression. Have them select one or two which might seem especially applicable and circle them. Ask members to write down or remember why they have chosen those particular words.

Announce that the next meeting will deal with powerlessness.

MEETING SEVEN

Topic: Powerlessness

Objectives: To understand that the loss of ability to control events is universal following a death

People generally go through life feeling a sense of having some control over events. When a loved one dies, that control seems to have gone, leaving in its stead a feeling of being bereft. Powerlessness can be among the most undermining of feelings.

Begin this session by asking members:

• The name of their special person who died
• What one word characterized their interpersonal dealings best

Go around again and ask members:

• Did they go through the list of depression words?
• Which word(s) held the most meaning and why?

If you notice that a number of members selected the same word or words note this and show them how their commonality of feeling is part of what makes the group function so well.

Explain to members that when someone is intensely grieving

the death of a special person, one of the most frustrating emotions he will experience is powerlessness.

Powerlessness is a sense of the loss of control of something as important as having a loved one continue living. Its components include every emotion in the entire gamut of grief.

The feeling of powerlessness comes because, despite trying with all your being to find the right doctors, to offer the best environment, to be as supportive as possible, the one you so deeply loved still died. The old nursery rhyme which ends with "all the king's horses and all the king's men couldn't put Humpty Dumpty together again" explains this powerlessness best of all.

After you have explained it, ask members whether they have felt this sense of powerlessness. Have they found their grief is heightened by the sense of loss of control? Do they feel captive to the whims of the universe?

All too often, grieving people equate powerlessness with failure. Not only do they feel angry, guilty and depressed, they also feel worthless. They see the death as a visitation of their own shortcomings and therein lies the potential for great tragedy. After telling this to the group, ask whether anyone is experiencing this sense of failure. Have other members contribute their own perceptions that might be helpful.

Explain that not only do people have to face the brutal truth of death, they all too often feel powerless because they think they should have been able to prevent it. Does any group member feel this way?

Tell group members that powerlessness works hand in hand with guilt but is actually a separate experience. The two come together when the survivor feels he should have been able to prevent the death but didn't. Explain that the word "didn't" is faulty and should be replaced with "couldn't."

Many hurtful feelings surround the sense of having lost control including anger, rage, frustration, fear, and hysteria. Ask each member if he has experienced or is experiencing any of these emotions and the wish to pound his fist on the desk or table. That, to many, is powerlessness.

Powerlessness also has the ability to make a grieving person feel very small, very insignificant. When this occurs, it is only natural to feel one has been sucked into a dreadful morass from which there is no escape.

Is any member of the group feeling this way? Ask other members what they believe might be helpful to solve such a problem. It is sad to hear someone describing themselves as so small, so insignificant. These people need some sense of being pulled back up to their original height, whatever that might be.

Tell members that being successful frequently contributes mightily to the problem of feeling powerless. Often a man or woman who has risen through the corporate ranks, carved out a successful business or in some other field achieved success feels an additional shock wave following the death of a special person. After all, such a person has created a world to his specifications but now his achievements seem meaningless. Ask those in the group if they understand and know this feeling.

Women who have given their lives to those around them and served as nurturers feel the same powerlessness with the loss of their special person. They bandaged cut fingers, comforted men who feared the next step up the corporate rung, mended and tended for the ill and terminally ill. Are there women in the group who fit this role?

Their positions were always fairly clear-cut and they worked well within them. Now, suddenly, they are faced with not only the death of someone they loved but also the end of a way of life. No longer is the person they were tending in need. It is all over and the woman feels bereft and, just as dreadful, she feels useless. No one can be comfortable when they do not feel needed.

Is a group member experiencing this? Do other members have suggestions that might help overcome this sense of powerlessness? Do you?

It is important to remember that although the woman was just described as the nurturer and the man the businessperson these roles are not limited by sex. Sometimes the male is the caretaker, the nurturer. Sometimes, the woman is the business dynamo. Sometimes each are both!

In most families, however, you will be dealing with traditional situations. Remind members that their sex need not stereotype how they functioned with their special person.

There are other issues involving powerlessness that lend themselves to great rage. Perhaps a special person was killed by a drunk driver who received merely a slap on the wrist. Perhaps a special person died as a result of a doctor's ineptitude. Yet another person may have been killed by a robber or accidentally became the innocent bystander. Has anyone in the group been bereaved in such a situation? Ask him to describe how the sense of powerlessness overtook him. Go from person to person in the group and ask for their reactions to what they have heard.

Suicide should be mentioned here although we are dealing with death inflicted by an outsider. Is the sense of powerlessness greater after a suicide than in the above situations? Ask the question and see how the group responds. If a member has been the victim of a suicide, the acknowledgment of his special problem may be helpful.

There are, of course, people who have not achieved in the business world. Remind the members that wherever their mark was made *they matter*. They are not worthless. It is *not* okay that life has dealt with them unjustly. Tell members this for their own benefit and for the benefit of someone they might meet down the line who might be helped by knowing everyone matters.

There are people with little money. Often they view the death of a special person as just another one of life's blows—just another kick in the heart.

This very negative type of "acceptance" can be fearful to watch. It is as if each of life's blows is anticipated—with just another one coming around the corner. If group members have been pounded by life in all its aspects, it is appropriate indeed to suggest they have the *right* to feel angry and hurt. They have the same rights others have. If someone who feels downtrodden by life can even remotely identify with this concept, you will have helped him not only through his death work but with his life work. Discuss negative acceptance with the group and how harmful it can be.

Powerlessness also contains the component of injustice. In fact, whenever someone dies and there is a second party involved, grieving people need to feel justice has been done. Tell group members you understand this. They feel it is urgent to their healing that this question be resolved: the criminal must be arrested, the drunk driver jailed, the doctor carefully investigated by his peers. Raise these questions with the group and ask for their feelings and suggestions. Unless some adjustment is made, powerlessness is heightened and the pain goes on.

The example was given earlier of the neurosurgeon who refused to meet with the family of a young woman who had died while in surgery, despite repeated telephone calls and letters from the parents. In order to begin rebuilding their lives, the family needed to know *why* the unexpected death had occurred. Ultimately, raging with frustration, they contacted a nationally known malpractice attorney. It took only one letter on his letterhead stationery from him asking for contact with the family to bring about a meeting.

The grieving family had no wish to sue or to berate. They merely wanted answers. They felt so powerless before the meeting because they had begun to feel, "My God, I am so insignificant even the doctor doesn't think I matter!"

Share this story with the group and ask for their responses.

You will hear other such experiences. The best way to handle this difficulty is to ask the person what he believes would be helpful in his *dealing with the issue of the death.*

In the case of an outrageously light sentence, you might suggest writing to the prosecutor, judge or media. In medical situations, the state medical association might prove helpful. The state bar association grievance committee can also be of help. Ask group members if they have other suggestions.

What you are in effect doing is letting those who feel powerless know they *do* indeed have some power. They can work toward bringing about a sense of justice to themselves and possibly even help some others along the way. Will the sense of feeling some power help those who are grieving? Ask the group.

There is one tragic reversal of powerlessness that has emerged during recent times—that is the question of "pulling the plug." When family members make this decision, they often are left with trepidation about whether they did the right thing. Although they can intellectually share the correctness of ending a loved one's suffering, not prolonging something that has most likely become obscene, deep down within themselves many people fear they have "played God" and they do not want this role. They suddenly feel they have too much power. Has this happened to anyone in the group?

It is best to listen to these people and work at reinforcing the deep sense of love such a difficult action displayed. If they need further support to reinforce the correctness of their decision, suggest they once again contact the doctor with whom they dealt.

After group members have expressed this dreadful sense of powerlessness, it is important to spend time concentrating on how each person can rebuild his life. Indeed, more than merely rebuilding, to show people they can still have a life that includes beauty and specialness. People may still learn to approach their jobs more creatively, become involved with organizations such as those for senior citizens, develop new interests such as woodworking, upholstery, knitting, paint-by-numbers, writing. Mention each of these; perhaps one might strike a responsive chord in a member.

Undertaking any of these activities can be exhilarating because they offer a fresh infusion of life.

Ask group members what else might be helpful. Have they tried anything new yet? Also, what has worked for them even for a little while? By examining the question of powerlessness from its negative aspects and then reexamining it from what people *can* do, you will have involved the group members to see the reverse of powerlessness: there will be a lessening of all the components that make one feel downtrodden; there will be at least a little ray of hope.

The opposite of powerlessness is power!

Ask group members to go back over their list of depression words and see if some changes should be made in light of this discussion. Have members use a different-colored pencil or crayon to underline what new feelings they are experiencing.

Ask members to begin a second list containing words of hope and promise that might help them go forward in their lives.

Announce that the next meeting will deal with acceptance.

MEETING EIGHT

Topic: Acceptance

Objectives: To summarize for understanding the components of mourning; to reinforce the positive steps to take; to reinforce that the contacts made within the group will continue to be meaningful to those who wish it

Working within the group has allowed you as a facilitator to offer members many insights into the dynamics of grief and mourning. By your presence and willingness to listen, you have probably allowed members to express themselves who otherwise might have been silent. Members have learned to understand and share their innermost attitudes about death and about their special person who died. This will become clear as you discuss acceptance.

Just as you did in the earlier meetings, go around the group and ask:

- The name of the person who died
- The relationship to the dead person
- When did the person die?
- What was the cause of death?

Point out to the group the greater ease with which they respond than when the group was formed.

Go around the group once again asking each member to share what changes he made in the "depression" list. Was he able to think of some positive words for the future? What were they?

Review in brief the subjects which have been covered in the previous sessions.

You have dealt with *denial*, the conditioned response to the news of a death.

You have talked about *funerals*.

Anger and the large role it plays in the death process has been explored in depth.

You have discussed *religion*. You have probably helped bring into focus many of the ambivalent feelings those who mourn experience.

You have explored the issue of *guilt* and how profound its impact can be.

Depression and its potential for great harm has been a focal point of at least one meeting.

You have reminded people who feel *powerless* that they can indeed still matter in this life.

You will now be dealing with the hoped-for stage in the grieving process and that stage is *acceptance*.

Acceptance is the result of a healthy grief process. It is the ability to recall one's special person without pain. Acceptance does not proceed from a denial of the death but rather through confronting the event. The only way around grief is through it.

Recognizing you have newly bereaved people within the group, it is important to explain that no one expects pain to completely dissipate after four months. That is not the way grief generally operates. However, if there are people who have been bereft for longer, they can share their insights. What they are doing is what you are doing—offering hope.

Because you have experienced the death of a special person, you, yourself, serve as a role model. To some degree you are the light at the end of the tunnel. Remember, acceptance does not mean liking the situation. It merely means one has come to understand it and hopefully be less frightened by it. Explain this to group members and ask if they feel comfortable knowing this.

Explain the definition of acceptance once again and then ask each member to offer his own definition. Does it vary? What do other members think of the new definition?

Do any members feel they have reached this stage? What steps helped them get there?

Was there a specific point during the meetings that a member felt he could after all make it through the nightmare?

Are there further issues any member wishes to share?

Suggest that members try the following:

• Go to a restaurant, even for coffee, or perhaps to a movie. Remind them that the first time is always the hardest. Suggest this social endeavor be a spontaneous thing the first time.

• Make plans in advance, although not too far in advance. The difficulties members have with thinking into "tomorrow" can be softened by knowing there will be something that needs doing tomorrow.

One of the greatest deterrents to healing and acceptance is the problem of feeling that by moving forward one is leaving the dead person behind—alone out there. Mention this to the group and ask if anyone has experienced this difficulty.

• Although members have worked, shopped, paid pressing bills, the time should soon be approaching when longer-range chores will be attacked. Have members balanced checkbooks? Bought that overdue gift? In other words, there is a time when we begin to tackle more than the necessities.

• Suggest trying new things. Rearrange furniture within the home. Remove the chair the dead person used at the table or change the position of the table.

• New hobbies, especially those that are creative, can be of real value. When someone is doing something creative he is bringing something forth. That something serves as a measure in the stage of "acceptance." He is no longer content with feeling it's okay for everything around him to be dead and spoiled.

Ask for reactions. Has anyone in the group made such attempts? How have these attempts been successful? Why? Did they not prove helpful? Why not?

Tell members that sometimes an attempt fails. The forewarning can be valuable. When someone has attempted and not succeeded (perhaps going into a restaurant and leaving in tears) it is important to know that the attempts *must* continue—perhaps the next time in a smaller, safer manner. Safer may mean shorter, going where there are strangers or visiting a friend's home.

Another stage of acceptance is the beginning of regrouping and the strengthening of the family unit. Ask if group members have paid much attention to how those around them are dealing with the death. Has anyone attempted something new and had it work successfully?

• Remind members that holidays and anniversaries will be difficult. Suggest they make some change in how they always did things because the truth is things *have* changed and that must be acknowledged as part of acceptance. What has worked well for group members?

• Have people note three good things—not great marvels— that have improved the quality of each week. Have them keep notes of these good things.

• Sometimes establishing foundations, giving grants, visiting orphanages, establishing memorials can be helpful not only for the recipients but for the grieving person. Down the road, they can see with pride that their loved one's name has been carried on. Has anyone in the group attempted this?

• Not everyone is financially able to do these things. There are other ways of commemorating a loved person's death. Some people take out advertisements in the personal columns of newspapers commemorating the date of their special person's birth or death. In that way, for very little money, people have a sense of having kept faith with the dead person.

You have used this entire meeting for closure. You have taken loose ends and put them together. There will be members who wish to stay on because they have benefited so much from the group experience. Do not turn them away. If they wish to stay and begin again, they are welcome. They may wish to sit in with another leader. People can gain perspective from doing so because each group forms its own personality; encourage them to.

Although certain topics should be dealt with in sequence at sessions, the group will sometimes move according to its own needs. You, as the facilitator, will have responded to those needs and directed the group accordingly. The latitude of forming your own approach is important.

If the group is desirous of meeting in a month or two just to check with one another and you are willing, by all means feel free to do so.